Hiring the Best

A Manager's Guide to Effective Interviewing and Recruiting

Fifth Edition

Martin Yate, C.P.C.

Adams Media
Avon, Massachusetts

Published by Adams Media, an F+W Publications Company
57 Littlefield Street
Avon, MA 02322
www.adamsmedia.com

ISBN: 1-59337-403-8

Printed in the United States of America
J I H G F E D C B A

Library of Congress Cataloging-in-Publication Data
Yate, Martin John.
Hiring the best : a manager's guide to effective interviewing
and recruiting / Martin Yate.—5th ed.
p.   cm.
Includes index.
ISBN 1-59337-403-8
1. Employees—Recruiting. 2. Employment interviewing. I. Title.

HF5549.5.R44Y37 2005
658.3'11—dc22
2005026451

This publication is designed to provide accurate and authoritative information
with regard to the subject matter covered. It is sold with the understanding that the publisher is not engaged in rendering legal, accounting, or other
professional advice. If legal advice or other expert assistance is required, the
services of a competent professional person should be sought.
—From a *Declaration of Principles* jointly adopted by a
Committee of the American Bar Association and
a Committee of Publishers and Associations

Design and Composition by Electronic Publishing Services, Inc., Tennessee

This book is available at quantity discounts for bulk purchases.
For information, please call 1-800-872-5627.

Dedication

This book is dedicated to your success in the ranks of management.

Acknowledgments

For their role in the continued success of this book, I'd like to thank everyone on the dedicated team of professionals at my publisher, Adams Media, and in particular Scott Watrous, Gary Krebs, Shoshanna Grossman, and Larry Shea.

Contents

You, Your Staff, Your Career 1

*T*here's a myth in corporate America that, upon promotion into management, you somehow become mystically endowed with all the skills necessary to manage a team that gets the job done on time and on budget. That is a manager's job, after all: To get work done through others, with you, as the manager, ultimately responsible for the productivity of your people.

However, you have to be careful to separate myth from reality in the workplace. Management skills don't come as a gift from the heavens; they mostly come hard won. If you are reading this book, you probably already recognize that it is impossible to *manage* productively without first *hiring* effectively; you are probably also aware that those managers who consistently make poor hires—and therefore have no chance to manage productively—ultimately fail.

No one knows how many managers have crashed their careers because they were unable to make the right hires. We have all heard about someone who is a great engineer (or accountant or salesman), but who failed as a manager, the translation being that he or she failed to get work done through others. Many management failures can be traced back to inability to recruit, interview, and select employees. In short, your ability to hire effectively is the foundation for your success in management.

With *Hiring the Best*, you will learn that employee recruitment and selection isn't brain surgery. It is a series of logical steps and sensible techniques that will enable you to make consistently good hires—and that, incidentally, will have ready application in other areas of your professional life where fact finding and communication skills come to the fore.

Although traditional accounting methodologies still largely deny that a company's work force is an assessable value, people are at the heart of every company's success. A company may have the best plant and equipment available, yet it is the *people* who make or break an organization, who produce and ship the product, who deliver the service. To talk of the body corporate is to talk of its lifeblood, those workers coursing through the halls. The more you realize that your primary responsibility as a manager is to get work done through others, the more effort you will make to secure your future with practical recruitment and selection skills.

A U.S. Labor Department study has shown that only 50 percent of new hires last more than six months in their new jobs. What happened to the other 50 percent? Even if we say that a few of these hires were rapidly promoted superstars, that still means a large proportion either quit or were fired. Actually, this is relatively good news: At least decisions were made in all these instances. What about the 50 percent who weren't superstars, didn't quit or get fired, the 50 percent who stayed in the job more than six months? No doubt some of them were dedicated and productive professionals, but common sense tells us that the survivors always include a percentage of clock-watchers who just scrape by over the years, missing deadlines, being out sick, spreading discontent, coming in two hours late in the morning and then leaving two hours early to make up for it. To paraphrase Gilbert and Sullivan, "A manager's lot is not an 'appy one." Again, it becomes clear that by improving selection skills, you can improve productivity and lessen your day-to-day management headaches.

Every manager has made bad hires and given worse excuses for them: "I dunno, boss, I learned him and I learned him, and I bought him books, but all he's done is eat the pages." Yet in almost every instance, the cause of a bad hire can be traced to one of the following reasons:

▶ Poor analysis of job functions, leading to recruitment of the wrong people

▶ Misguided recruitment strategies, leading to an inadequate pool of talent

▶ Poor analysis of the necessary skill sets and behaviors, leading to inappropriate selection criteria

▶ Inadequate initial screening, leading to wasted time and the wrong candidates on the short list

▶ Inadequate *interviewing* techniques, resulting in less access to the facts

▶ Inadequate *questioning* techniques, allowing candidates to commit "snow jobs"

▶ Poor utilization of "second opinions," compounding all of the above errors

▶ Overselling of company and career/money expectations, leading to frustrated and unmotivated staff

▶ Not checking references, leading to troublemakers (and worse) sneaking onto your payroll and damaging your professional reputation.

Hiring the Best will allow you to avoid these nightmares. It is a proven and practical approach to recruiting and selecting the right people for the job. This book was first published in 1987, and so the approaches in it have been used by managers around the world for almost twenty years. This new edition comprises a complete revision to serve the changing needs of the twenty-first-century manager.

The first part of the book will help you define the real deliverables of the jobs you fill, and give you a solid grounding in all of the most effective recruitment strategies. We'll cover how to build and generate referrals from your personal networks as well as Internet advertising and other online recruitment strategies; how best to leverage job fairs and internal referral programs; and how to decide which type of headhunter to use and how to get the most out of that resource.

You'll then learn to meld these and other techniques into a comprehensive recruitment approach that helps you fill today's urgent need, while creating the visibility and credibility that connects you to the best players throughout your profession. This not only helps with tomorrow's staffing needs, but also provides the networks to leverage your own career most effectively.

Understanding effective recruitment strategies will be a career booster whether you work for a company with an organized Human Resources function (in which case your HR relationships will be more productive), or for a smaller company without such organization, where you will be seen as just that much more knowledgeable and connected with the needs of management.

You can connect the lessons from *Hiring the Best* to your personal overall career management strategy. As a manager, an integral part of your success in each job that you hold in your career will be having an adequate supply of the right talent on tap with which to staff your departments. Let's develop that thought.

You recognize that the management path is the one most likely to deliver you the American Dream of success and a measure of financial independence. In other words, you understand the equation that:

Successful management = financial success

And you recognize that at the heart of this equation lies another, namely that:

Management = getting work done through others

Getting work done through others means hiring well, and that in turn depends on your having an adequate supply of talent. When your very success depends on it, ensuring that supply is not something you can leave to the HR department or the salespeople at Hotjobs.com. When you become involved in the recruitment process by becoming better connected to your professional communities, you not only satisfy this need, you also build networks that will help ensure your own employability. Knowing and being known within your professional community is the most effective and cheapest way to find good employees, and it is also the best way to secure new opportunities for yourself.

You can express this understanding in a third simple equation:

Professional connectivity = career resiliency

Now let's take these three equations together:

Successful management = financial success

Management = getting work done through others

Professional connectivity = career resiliency

So learning to recruit and hire effectively has ramifications far beyond doing the best possible job for your company. If you do well in management, you will be successful financially; to be successful you have to get work done through others; and the best way to accomplish this is by being connected to your profession to ensure a constant supply of talent for your employers as well as professional know-how for yourself.

In the second part of this book, you will learn a practical approach to interviewing that you can read tonight and use tomorrow, although more careful study will always repay greater dividends. You will find out how to look beneath the surface of those shiny resumes and discover what they are trying to hide from you. You'll also learn how and when to use the telephone as a screening device; it's a time management technique that effectively generates a worthwhile short list to meet in person.

To ensure that you only choose the best from those short-list candidates, you will learn the best ways to structure standalone or sequenced in-person interviews; how to use the most effective interviewing approaches and questioning techniques; and how to get the best out of second opinions. You'll find more than 400 questions to ask, as well as explanations of what the candidates' answers reveal about their skills, professional behaviors, and personalities. Perhaps most important, you'll learn how to do all of this while staying on the right side of the law.

Hiring the Best synthesizes all of the most effective recruitment and interviewing techniques currently available. After reading it and following its principles, you can always have access to a wide selection of candidates and will never again be fooled into making the wrong hire for the wrong reasons.

How to Define Your Needs

*I*t has been said that if you do not know where you are headed, you have no way of knowing when you have reached your destination. In the first chapter, we confirmed that making consistently good hires is vital to your overall success as a manager; now we are going to look at the essential criteria that will help you correctly define the needs of individual jobs.

Describe the Job First

The first step you should take when filling a position is to take the time to generate your own job description (JD), rather than relying on the company's existing JDs, which might not accurately define the job in terms of your current needs. The JD you create will:

- ▶ Profile the job's functional requirements and the skill sets necessary to discharge those duties.

- ▶ Profile the job's performance responsibilities, or its deliverables, and the analytical skills and other supportive professional behaviors that allow successful execution of the work and the working and reporting relationships.

- ▶ Define realistic educational and professional credentials.

Additionally, you will get a handle on the type of professional who will function most effectively as a member of your team (and, most important, the type you will be able to manage).

Some recruitment and selection experts will tell you to focus on performance, or deliverables and motivation, over explicit skill sets and the expertise that comes with their application over time. It's true that the best hires will always come from the people who are the most motivated to perform, but you must nevertheless first identify a job's functional responsibilities and the skill sets required to execute them. These are the foundations upon which you will develop your job description. In this process, you will also differentiate the essential skills for the job from those "nice to have" skills that you can use when evaluating your final candidates.

This definition of functional responsibilities and skill sets will not only give you a firm foundation for the rest of your job description and a more complete picture of the job; it will also keep you on the right side of federal law. The 1990 Americans with Disabilities Act requires that you identify the essential functions of each job.

An effective job description—one that you can share with recruiters and members of a selection team, and one that will provide an intelligent starting point for interview questions—clearly defines the responsibilities of the job as well as the results a worker will be expected to deliver. As a way to begin:

List the five (or so) major functional responsibilities of the vacant position, those areas in which the employee will spend the majority of time every day.

For example, a couple of those ongoing responsibilities might be:

▶ Achieve and maintain sales quota within 90 days of start date

or

▶ Add four new accounts each quarter

Notice that this has nothing to do with years of experience or educational attainment, which is where most job descriptions start—and fail. When you instead start with the functional responsibilities, you focus on the performance criteria, the deliverables an employer has every right to expect in return for a paycheck. That is what will keep the employee—and you—productively employed.

When you define performance criteria specifically in this way, you will have an effective blueprint for the interview process, for new employee orientation, and subsequently for managing productivity. Most important, a focus on expected performance will help your objective evaluation of a candidate's ability to deliver in your areas of need. This will always generate better candidates—and employees—than will going out to look for someone with a degree in communications and five years' experience in sales.

Wanted: A Problem Solver

Employees are never added to the payroll for the love of mankind; they're added because they will contribute to the bottom line. Essentially, all jobs do this by helping to make money, save money, or save time. Workers accomplish these goals largely by anticipating and preventing problems in their area of responsibility, and by solving problems when they do unexpectedly arise. So at some level, every job is that of a problem solver who exists to solve problems and to prevent their occurrence in the first place. This concept applies to any job, at any level, in any organization, anywhere in the world, and it is the key to making successful hires. If there are no problems to solve, or problems to prevent, it could mean that there really is no job to fill, or that job has not as yet been clearly defined.

Thinking about the job in terms of its problem identification/avoidance/solution responsibilities will clarify your focus during the recruitment phase *and* the selection process; it will also help with managing performance on the job after a candidate is hired. Once you have identified the particular problem-solving business that a job title is engaged in, you will have gone a long way toward isolating the additional criteria that define ability and suitability.

To this end, identify and list the typical problems that the target job handles on a daily basis, the problems it is there to avoid by timely execution of duties, and the problems/challenges that naturally arise, and therefore must be solved, because of the nature of the work. Once you have identified a job's areas of functional responsibility, its deliverables, and in turn the problems that it is there to anticipate and to solve, the next task is to isolate the professional background most likely to be supportive of these goals.

Defining Education and Experience

It is helpful to define the special knowledge, experience, and education that a candidate is likely to have under his belt to enable proper execution of your defined responsibilities.

The first step is to determine what educational background is necessary to do that job and what educational background is desirable, *being careful to differentiate between the two.* Unless you intend to verify that degree (and have done so historically), don't put too much store by one. When educational backgrounds do get checked, the chances can be as high as three in ten that the claimed level of educational attainment isn't what it appears to be. Somehow, during the writing of the resume, the high school diploma becomes an associate's degree, the community college degree becomes a bachelor's, and so on. Exaggerating education is the single most common deception that job hunters at all levels make. Always ask yourself whether a specific degree or level of educational attainment is absolutely necessary, or just whether it is a desirable asset, a "nice to have." Perhaps there might be room for flexibility here; for example, can on-the-job experience be substituted?

If you determine that a certain level of education or specific type of degree is mandatory for the job, be aware that deception is so rife that you will need to make a point of credential verification as part of the selection process. Use educational criteria as a signpost of commitment and a determinant of the ability to learn, which is an essential skill in itself in an ever-changing workplace in which learning new skills is an important responsibility for most high-performing workers.

If you are not going to verify levels of educational attainment, the importance of educational levels necessarily moves from a "must have" to a "nice to have."

Beyond the question of education, the next step is to *understand the depth and kind of experience you need a candidate to possess.*

Defining desired experience is fraught with challenges. It might be easy to say "five years' experience required," because you had five years of experience when you landed this job, or because other people who have been successful in the position also had about five years of experience, but it is dangerous to make such criteria hard-and-fast rules. A sharp youngster with three years of progressively diverse experience could often be a better bet than the ten-year seasoned pro, who has in reality simply repeated one year of experience ten times, not progressing and not learning from his mistakes.

Additionally, you should define exactly what you mean by "experience." Do you mean experience delivering on the individual performance criteria of your job description, experience in the profession, in your industry, and/or experience in a company of similar size and culture? To some degree, all of these considerations are relevant, but some more than others depending on your situation. For example, industry experience will come to the fore in a business-to-business marketing or audit position, while it might have lesser importance for a customer service job.

Hard-and-fast rules regarding experience can cause you to miss out on good people, so it is always helpful to allow yourself some flexibility. If you do demand "five years of solid experience," take the time to quantify what it is that those people will be able to deliver as a result of that experience that a candidate with three years' experience could not. It's one thing to say that you need someone with fifteen years of manufacturing experience; it's another to say that you expect the employee to run a 24/7 four-shift operation and then move it lock, stock, and barrel to the Philippines in fifteen months.

Determining Supportive Professional Behaviors

Once you define the job in terms of responsibilities, experience, education, special knowledge, and deliverables, you are in a position to analyze the professional behaviors that allow a worker to deliver on those performance requirements.

I emphasize these *learned professional behaviors* because, to a large extent, the professional behaviors that are most desirable to you as an employer are developed as a result of our experiences in the workplace; they are not necessarily the behaviors we developed growing up. From that first day on your first job, once you noticed how different the world of work was from the relatively cozy life at home or school, you began to observe and emulate the more successful professionals around you. Slowly, you developed a whole slate of learned behaviors that helped you succeed in your professional life. Now that you are responsible for hiring, you need to examine each of the functional areas of responsibility and each of the deliverables to determine which specific professional behaviors are most relevant to your needs.

Over the years, I have identified a group of professional behaviors that seem to be common to all professionals in the successful execution of jobs at all levels and in all professions. Read through the following list, thinking about the professional behaviors that would encourage the successful execution of each of the performance criteria specific to your job opening. When you do this for each functional area, you will not only get a good idea of the behaviors that are most relevant to the job, but which of those chosen behaviors are most important because they crop up most frequently. This will give you a more comprehensive picture of the ideal candidate, and offer additional lines of investigation for the interview process.

Communication Skills: The ability to communicate effectively with your employees, with coworkers throughout the company, and perhaps with customers, is critical to the success of most jobs today.

Verbal, listening, and written communication skills, along with technological adaptedness, apply to all jobs; additionally, dress and body language are communication skills relevant to some jobs throughout the hierarchy, and to most jobs at higher levels.

Time Management and Organization: Application of time management and organization practices allows a professional to work efficiently and productively. Without them, it is difficult for any professional to be successful on a consistent basis.

Team Orientation: No one is successful in the professional world operating as a lone gun; you need people who understand their work in terms of the role it plays in the larger picture, and for the common good. Candidates who can think and talk in terms of group good, cooperation, and shared goals are going to add to the strength of your team, and will be more cooperative from a management perspective.

Energy: As a manager you can't succeed with players who can't or won't make an effort. You need people who will always expend that extra effort in the little things as well as more important matters. A person should be obviously healthy enough to maintain that energy over the length of the working week. This is a behavior for which posture and grooming can offer you useful input, because people who express a positive self-image in these ways are likely to be engaged with their work.

Motivation: Enthusiasm and a desire to make a difference, an eagerness to learn, and a willingness to take the rough with the smooth that goes with every job all show that a candidate is engaged in a meaningful way with his or her work. A motivated employee will do a better job on every assignment, and, all other things being equal, a motivated candidate will always be your best choice come decision time.

Determination: Even in the best-run operations, things go wrong; that's why the presence of a problem-solving attitude is so critical in your hires. The job you are filling will likely benefit from someone who sees difficult situations through to their proper conclusion, and who does not head for cover when a problem or situation gets tough. You will learn about determination when you ask questions about difficult situations that a candidate has experienced, and how they were resolved.

Confidence: A degree of confidence is required in all jobs to look at challenges calmly, and to develop the skills and strategies necessary to fully contribute to the team's success. Confidence comes when a candidate has been actively engaged in his or her work, building a wide frame of reference for the work and its challenges. You are looking for candidates who exude confidence in their skills, and confidence in their ability to learn new skills, because they are engaged in the quest for constant improvement.

Confidence comes with success, and success comes with the application and interaction of each of these learnable professional behaviors. For this reason, when you find applicants with one of these behaviors, you will see that behavior interacting with others in the group.

Reliability: It is said that showing up is half the battle, so seeking reliable behaviors means that you look for people who demonstrate a personal commitment to their work's success. You'll see reliability expressing itself as a different aspect of determination, and vice versa.

Honesty/Integrity: A thorough professional makes decisions in the best interest of the company, and never based on personality, or on a whim or personal preference. You will see that those who demonstrate honesty and integrity in their professional lives are people who know what to do, because they understand that it is the "right" thing to do professionally. When you can rely on an employee's integrity, you have one less worry.

Pride: Pride as a professional and in a job well done is an expression of all these behaviors interacting with each other. This can become apparent on a day-to-day basis when a person makes the time to pay attention to the details that guarantee the integrity of that work, rather than just getting a job onto someone else's desk. In many jobs, the devil is in the details. Get your candidates to talk about their work and their profession to see how deeply professional pride runs in their veins.

Dedication: Dedication, or commitment to professional excellence, is a behavior you will find expressed in a candidate's respect for the job's role and the profession. You will see it in the extra effort a candidate puts into his or her career, via books, classes, education, and membership in professional associations. For a job in which surprises and new challenges are the norm, rather than the exception, such dedication is worth its weight in gold.

Analytical Skills: Analytical skills play a role in every job today, and coupled with a wide frame of reference for the job and the role it plays in contributing to the bottom line, they are invaluable in an employee, and probably relevant to the job you are filling. Look for candidates who weigh the pros and cons of a given situation rather than jumping at the first or easiest solution to a problem, and who are able to weigh the potential negatives, as well as the positives, of a proposed course of action. You will see the presence of analytical skills when you talk about the day-to-day problems that are faced in a particular job, and how a candidate analyzes and solves them.

Goal Orientation: Employees basically come in two flavors: the task oriented, who let each job expand to fill the time allotted, and the goal oriented, who are galvanized by a challenge and eager to bring it to a successful conclusion. So if the word *productivity* is ever mentioned at your company, you need the second flavor, and you need to avoid the first.

Goal-oriented people tend to break down tasks into small doable steps tied to specific timelines; this in turn most likely means that they have a grasp of time management and organization techniques. If you find a goal-oriented candidate who for some reason lacks those skills, you'll probably find that he or she will be able to apply them in a flash.

Profit Orientation: Your bottom-line concerns as an employer are really quite simple: to increase productivity, and thereby, profit. So a candidate's awareness and orientation toward saving time and money, and finding ways to make more money, will let you know whether that person shares a necessary awareness of productivity and profit. This profit awareness is likely to be present with the goal oriented, and additionally becomes visible in the way a worker understands efficiency and the importance of systems and procedures.

Efficiency: All the behaviors discussed here ultimately relate to productivity, and efficiency is no exception. Productive workers are also efficiency minded, always keeping an eye open for wasted time, effort, resources, and money, and constantly looking for a better way to get the job done. Ideas of efficiency and economy engage the goal-oriented mind in ways the task oriented might not consider.

Procedure Oriented: You need people who understand the need for systems and procedures, and who willingly follow the chain of command. You do not want to hire workers who implement their own "improved" procedures or organize others to do so, or who go around you to others in management.

Together, these learnable behaviors spell long-term career success for the manager who develops them as a personal skill set, and who seeks and encourages their development in others.

The question now becomes whether it is possible to find someone with all these behaviors. A couple of years back I was in Mexico City for six months with Elektra/Groupo Salsa (a 19,000-employee conglomerate), working on an employee selection–revamping project. One day, in a recruitment and selection workshop, a manager complained that searching for all these professional behaviors was setting the bar too high, that in his particular job market he was never going to find someone who matched all his needs. I explained that once you create a master list of performance criteria, you can review each responsibility against the list of desirable professional behaviors that are supportive of proper execution in that area. At the end of your analysis, I explained, you will have a weighted list of all the relevant professional behaviors and an idea of which are most important to the job. Will you find candidates with all the desired professional behaviors? You probably will, more often than you would think. It is also certain that if you do not look for these behaviors, you most certainly will not find them. When you do seek the presence of a relevant professional behavioral profile as it relates to the needs of the job, you are developing a valuable tool with which to objectively evaluate one candidate against another.

Once you have defined the open position in these steps, it can be useful to have a check and balance, with some members of your team developing their own job descriptions for the position. You might give them your freshly developed job description and ask what they might add to it, or subtract from it. With the additional insight from those closest to daily responsibilities, you should have a comprehensive overview of the abilities and behavioral profile needed to make a success of the job's deliverables.

Finding Motivation

It is never pleasant to work with people who cannot do their jobs, and it is worse to work with those who can do the work but won't do it, or let the tasks take up all the time allotted simply because they can. Consequently, every hire you make has an impact on the rest of the work group.

Obviously, you want to hire people who are able to do the work at hand, and you also want to hire only those candidates who are motivated to do the best they can in their own professional lives. This makes identifying motivated candidates an important consideration that benefits everyone.

In fact, in the final analysis, when there are no other differences between two equally qualified candidates, you can safely make a decision based on which one is most knowledgeable about the profession, the company, and the job, and the one who is openly enthusiastic about joining the team.

Later in the book, you will find questions specifically designed to evaluate motivation, but for now it's enough to know that you will find its presence expressed in the degree to which a candidate is enthusiastically engaged in his or her work. Motivation will similarly make its presence felt in the way a professionally engaged candidate changes the job interview from a one-sided examination of skills into a two-way conversation between colleagues.

It is no good to hire someone who can do the job, but won't give his or her best; you only want to hire the candidate who "can do" and "wants to." This order of "can do" first and "wants to" second is relevant, not only in understanding your needs and getting a three-dimensional picture of the person you want to hire, but also in prioritizing your evaluation procedures. A candidate's degree of motivation only becomes relevant as it becomes apparent that the person is able to do the work or is able to learn to do the work in an acceptable time frame.

Determining Manageability and Teamwork

There isn't a manager in the world who enjoys a sleepless night caused by an unmanageable employee. Avoiding such nights is a major concern for successful managers, who develop a remarkable sixth sense when it comes to spotting and cutting out mavericks. This sense grows with an awareness of the role that personal motivation, manageability, and team orientation play in the success or failure of a department.

Manageability can be defined in different ways: the ability to work alone; the ability to work with others; the ability to take direction and criticism when it is carefully and considerately given; and, perhaps dearest to a manager's heart, the ability to take direction when it *isn't* carefully and considerately given, perhaps because of a crisis.

Equally crucial to manageability is the willingness of an employee to work as part of a team, to get along with others regardless of their sex, sexual orientation, age, religion, physical appearance, abilities or disabilities, skin color, or national origin. In other words, having the emotional maturity to deal with others as professional colleagues, rather than allowing negative social preconceptions to color those relationships.

As you define the position to be filled, ostensibly for the needs of the recruitment procedure, you will also benefit by creating a profile of a candidate who is motivated, a team player, and who is manageable by you . . . even with all your warts and blemishes. It's best to do this now, while you are objectively focused on the nuts and bolts of the job, because it will help you in developing the right questions and evaluative frame of mind for the interview and selection cycle.

Later in the book, we will delve deeper into the ways to establish manageability, teamwork, and motivation. For now it is enough to consider:

▶ The best people you have ever seen doing this work, and what made them stand out and succeed. For example, you might note that all the success stories you recall were people who never left work without planning for tomorrow, based on the activities of today.

▶ The worst people you have ever seen doing this work, and what made them stand out in this way and ultimately fail. For example, you might note that the failures you recall all seemed to react in a vacuum, to the events of the moment, rather than having a plan of action in place, or a frame of reference to similar past events.

Try to break down the reasons for success or failure into component parts of experience, skills, attitude, and behavior. When you put such considerations together, you might conclude, for example, that successful people have good time management and organization skills and that people who fail in this job often lack application of these learned behaviors. This will either give you a valuable new insight into your needs, or reinforce conclusions you reached when evaluating the importance of learned professional behaviors.

Special Considerations

Almost every job you fill will have special considerations that will impact the position profile.

As one example, if you are working toward a promotion for yourself, you might need to include succession planning in your recruitment initiative. After all, you cannot move up without finding a replacement, so you may want to hire strength, and therefore won't rule out seasoned professionals. At the same time, because it is always best to promote from within, you would only hire from the outside if there were no one within your department who could be groomed to step up.

Communication issues are also a somewhat nebulous, but nevertheless important consideration in many jobs. You will need to consider with whom this employee will be interacting, in terms of coworkers, other departments, other management ranks, and customers. In all of these areas you then need to define what that communication will be and how that might affect selection criteria. Will the communication take place by telephone, in person, in meetings, at the dining table? Each of these instances can increase or decrease demands on the position holder; telephone communication with other departments requires far less in the way of hard business skills and social graces than do formal meetings and dining with clients. If the latter will be required in the position, you might want to require candidates to make a formal presentation, or at least discuss the tactics and pitfalls of client relations, and you might choose to have them do this over lunch so that you can see your top candidates functioning in an on-the-job situation. This also allows you to see whether any of the candidates wields a steak knife like a machete.

Technology is another consideration that plays a role in every job today, and changes the very nature of all our jobs almost as rapidly as do the pages on your calendar. You should select candidates who are either technologically up-to-date with your company's operational platforms or can get up to speed in a reasonable time frame. You also need to identify some of the learning challenges that will be coming to your department over the next year or so. Understanding these challenges now can help you look for people who might have experience, or a track record of being able to learn new skills on an ongoing basis.

Finalizing the Job Description

Once you have analyzed your needs for the position and separated them into "must haves" and "nice to haves," you need to finalize them (with sensitivity to HR's needs for defensibility in lawsuits) in a format you can use for the recruitment and selection process. Use simple terminology that makes the performance expectations of the job easy to grasp. If you can't explain the job in simple terms, you probably don't understand it well enough yourself, and need to give additional thought to the job definition. Think and write in terms of the key responsibilities, the core competencies and what needs to be delivered in those areas, and the attitudes and behaviors that guarantee that the work will be done efficiently. Include the acceptable variables of experience and education so that everyone on the recruitment and selection team will be on the same page, and give them the opportunity to see and comment on the final document.

Involvement of others in defining the position makes them stakeholders in a successful outcome, and for staff members it is also a reward for performance with recognition and new skill development. A clear job description is the foundation for successful recruitment, selection, and also management of the chosen candidate. You can see a couple of examples of how all your work translates itself into powerful recruitment ads in the next chapter on pages 43-45. We will also come back to your analysis of the job description in the second half of the book, when we examine how all this work arms you for the interview and selection cycle.

Deciding on Compensation

There is just one more outstanding issue to consider in completing a recruitable job description, and that is compensation, including benefits. Workers are far savvier about compensation today than in years past, because they talk to peers about money and have all the tools of the Internet with which to compare their wages with regional and national norms. While pay and benefits are not typically considered the number-one reason to accept or reject a job, noncompetitive offers will usually result in rejection of a job offer, unless you represent a particularly high-profile company or your outfit has some other overwhelmingly unique attractant.

Your compensation must be competitive with other companies in the profession and within your geography, and, needless to say (I hope), with similar jobs within your own company. It's ideal if the compensation package can accommodate an appreciation for superior performance, and along with competitive benefits, if it includes some incentive for individual and group efforts.

Exactly what to pay is the focus of a professional field all by itself, with compensation professionals swelling the ranks of all but the smallest HR departments. It also is the subject of many useful books on the subject, with perhaps *Basic Compensation*, by Robert Jones, being the best in the field.

Unless you manage in a very small company, there will likely be HR professionals who have already determined the salary ranges for all open positions within the company. If your company does not have an HR department, you can still find plenty of reliable resources for compensation; you will find compensation consultants as active members in professional and management associations, the local chamber of commerce, and area employer coalitions. Headhunters can also give you a good handle on what are locally competitive salaries.

In addition to these resources, you have the Internet at your fingertips. Start with *www.bls.gov*, *www.careers.wsj.com*, *www.salary.com*, and *www. dbm.com*. You can also go to the employer sections at Internet job sites. Rather than go to the big sites, you are likely to get better information by going to sites that specialize in the profession within which your particular job opening resides.

Benefits

This is another area that is probably handled by HR specialists, or by an external benefits consulting company. Because workers increasingly feel the pinch as raises get smaller and contributions to health care increase, they increasingly have a clear perception of the dollar value of benefits, which means that it is a topic with which your company should be completely up to speed. Again, this is an area that has its own consultant industry and generates new book titles every season, and for which there is a wealth of information on the Internet (see Human Resources Services in Appendix B).

Performance Incentives

All jobs can be incentivized to one degree or another, although sales, technology, and management are the areas in which incentivizing is most visible. Performance incentives can increase earnings quite dramatically for workers in sales, where the incentive structure defines wages, and also in technology and management, where wages are often significantly enhanced through incentives.

These three particular areas of professional endeavor are more highly incentivized because individual contributions can be seen to have a more direct impact on the bottom line. Consequently, when you recruit in these areas, reward for performance should be part of the package if you expect to remain competitive.

You don't have to have the best pay, benefits, and incentives to get the best people—although it does help—but you do have to be competitive with regional norms for your profession. Also, because we typically spend more of our waking hours with our coworkers than with the people we love, you need to be able to present your department and company as a rewarding and positive environment in which hard work, competence, professionalism, and commitment are recognized and rewarded.

A Last Consideration

Defining a performance profile for each of the jobs under your control is an important step toward giving you an objective means by which to choose job candidates and subsequently evaluate employee performance, and in the process provide your staff a ready yardstick against which to measure themselves.

The issue of skill versus compensation gives us one last consideration before moving forward to effective recruitment strategies.

Sometimes managers have a perception that their best hire will be the person with 100 percent of the skills demanded by the job, but hiring such a candidate is not always the best decision and can create problems.

Unless there is opportunity for further professional growth, a candidate with 100 percent of the required skills for the job is more likely to become demotivated because he or she is not challenged by the work.

A candidate with 100 percent of the skills is also likely to command compensation at or near the top of your approved salary range. This makes it difficult to provide reasonable raises, no matter how productive the person is, without promotion into another level, which isn't always possible.

This means that the person who seems most qualified may not be the best person for the job; lack of opportunity for professional growth and increased earnings are major reasons for workers leaving one job for another. Often you will build a more effective team by hiring people who can do, say, 60 to 80 percent of the job and who are motivated by their work and by the opportunity for professional growth. Such candidates can be hired lower in the approved salary range, allowing for good raises without the need for imminent promotion into another category.

Now that you have a logical approach to defining open positions, it is time to move on to creating recruitment programs that will generate an adequate flow of suitable candidates.

Recruitment in Today's Marketplace 3

*T*here are going to be plenty of workers looking for jobs in the new world of work, but not always with the qualifications and professional profile you might need. No matter what the job, it has been created to have a positive effect on productivity, and only when you have the widest selection of qualified candidates can you make the best choice. Simply placing a recruitment posting on Careerbuilder.com or in your local paper will not allow you to make that kind of privileged choice; you'll have to stretch beyond the average approach to get superior performance.

In this section of the book I want to give you a solid grasp of all the different techniques that companies use to recruit staff, and to show you ways that allow you to personalize these techniques for your own ongoing use, so that you can take them, and the contacts you make through them, with you from job to job and company to company. When you use this approach, you'll find that the candidate who wasn't right for today's need is exactly the right person for a slot a year from now. Remember, a manager's job, first and last, is getting work done through others, and knowing where to find those "others" is key to that prime responsibility. The trick is to accomplish this in ways that don't overwhelm your whole professional life.

People Power

Henry Ford once said that you could repossess all of his factories and burn all of his warehouses to the ground, but as long as you left him his people he could rebuild everything that had been lost. As a manager, Ford recognized that employing productive people and knowing how to find them were the tools of his management trade. His famous statement also acknowledges how hard it is to find good people.

Of course Ford needed little in the way of the workplace skills that are demanded of even the simplest jobs today; essentially, he needed warm bodies to show up to work, and he needed them in a time when much of the nation was eager to move from farm work to factory work. You could say that Henry Ford had it a sight easier than you do, but then again, he didn't have the recruitment tools available that stand ready for your use.

Hiring from Within

There is a story frequently told in the world of executive recruitment of an outfit with an important position to fill. An eminent, retained search firm convinced the company that the "quiet confidence of a retained search" was the route to take. The company was advised that this search for a senior executive would be a difficult one, and would require a $25,000 retainer and six months to complete. The search firm, true to its word, came back with a recommendation six months later: it said the company should promote the current assistant to the vacant position into the job.

Often we go outside to find that "special someone" who has one key skill we covet, and then cheerfully invest vast amounts of money, time, and effort to bring that person up to speed on the other nine critical aspects of a job for which the employee may have no particular aptitude.

Whenever you have the opportunity to fill an existing position, or to open up a new slot within the area of your authority, look first within your own ranks. It saves time, money, embarrassment, and start-up time. Further, you will improve morale among current employees, because promoting from within demonstrates that you encourage and reward honest effort and competence.

In an age when we can't guarantee long-term employment, employees are increasingly demanding that we at least maintain their employability. Modern times demand increased productivity from us all, and today's professional, unlike his more docile forebears of years past who could look forward to long-term employment, is dissatisfied without meaningful recognition and professional growth opportunities. When you can hire from within, you motivate every single person in the department, because they see that there is opportunity where they work today to achieve their own professional goals for tomorrow. The result is that you keep better people longer.

Always start a job search by looking within your department and then within the company to see who would welcome and benefit from increased responsibilities. Show yourself to be a manager who helps people grow, and your team will walk over hot coals for you. Too many managers fail to realize that each staff member has personal goals and will only remain loyal and productive when management supports those goals. Show yourself as a more typical manager, one who demonstrates a lack of faith in his or her existing staff, and you will find yourself managing a succession of empty chairs, because those potentially loyal employees will find themselves a manager who *will* help them grow.

Having looked within your own department, you can, if you feel it is appropriate, canvas colleagues in other areas of the company for suitable candidates. However, because gifts are usually worth what you pay for them, you should be wary of hiring an employee from another department simply on recommendation, as you could be inheriting someone else's headache.

With "internal hires" you will need to apply the same rigid evaluation procedures as you would for an outside hire, carefully evaluating the needed skill sets and professional behaviors along with relevant real-world experience and then conducting structured job interviews, just as you would with an outside candidate. At the same time, HR can give you access to the personnel file for review. Finally, of course, you will want to check references, and the best ones in this instance could well be your own people and what they know of the candidate's behavior and performance.

When dealing with internal candidates, you should be aware that a proportion of them might be on the verge of looking for growth opportunities outside of the company. They need to be treated with the same consideration that you would offer an external candidate. This is especially important if it is one of your staff members who has responded to an internal posting; if the person doesn't get the job sought, you need to be alert for changes in attitude and commitment.

If searches within your department and the company at large do not yield the right candidate(s), examine your personal files and then your company HR database for suitable candidates. If this involves the Human Resources department, you can (and should) do more than just put in a formal request.

Helping Out Human Resources

Human Resources is perhaps the most notoriously overworked depart-ment of the contemporary American corporation. Its resident profession-als deserve your consideration, understanding, and help.

By the way, lest you need further encouragement to pay careful atten-tion to this section, remember that the HR function of your company is intimately involved with every single available opportunity, up and down the corporate ladder. That you understand the recruitment process and are able to work productively with HR will put you on that department's radar when another opportunity, perhaps suitable for you, comes along.

To gain HR's best efforts, become knowledgeable in the recruitment and selection process and do whatever you can to get involved with the search yourself. Naturally, you will make every effort to understand and work with the established procedures. All too often in larger companies, Human Resources recruits for managers whom HR staff have never met; you, on the other hand, want these good people to know you on sight, and not scurry in the other direction when you do heave into sight over the horizon. Make yourself known as a professional, motivated manager willing to carry his weight in job searches, rather than just another insistent, gray, disembodied voice whining orders and making complaints.

Sometimes even your best efforts may result only in your being pre-sented with a daunting database of dog-eared resumes, but nevertheless make due diligence, as your ideal candidate could be hiding somewhere in there. We'll talk about techniques for screening piles of resumes without going blind or driving yourself mad a little later.

Once these internal searches are in process, you'll next need to take advantage of your professional network.

Networking

Most people lack networks of depth and relevance, so you may need to build the strength of yours. The effort you put in will help your recruit-ment activities, and it will also get you better connected to your profession for your own personal growth. (By the way, if you go to my Web site at *www.knockemdead.com*, you will find my forty-five-minute Networking Workshop, where you'll learn everything you need to build deep, wide, and relevant networks.)

An important key to overall success in management is the possession of usable knowledge relevant to the situation at hand, and when you don't have it, knowing where to get it.

Employers favor the introductions and referrals that come from networking because these hires are seen to be faster, cheaper, and they result in an employee who is productive more quickly and who stays with the company longer. Nevertheless, networking is easier said than done, because most professionals do not have nearly extensive enough networks to serve their needs. Building productive networks takes time and effort.

The Company Web Site

One of the few things I have taken as given in this current edition of *Hiring the Best* is that your company has a Web site, and that it is used as a recruiting tool, with all openings posted automatically. If not, somebody needs to wake up and smell the coffee, because this is another powerful and low-cost recruitment tool.

A company Web site that is oriented not only toward potential customers but also toward potential employees is a must in this day and age. There is no cost to post job openings on your Web site, and with Internet search engines your job openings become visible to the whole world.

Using the Web site as an effective recruitment portal to your company will be most effective if the site is user friendly. The Internet allows fast access to countless job opportunities, and it has led to an online culture that demands instant gratification. A site that is slow to load, difficult to navigate, and includes a cumbersome application process will drive potential candidates away.

It will help the recruitment process if tools on the site allow visitors to forward information about a specific opening to others, and if the site can notify them whenever a suitable opening is posted on the company Web site. If the budget doesn't stretch to making these changes in-house, many of the bigger job sites will happily host a recruitment-friendly site for you.

Professional Networks

Just as you will use professional networks in your own job hunts, with a little effort you can use them just as effectively when you are the one doing the recruiting. The benefits to this are that:

- You will be able to network effectively, which is a great recruitment tool.

- Your obvious connectivity makes you look good in the eyes of upper management.

- Your involvement will make you known as someone worth knowing, which will expand your network of helpful colleagues for the next time you need to make a strategic career move.

- You stay attuned to what is going on in your profession, and you get the benefit of training that makes you a more knowledgeable and productive manager.

- You will be able to develop sources for useful information and advice for the time when you'll need it, and from those sources, develop mentors for your own long-term professional growth.

Obviously, being able to tap into diverse professional networks is worth your commitment, so the question becomes, "How do I get professionally connected?" The answer is to become an involved and active member of at least two, and perhaps three professional associations. Membership in a management association and an association serving your industry or profession are the two obvious choices.

If you fit the profile of a special-interest or minority group, you might also consider professional associations that cater to another dimension of your professional life. These include—but are by no means restricted to—associations for African-Americans, Latinos, Asian-Americans, professionals with disabilities, and women. If you do not fit such a profile but want to tap into the diverse talent such associations represent, you might still apply for associate membership.

Your employer is likely to cover your professional membership dues, and if not, you can probably easily afford them yourself. Active association membership puts you on the radar of the best qualified and connected professionals in your area, all of whom maintain membership, at least in part, to support their career progression goals (making them more committed than the average bear). As a member representing the management ranks, you automatically initiate a passive recruiting presence among motivated and committed professionals in your field, just by being a member and a manager.

You become even more visible when you attend the meetings that occur monthly in most major cities, and the regional and national get-togethers that occur throughout the year further increase your visibility and credibility. When you attend association activities, you get to know, and get to be known by, the most committed professionals at all levels of your profession. You can go further than just attending the meetings; you can also volunteer to get involved in upcoming and/or ongoing activities.

Becoming involved as a volunteer is very easy. There is always a need for someone to set out chairs, or hand out paperwork and nametags. Initially, the task itself doesn't matter, but your willingness to help in a community in which everything is achieved by volunteer work most certainly does. Your energy will get you on first-name terms with people you would probably never otherwise meet.

You should also consider volunteering for one of the many committees that help associations function. Any committee will do, although the membership committee is usually the biggest and will get you in touch with all existing and new members.

Professional associations all have online newsletters. Many have a help-wanted section, where companies love to advertise because of the quality of response. If your company doesn't currently invest recruitment dollars in such venues, it is probably because it is not aware of the benefits. Of course, you won't get the enormous volume you might get from advertising on, say, a Monster.com board, but the responses you do get will invariably be qualified.

The association directory, which comes with your membership package, provides you with a superb networking resource. Of course, it is best if you already have a face-to-face relationship with people, but if you don't, the membership directory will open many doors for you. You can feel comfortable calling any other member on the phone and introducing yourself this way: "Hi, Jack Larsen? My name is Martin Yate. We haven't spoken before, but we are both members of the Teachers Federation. I need some advice; can you spare me a minute?" Then go on to ask for directional guidance and perhaps a referral. Your mutual membership, and the commitment it bespeaks, will guarantee you a few moments of anyone's time. You will, of course, need to abide by the associations' guidelines on recruitment activities with members, which sometimes request that no direct recruiting be done, as in "Can I recruit you for this job?" Instead, you are just passing the word that you're looking for a good so-and-so; do they know anyone? Remember to invest forty-five minutes in the knockemdead.com Networking Workshop, and establish the most effective recruitment resource known to man.

Networking on the Internet

While not quite as effective as the relationships you can nurture with your in-person networking activities, the Internet allows you to connect more quickly and to many more people over a much wider geography, so on balance it is another powerful networking tool.

Professional Community Sites

The Internet has become an effective way for geographically dispersed people with similar interests to establish community. You will be mostly interested in connecting with communities that share similar professional, skill, or industry interests, rather than those groups that are connecting primarily for social reasons.

You can find online networking opportunities with sites catering to the following interests.

Professional Associations and Alumni Groups

All professional, business, and alumni associations have a Web presence, and many host community forums in which members can exchange ideas and ask questions of each other. Most associations and alumni groups will also have their membership directories available online, which can help you identify people quickly and easily.

Web Forums, User Groups, and Discussion Groups

With forums and discussion groups, the primary focus is the exchange of information. People go to these sites specifically to post and answer questions in a specific area of interest. These sites are often hosted by industry news and trade publication sites and motivated individuals; they can be especially useful in reaching technical professionals.

It is wise to contact the site's moderator to get an understanding of the character of the group and the topics addressed; some sites seem to focus mostly on jokes and griping. When you do find relevant groups, you have to become a member of the community before you start recruiting, just as in the real world, so your involvement should always be partly based on your personal commitment to growth and knowledge.

Industry Destination Sites

These will include sites that offer industry and skill-related news, such as trade publications and industry/skill/local *vortals*. While a portal site such as Yahoo.com is a doorway into a wide world of interests, a vortal is a doorway into a narrow or vertically integrated world of interests that are specific (in our usage) to an industry, profession, locale, or skill set. Such a doorway is filled with information and links relevant to its specific audience.

Locating Online Networking Opportunities

For recruitment purposes you'll need to think about whom you are trying to reach, in order to develop a list of keywords to pump into your search engine of choice:

- Where do they live? For example: *Denver*

- What are their job titles? For example: *Accountant*

- What skills do they have? For example: *Public Accounting*

- With what tools do they work? For example: *Excel*

You will then mix and match these keywords with phrases such as discussion group, forum, and so on. I keyed in "public accounting" and "discussion groups" on Google and got 1,550,000 results. I visited the first ten, seven of which had relevant groups.

Your challenge won't be in finding opportunities for online networking; it will be in narrowing down the field to your specific needs and geography. You may come across groups where recruitment is frowned upon, or where you have no personal impetus for involvement. We'll discuss how to leverage these when we discuss advertising.

Professional Networking Sites

A new rage on the Internet that has real relevance to all of us in building deeper, more relevant recruitment networks is "social networking." It revolves around online networks built on professional expertise and incorporating common experiences or interests.

These professionally oriented sites allow users to post profiles that include skills, employers, work history, and educational attainment. From a recruitment standpoint, these profiles work just like a resume. Professionals who want to be visible and are available to opportunity are flocking to these sites, enabling you to reach out to an endless horizon of potential candidates.

It works quite simply: you join a social networking site (with a few you have to wangle an invitation), fill out a profile for yourself, and you are ready to go. Most sites encourage you to identify topics you wish to hear about; for example, you can announce that you are interested in hiring people.

Networking sites offer a reliable pathway to both active and passive job seekers. You can search a site's database by zip code, job title, company, or other keywords of your choice. The resultant search tells you how many people match your requirements and then allows you to initiate contact directly, or through the chain of people who connect you.

You can then approach people directly, or through the network that connects the two of you. It's a simple matter of stating your business: "I am an accounting manager in the beverage industry, looking for an _____. I saw your profile and wondered if we might talk. Let's exchange telephone numbers."

Recently I plugged in the phrase "Information technology" for a general area of expertise so that I could isolate people in a particular profession, and I got 39,000 profiles. I could then proceed to narrow down this list by applying other words to my search phrase. In this hypothetical instance, because I wanted someone with a sense of commitment and determination, and someone who was a team player and used to taking the rough with the smooth, I decided to add the word "army," reckoning that asking for a military background would increase the odds of finding those behaviors. The search phrase then read, "army and information technology." When I combined both of these keywords, I got 980 profiles that matched my search criteria, and in the majority of instances these people had moved from the army into information technology.

You can refine your searches endlessly by the keywords you use. It took ten minutes for me to sign up and thirty minutes to understand how it works—this isn't brain surgery!

Networking sites also offer an array of useful services that enable your networking activities. Two of special relevance to recruitment are:

▶ Message boards and forums for common interest groups.

▶ Offline social events so you can meet and mingle in person.

There are more than fifty sites catering to professional networks. You can find links to a comprehensive list of social networking sites in Appendix B or online at *www.knockemdead.com*.

Networking for the Long Term

The cycle of recruitment and selection is ongoing for every manager. If you are hiring accountants today, you will probably be hiring them six months and a year from now. This should lead you to invest in your networking activities as part of your manpower planning. If you only network and recruit when you have an urgent need, you will be reactive and feel pressured to hire the first warm bodies that come along. When you think about your needs over the coming year, you can start sourcing and building contacts now for when you need them. When you need to hire again you won't feel pressured, and you'll have a ready pool of candidates to work from.

College Career Services and Alumni Associations

When you're looking for entry-level people, the career services office at your alma mater, relevant national institutions, and local schools can offer you a ready supply of motivated entry-level professionals. With people changing careers more frequently today, that entry-level person need not be someone still suffering from terminal acne; you can find people who are at entry level in the profession but who also have some real-world business experience, which can be a nice plus. All you have to do is introduce yourself to the career services department, and those professionals will take it from there. You can also go to the Internet Resources page at the knockemdead.com Web site and link directly to resources from there.

People like to work with people with whom they share something in common. Your alumni association is a complete and valuable network just waiting for you to become involved and leverage the contacts. As an alumni member, you maintain relationships with other professionals in your field and also get a copy of the alumni association membership directory, packed with qualified people you can call with a certainty of a warm reception.

Alumni associations all have online newsletters and carry job postings, frequently with little or no cost involved. Some alumni associations even have semiformalized job search networks, and alumni are encouraged to pass along their companies' needs. Even when your school days are in the misty past, don't forget the school's alumni and the valuable resource they represent.

References

References are a powerful but usually overlooked recruitment tool which, when properly used, will also expand your network of professional contacts. We'll talk about reference checking a little later in the book; right now let's think about how references can be used in recruitment.

Get in the habit of checking both management and peer references personally. You'll avoid problem hires, get leads on other candidates for other jobs, and have the knowledge to get the very best out of your new hires.

You can get even more return for your time investment by tagging another dimension on the end of the conversation. After the reference call itself is completed, take a few moments to talk to your management peers about what they are involved with right now, and tell them a little about your own activities (being careful not to leak any confidential or competitively useful information). You might also ask if they are active in any of the same associations as you are, and if so, suggest you look out for each other to "put a face to the name." Then, as a postscript to the conversation, you can ask for advice about other current or imminent staffing needs: "Clare, I'm just about to start a search for a five-year engineer who can . . . Have you run across anyone who could do that?"

It takes no time to ask the question, which may well deliver a qualified candidate, and it gives you more experience in multitasking your business conversations, thereby improving your productivity. If you do get a referral, see if you can return the favor, either now or later.

Employee Referral Programs

Employee referral programs (ERPs) are a company's way of getting formally involved with the networking abilities of its employees as a low-cost recruitment option. Because ERPs are corporate programs, it is unlikely that you are going to develop one on your own, so we are going to restrict ourselves to a brief comment about how you can maximize them if they already exist in your own company.

ERPs typically offer a cash incentive for successful referrals that is awarded to the referring employee, and from which you as a manager are understandably barred. Incentives can vary, and may include prizes (a household appliance, for instance, or a paid vacation) and monetary compensation—from a token sum for help in filling a clerical position, up to several thousand dollars for successful referral of a key professional or management employee.

These programs are usually very effective when first launched, but after a year or so they seem to slip off workers' radar, most often because people forget about them. To be continually successful, they require consistent promotion.

If you do have an ERP at your company, make sure that you have a clear understanding of how it works and are able to explain the submission process to your employees. Then when you have approved openings within the area of your responsibility, you can boost the programs at departmental meetings, with a reminder of the incentives the company offers for successful referrals. It costs you nothing to promote the program and may well put some money in an employee's pocket, for which that worker will be thankful.

However, a degree of caution is suggested. There are quite a few horror stories about employees neglecting their normal duties to become full-time recruiters without anyone asking them to do so. In extreme cases, employees may steal referrals from headhunters and offer them as their own, forcing the employer into a difficult position if the ruse is discovered. On occasion, you'll even hear of an employee who, dissatisfied with the referral bonus offered, channels his or her referral on the sly through an unscrupulous headhunter and ignores the employee referral process completely.

Beyond cloak-and-dagger maneuverings such as these, confidentiality is another stumbling block. When friends and colleagues are referring one another, it's essential that sensitive information, such as salary, be kept strictly confidential.

Keeping all of the potential pitfalls in mind, explain your employee referral program to everyone from the beginning. Address the rules in such a way that misperceptions and opportunistic episodes are kept to a minimum.

If your ERP is fading, you can sometimes give it a boost by using the Grand Prize concept. Every time an employee makes a successful referral, give a nominal financial reward, and enter the name of the person referring the new employee in a drawing for a prize of very high perceived value. At the end of the program, draw the name of the Grand Prize winner.

All parties must recognize that when monetary rewards are paid, the Internal Revenue Service will consider the sums taxable income. Make sure that employees are aware of any deductions well ahead of time. If the company does not make the deductions, inform the employees that the income is taxable and must be handled accordingly. If you ignore these details, the best-intentioned program in the world can lead to misunderstanding, conflict, and morale problems in the work force.

Ex-Employees

Ex-employees can also provide an effective source for networking. When you hear about a much-respected ex-employee, find contact information and get in touch with that person. These people know better than anyone else who might be suitable for your job, and you may even find that some are interested in returning to the fold. Before making contact, though, check with HR about company policy on rehiring and any information about the individual that might be relevant to your recruitment and decision-making process.

This option is gaining such credence that forward-looking companies are now beginning to sponsor online corporate alumni networks.

Customers and Vendors

Managers often have ongoing relationships with customers and vendors as an integral part of the execution of their duties. These customers and vendors might be exterior to the company, or they might also be internal.

The customer/vendor relationship provides opportunities for recruitment networking, and because the parties involved also have a stake in the success of your endeavors, they can be expected to listen with a sympathetic ear. Also, because their professional involvement is contiguous to yours, they can reasonably be expected to come into contact with the kind of people you might need. It is simply a matter of being aware of the multitasking potential of your business interactions.

These are the low-cost, and no-cost, recruitment strategies that everyone can apply to their recruitment needs. From here we move on to recruitment tools that have a price tag attached.

Advertising: Newspapers and the Internet

Recruitment advertising is the logical next step to reach potential employees when existing databases and networking fail to deliver the goods. This is the logical next step because, up to this point, the recruitment process relies entirely on goodwill, unless your company uses an ERP program to reward referrals with cash or gifts. Recruitment advertising marks the first time that you use third-party resources, and advertising is the first of those outside resources to be used because it tends to be cheaper than the alternatives. For your recruitment advertising to be effective, you have to ensure that you have an effective message that reaches the correct audience.

Recruitment advertising usually means newspaper and Internet advertising, although we will address the special uses of radio later in the section. Which of these delivery vehicles you use, and in what proportions, will depend largely on the types of people you are recruiting and the geographic scope of your search. While all companies advertise in both online and print media, with some preferring one over the other, this is a decision that might well vary depending on the position and the recruitment challenge. To give you the most comprehensive overview, we are going to look at recruitment challenges that use both print and the Internet. Some examples:

A national search for a senior professional or management position when relocation has been approved for the position might well include recruitment advertising in one or more of the nation's three newspapers with true national reach to the professional classes: *The Wall Street Journal*, *USA Today*, and *The New York Times*. Such a search would probably also include postings on job sites such as 6figurejobs.com, Netshare.com, and TheLadders.com; the site of the American Management Association; and a site specific to the profession.

A national search for a professional information technology position where relocation has been approved for the position is far more likely to place the print budget with professionally oriented magazines such as *Technology Review*, *Information Technology Advisor*, and *Hispanic Engineer and Information Technology* rather than the big-reach national newspapers. Such a search would probably also include postings on job sites such as dice.com, computerjobs.com, and computerjobsbank.com; the site of a relevant professional association such as the Information Technology Association of America; and perhaps one or more of the nation's three major job sites—Careerbuilder, Hotjobs, and Monster—although you might find such placement gives you too many unqualified candidates.

A national search for ongoing mid-level finance positions where relocation has been approved for the position is likely to include recruitment advertising in one or more of the three national newspapers mentioned previously. It also would include postings on one or more of the nation's three major job sites—Careerbuilder, Hotjobs, and Monster—and a site specific to the profession, such as the American Accounting Association. If postings on the "big three" sites generated too much unqualified response, you would probably migrate to specialist sites such as jobsinthemoney.com, careerbank.com, and accounting.com.

In all instances where technological adaptedness has a role to play, Internet advertising should figure prominently, because it is a self-selecting medium.

Nevertheless, the vast majority of job growth in the country is, and has been for some time, in lower-level in-person-service and construction jobs. So with an example for a customer service position that requires basic phone skills and a high-school diploma, and where relocation is not an issue, your advertising will exclude the big national daily papers, and is likely to focus on your local and local alternative newspapers and penny-saver. It might not be necessary to have an Internet posting at all, unless of course you are a national company with customer service positions available throughout the nation, in which case you naturally choose the "big three" job sites, which are likely to give you the widest coverage.

Print or Internet

Actually, it isn't an either/or decision, because you don't automatically advertise on Hotjobs or in *The Wall Street Journal*; rather, the position you are trying to fill dictates the advertising vehicle(s) most likely to deliver consistently qualified candidates.

With print advertising, you get an ad published, and that is about it; with advertising on the Internet, other recruitment tools are available that might have special value to you in terms of time management and/or managing the recruitment process. The following tools are all available on Internet job sites, but by no means are all tools offered on all sites. As a rule of thumb, the bigger the site, the more recruitment tools will be available. All of these services typically have a price tag attached to them.

Resume Databases to Search by Job Title and Skill Sets

The search engine can be programmed to push resumes matching your needs over a period of time. This is one of the most valuable additional services. Most job sites purge their resume databases every ninety days or so, allowing them to tout the "freshness" of available candidates. Some sites have archives of older resumes available to your search; though overlooked by many, this can be a great recruitment resource.

Advanced Screening

This ranges from applicants completing onscreen prompts in answer to your tailored screening questions to a dedicated counselor who will prescreen and rank, based on your requirements, a couple of handfuls of the best available qualified candidates for that week.

Background Checks

An automated process that, depending on the service, can verify identity, education, driving and credit histories, and criminal record. Note that this is different from a reference check, which requires voice contact and which you should strongly consider doing yourself.

Mass, Targeted E-mails

These are sent to qualified job hunters in the site's resume database, encouraging them to apply for your job opening. Note that most job sites have free push technology for their job hunters, which allows a job hunter to receive notification of all suitable jobs that are posted by employers.

Job Posting of Your Recruitment Ad to Any Number of Other Job Sites

Some sites offer to post your needs to other sites automatically, thus saving you time. You might try this, but if you get too many unqualified responses, you might wish to de-activate this option.

Pre-Employment Testing

Increasingly, psychological and aptitude tests are becoming part of the screening process, and job sites are starting to partner with providers of these tests.

Given your circumstances, any or all of these services can be valuable to you, but before shelling out additional dollars for these services you should verify that they actually deliver the service they promise. Any service is only as good as the provider, so you might want to check the experience of other advertisers on that site.

America's FREE Job Bank

No commentary on advertising and the Internet would be complete without mention of the nation's largest job bank. Run by the Department of Labor, America's Job Bank includes online postings from every local Department of Labor in the nation. You get national coverage for no cost.

There used to be a feeling that posting jobs with the Department of Labor would only generate applications from the terminally unemployed or unemployable, a feeling I once subscribed to, but this is no longer the case. We now live in a world in which every one of us can expect job dislocation at some point, and this site is heavy with traffic from across the professional spectrum. It's a smart cost-free move to post your needs at *www.ajb.dni.us.*

Appendix B at the end of this book gives you a wide selection of tried and proven sites that will be helpful for most of your manpower needs. Your unique requirements will determine exactly which site is best suited to you; this is a decision that might take a couple of hires to clearly determine. Of course, recruitment networking will always give you an edge, while saving time and money.

Creating the Message

Now that you understand that advertising vehicles can change radically depending on your particular needs of the moment, we progress to the recruitment message. Here it becomes a case of the more things change, the more they stay the same.

While you may be advertising in print, on the Internet, or both, your message still needs to stand out from all the other companies that are looking for the same kind of employee. Both media are crowded, and in both media it comes down to creating an arresting message.

An average Sunday newspaper can carry a dozen pages of employment-oriented advertising, and each of those pages is likely to feature more than a hundred advertisements. Advertising on an Internet job site presents the same challenge, though instead of initially flipping newspaper pages, the user keys in a job title and is subsequently presented with pages of competing ads. While these advertising media are different in the way they deliver the message, the message shared is still the same: "Hey you, come work for us!"

Recruiting for Today and Tomorrow

Your recruitment ads are typically going to be in competition with those of many hundreds of other companies, so how will your needs stand out in the crowd?

Your challenge is comparable to that faced by the proprietor of a single boutique situated in a suburban mega-mall. While being situated in the mall (or, in your case, a newspaper help-wanted section or Internet job site) is a sensible marketing decision because of the volume of foot traffic, the challenge is to find a way to draw both the serious shopper and the casual browser through the door. Always remember that today's casual browser is tomorrow's serious shopper. That highly qualified candidate who contacts you in the midst of a serious, systematic job search may be of greatest interest to you now, but the one who is "just looking" at the opportunities you have to offer may also prove valuable to you a few weeks or months down the road.

Critics of advertising have claimed that only the unemployed and employed but chronically dissatisfied read recruitment advertisements (either in print or online), and that all the advertiser can expect to hear from are the dregs of the work force. This is not true: we live in an insecure world of work, in which savvy professionals increasingly keep a weather eye on suitable opportunities in the job market.

Advertising agencies recognize the importance of recruitment advertising as a way to reach today's job hunter, and also point to it as an effective public relations tool and promotional device to identify and brand the company as a desirable place to work, and in the process attract tomorrow's job hunter.

With a primary focus on attracting today's job hunter, but with an eye cocked at tomorrow's, it all begins with grabbing the reader's attention and getting your message read with something like serious attention.

Grab the Reader's Attention

The first step in getting a response to your advertisement is to get it read, and that can depend in a large part on the headline: a good grabber will win readers. Advertising copywriters who specialize in recruitment advertising follow three headline rules:

▶ While the headline doesn't have to be witty, it must address your audience.

▶ The headline must promote qualities that are likely to appeal to the reader.

▶ The headline must mention the job title.

For example:

Executive Administrator to CEO—Core of the Executive Team

---

or

Financial Stock Administrator—Right Place, Right Time

Neither of these examples is witty—best to leave that to the professional copywriters—but both do mention the title, and both speak to the individual's sense of professional self.

In print, you may have the option to use a distinctive type that helps your ad stand out. Online, you are more likely to be restricted to the use of caps and the bolding of your headline to draw attention to your ad.

The Message

The headline wins attention, but it is the message in the body copy that encourages the reader to take the next step of applying for a chance to work at your company.

To write an effective advertisement, you will need all the facts at hand: all the "must-haves" and all the "nice to haves" that you'd like to see in the candidate, as well as all the pluses about the job and the company. Writing one or two sentences about each of the following headings might help you focus.

- Job title
- Type of work
- Major skills required
- Educational requirements
- Location
- Company selling points
- Training
- Personal development/career progression opportunities
- Equipment
- Environment
- Work conditions
- Salary, benefits, and other incentives

The end product of this exercise will give you the information you'll need to craft compelling print or Internet recruitment ads.

The Job

The description of the work to be done is of major importance; the reader wants to know if a good match exists just as much as you do. You need to include information about the responsibilities, of course, but at the same time you can excite the reader by talking about what he or she will be doing, rather than what experience is necessary. In the following examples we are going to use Internet recruitment copy because it is less word restrictive. Be aware that you will have to considerably pare down the copy for newspaper and trade journal advertising.

Experienced Exec Admin to CEO—Core of the Executive Team
Give your career a change in latitude! As the extension of the CEO you will take ownership of the executive support process with your never-ending can-do (and must-do) attitude.

---

or

Financial Stock Administrator—Right Place, Right Time
Direct the successful administration of global stock option programs, employee stock purchase plans, and director equity plans at a time when _____'s cutting-edge information retrieval technology has never been more in demand.

The more "must-haves" you put in an ad, the more potential respondents you will lose. Even the "minimum standard" of a degree is somewhat suspect. Why rule out those competent professionals who might otherwise be acceptable, especially considering that some will be engaged in gaining that degree?

To find the best employees and have the best candidate pool, cast your net wide and use an exceptionally fine mesh. Make advertisements "specifically vague" and future oriented, as we see in the following two examples. Recruitment ads draw best when they are specific enough to whet the appetite to know more, but vague enough to keep people from ruling themselves out; they work best when talking about challenges and opportunities rather than those imposing "must-haves." There will be time to separate the winners from the losers later, and remember, the losers for this particular position may be shoo-ins for next month's openings.

The copy can be enticing, talking about what the new employee will be doing and how that person's presence can make a difference to the company. From the Stock Administrator position:

> Your impact on our organization will be significant in several ways. From an accounting perspective, you'll play a key role in quarter-end financial preparation. From a communications standpoint, you'll ensure that all employees understand the value of the stock benefit plans that can be a significant part of their total compensation package. There will also be opportunities for you to stretch your skills by contributing to treasury activities such as cash management. Attendance at yearly NASPP conferences and monthly lunch meetings focused on professional development will further enhance your expertise and ensure your success in this career opportunity.

And from the Executive Administrator:

> You will wear countless hats—executive communication, human resources, investor relations, and numerous others. You are not just a schedule keeper, but a true part of the executive team. Your responsibilities and compensation will reflect your value to the CEO and CFO.

The body copy of the advertisement, then, should address the job in terms of the opportunities it offers. It's okay to include mandatory requirements once the reader is engaged with reading about the opportunity.

From the Stock Administrator position:

> You'll leverage, ideally, a Certified Equity Professional (CEP) designation, plus deep skills in accounting and a strong aptitude with Equity Edge software to drive financial reporting of _____ equity compensation plans. To hit the ground running, you'll need very strong Equity Edge, OptionsLink, and MS-Excel skills, including the ability to run macros and system imports and exports. Bonus points for those who have worked with Oracle Discoverer and MS-Access.

And from the Executive Administrator:

> Strong organizational skills and expertise in Microsoft Office skills are just the basic requirements of the position.

The ad should talk up the company as a desirable place to work. Never assume that your company is either a household word or is generally recognized as a great employer. Instead, consistently use your help-wanted advertisements as a public relations vehicle to send the message that your company is progressive, professional, and a terrific place to work.

From the Stock Administrator position:

> There will also be opportunities for you to stretch your skills by contributing to treasury activities such as cash management. Attendance at yearly NASPP conferences and monthly lunch meetings focused on professional development will further enhance your expertise and ensure your success in this career opportunity.
>
> _____ is a leading enterprise solutions provider helping organizations maximize the return on their investment in "intellectual capital." This is a tremendous opportunity to join a stable, financially profitable company, while expanding the breadth of your skills into what normally are treasury-related functions.

And from the Executive Assistant position:

> You will support the Executive Leader of a visionary, high-profile, whirlwind-paced company. You will often serve as the "face" of _____ as you work with our customers, investors, and management, and your understanding of the CEO's style and direction will keep the company's message on course.

The body copy of your print and Internet advertisements should address the job in terms of the opportunities it offers, and the performance expected. When you emphasize performance over skill sets, you will self-select the more results-oriented candidates.

In writing your advertisement, get the copy down and then edit to remove repetitions and redundancies. While online advertising allows you all the space you need to sell the job and the company, print advertising has more stringent space restrictions, so you'll need to edit your copy down to the fit number of words or the amount of space that is affordable.

Whenever possible, cut impotent words and phrases. As you read the first draft of your ad, you may come across phrases such as, "Applications are invited for the position of . . ." This is a waste of space, advertising money, and the reader's attention. Of course applications are invited for the position in question; why else is someone paying to have a recruitment ad published?

Never use gender-specific structure, such as "the right applicant will find his salary and benefits package extremely competitive." Not only is this sexist and illegal; it also turns off precious potential applicants. Better to make it personal and talk in terms of "you."

In the process of identifying how you will sell the job via advertising, you have also helped yourself prepare for selling the job when you meet that ideal candidate. By becoming engaged in the recruitment process, you have more clearly defined your needs and enhanced your ability to sell the job when the time comes.

Money Talks

Whether or not to include salary in the ad is a difficult question. Doing so can be imprudent: If current employees earning considerably less see the ad and realize that you are prepared to pay more for outsiders, you may have trouble in the ranks. In these situations, the position you are trying to fill has, all too often, been vacated by someone who was unhappy and moved on to greener pastures. Whether or not this is the case, though, there is little point in losing the goodwill of the people you have trained and nurtured. If, however, everyone works within fair and equitable salary guidelines, and assuming that salary is competitive, mentioning it can only help attract candidates.

Remember, too, that advertisements that do not include some mention of remuneration are thought to get only half the response rate of ads that do mention money. While you can improve the number of inquiries by specifying an exact salary, you can include something such as "Salary range starts at $30,000; the right candidate can expect a salary and benefit package commensurate with experience."

Other options would include "Competitive salary," "Salary dependent upon experience," and "Excellent salary for the right candidate." While these are not as effective as mentioning specific dollar ranges, they are infinitely preferable to making no mention whatsoever of money. Ultimately this is a judgment call based on your particular circumstances.

Encourage a Response

Of course, your advertisement can include all the right inducements about the job, money, and opportunity, and still not get the kind of response you want and deserve. You can increase response rate by how you ask applicants to respond. If you want to keep things nice and quiet around the HR office, use something along these lines: "Send resume with six references to Box 983452."

On the other hand, if you want applications, consider: "Let's get together. Call Sam Corker at 617/755-3465 to arrange a meeting, e-mail to *jobs@acme.com*, or send a resume to Acme at PO Box 98345, Ocean Point, NY 11759." Options for contact not only increase response; it also keeps you on the right side of the law. Featuring only one means of application in your advertisement can be problematic from a legal standpoint (not that it always will be, but it may), as it does not take into account the new requirements of the Americans with Disabilities Act, which mandates equal access for hearing-impaired and other disabled workers.

When Should You Advertise?

The answer here is really very simple. Online you purchase an ad (or posting, as it is often referred to in the online world) to run for thirty, sixty, or ninety days. In print you can do the same thing, but you pay in multiples of the editions of the publication in which your advertisement appears. Job hunters always read the Sunday editions of newspapers, which carry the heaviest recruitment advertising. There may be one additional day that pulls exceptionally well for recruitment in your local metropolitan newspaper. In New York City, for instance, Wednesday is a big day for secretarial advertising. Tuesday, Wednesday, and Thursday are usually your best candidates for the add-on day. The advertising sales staff at any newspaper or magazine can tell you which editions pull the heaviest readership.

Other Print Advertising

There are alternatives for print advertising, including pennysavers and association and trade publications.

Pennysavers are the independent classified and help-wanted publications that are usually distributed free in and around major metropolitan areas. They include a significant amount of recruitment advertising, and can be effective recruitment tools for low skill-level jobs, but beyond this they have little relevance. On the other hand, *professional association and trade publications* in print and their sister sites on the Internet can be very effective tools for filing professional positions; you won't get the same volume of response, but it is likely to be far more targeted.

Placement on the page is vitally important in print media, especially when you are placing ads outside of the recruitment section. Following is a list, in descending order, of the best page positions to have in magazines:

> First right-hand page

> Back cover

> Inside front cover

> Page facing contents

> Inside rear cover

> Page facing cover article

> Page facing inside rear cover

> Early right-hand page

> Early left-hand page

Alternative Internet Advertising

We spoke earlier in the chapter about networking on the Internet with communities that share similar professional, skill, or industry interests as an effective way for geographically dispersed people with similar interests to establish community. If you keep your eyes open while networking via the Internet, you will find groups where you can advertise for a fraction of what it might cost you to advertise on one of the big job sites or in a national newspaper. Specifically, we talked about professional associations, professional networking sites, alumni groups, Web forums, user groups, and discussion groups.

All of these groups can offer traditional and nontraditional recruitment advertising opportunities. With most of these sites you will find an established procedure for posting jobs, almost always under the aegis of a commercial agreement.

At these sites you will also find many, but not all, of the sponsored user and discussion groups. You should never post job openings in any of these venues without permission, as many of them are concerned about turning into yet another job board.

When you are a member and active participant in these groups, there will also be a couple of options available to you through the moderators. For example, they might mention your need in their regular or special posts, or send an e-mail to members on your behalf.

Much depends on the nature of the group and your relationship with the group. You may be seen to be involved and a good citizen, perhaps through volunteering on group projects that have a professional payoff to you outside of your involvement, or by encouraging other experts to bring special knowledge to the group. Many things become possible when you are seen as a productive member of any professionally related community.

If you take your profession seriously, you will find one or two groups that help advance your professionalism and thereby your career, and in this way you will become an involved member. When this happens, you can nurture those groups as ongoing recruitment resources and, when the time comes, as networking resources for your own survival and advancement.

Radio

Radio has proven effective for many companies as a recruitment medium, but only when the objective is to fill multiple openings. It is prohibitively expensive for single hires. If you are not involved or likely to be involved in mass hiring, this section will best serve you when some idiot suggests using the local rock station to hire three customer service reps, "because Acme did it last year."

If your company is involved in a mass hiring, which these days will be big news in your community anyway, the most attractive aspect of radio is its ability to help you target your market precisely. A radio station's format is carefully structured to attract a certain type of listener for the specific purpose of selling air time to advertisers. This means that if you wish to reach people over the age of eighteen and younger than twenty-five with at least a high school diploma (or any other similar profile), radio can do it for you. Radio advertising can be a great recruitment method when you want to call the audience to action; specifically, it is effective if you want to invite people to an open house, to see you at an upcoming job fair, or to direct potential applicants to your advertisement in a newspaper or on your company Web site. Bear in mind that radio often catches the listener at a time when jotting down a telephone number is impractical (for instance, during the drive home). You can make your telephone number more memorable by obtaining a vanity number; typically, this costs only around $40 a year. Which is easier to retain: 312-555-9873 or 312-555-JOBS?

Are radio campaigns expensive? They certainly can be. The price per minute may not seem overwhelming, but the problem is that one radio spot is more or less useless. Radio advertising requires constant repetition if it is to be effective. Even considering the costs involved, however, it is a good vehicle for many firms. The rule of thumb is that a campaign should last a minimum of a week and feature no fewer than thirty separate spots. The accepted technique is to blitz the audience, rest, then blitz again. It is worth noting here in passing that television has yet to prove itself as an effective recruitment medium, although some cities do have free postings on their community access programming. It's great that it's free, but don't hold your breath waiting for results.

Job Fairs

Job fairs or career fairs are real-world or Internet-based events where groups of companies with multiple openings gather together for a limited time period, often for just one day. When you key in "job fairs" on an Internet search engine, you get leads to local job fairs and also invitations to visit job sites where "there's a job fair every day." These fairs may be set up as a cooperative effort among a group of companies, by a newspaper, by an Internet company providing an additional service to their clients, as a profit-making enterprise by a professional job fair company, or even by the local chamber of commerce.

Job fairs may be geared to a particular profession, to diverse employers in a particular geography, or to a level of employee. The most effective job fairs seem to be those geared toward recruiting entry-level employees.

When you rent a booth at a job fair, what are you getting for the $500 to $5,000 you will pay? Essentially, you are buying into a giant advertising campaign in the hope that it will draw enough attendees to justify your participation.

Job fairs do a ton of repeat business, which is evidence enough of their success. However, the fact that these fairs are successful for the proprietors does not mean that they are necessary right for finding the types of people *you* are looking for at any given time. It isn't enough to ask the promoter, "Say, do your fairs tend to pull swamp gas reciprocation engineers and methane throttle specialists?" The answer will invariably be "yes"; the promoter is out to make things look as good as possible to you, and, with 2,000 to 10,000 people wandering through the door, those types of applicants may occasionally show up at the fair. The question is not whether *any* of the types of applicants you want will attend, but *how many*. Fairs geared toward a specific type of worker are usually the most successful, because they make it easier to reach a clearly definable type of worker.

The secret is to look at the types of positions you have recruited for successfully *without* using job fairs. If the task at hand requires you to recruit outside that area, then consider attending a job fair, but make sure it is one at which these types of people have been recruited successfully in the past.

It is also advisable to ask what the promoter will do to attract the types of people you need. Virtually all job fair companies have developed extensive mailing lists; in fact, a part of their budget is always set aside for direct mail and e-mail campaigns. You can ask the promoter to insert something for you in the mailings that are sent out to promote the fair.

Bear in mind that while smaller job fair companies may promise you the moon and give every good effort, they often don't have the resources necessary to mount a sustained campaign and build a good following. Local radio is often used to drive potential attendees to the fair, and that can be expensive. Established companies, by contrast, will have larger client bases, extensive mailing lists, and comparatively deeper pockets (an important consideration, since you are buying into a promotional event). The exception here would be the job fair put on by your local chamber of commerce; these organizations have been known to sponsor high-visibility fairs that are quite cost-effective.

When attending a job fair as an exhibitor, you must present your company attractively, and with exactly as much attention to concerns of buyer perception and public relations as that of any consumer products or advertising firm. A handmade paper banner and a pile of application forms simply won't do the job; you and your company must be packaged for the event.

Make sure that your booth looks top-notch, that the people representing your firm are articulate, polite, and professional, and that everyone involved understands a clear approach to the recruitment process. It's worth noting that few if any hires are made at the booth, as the objective is to generate applications and resumes and follow up on them later. You will nevertheless be screening potential employees into, or out of, consideration in the short conversations you have at the booth.

Disadvantages to job fairs include their occasional logistical problems. These fairs can be (and often are) adversely affected by the weather. Even with an indoor facility, attendance may plummet when there is a thunderstorm or snow. Because the advertising is usually geared toward a specific time and place, it is highly unlikely that rain dates, guarantees, or refunds will be part of the package.

Job fairs, then, can be effective, but even insiders agree that they are not the be-all and end-all recruitment solution some might suggest. They should be considered one part of a balanced recruitment program; used intelligently, they can enhance your company's image and recognition in the marketplace at the same time that they are generating resumes. As one participant told me, "The best reason to exhibit at a job fair is not so much to get employees—although it does do that—but rather to get exposure and let the workers in the area know that my company exists and is a good place to work. That way, when they read my ad, or when my recruiter or headhunter calls, they know who we are. We're no longer an unknown quantity."

University Internship/Co-op Programs

For the prudent manager eager to enhance company stability over the long term, campus recruitment and organized co-op/internship programs offer extremely attractive recruitment opportunities for entry-level positions.

Traditionally, co-ops have meant major companies visiting campuses and selecting students to work for them through a semester or more, part-time throughout their entire college experience, or maybe just through their vacation breaks. You really can tailor these programs to your precise needs. The intern experience benefits both parties. The student gets work experience, a more competitive resume, references, and eventually, a higher starting salary that reflects work experience. You get the opportunity to handpick key future players, after having them under close scrutiny for a considerable period.

These days, it is not just the larger companies that stand to benefit from the flexibility of these programs; they are available to companies of all sizes.

If you decide to start an internship program, the career services offices of colleges and universities will be eager to help you get things moving. Whether the institution in question is a prestigious Ivy League school or a local two-year community college, the administrators realize that their ability to place their alumni when their studies are finished will dramatically affect the school's ability to attract future students. You are virtually assured of a warm reception and a helping hand from the schools you approach.

Even if you need only one or two people a year, virtually any college or university career planning officer will work with you. All it takes is a telephone call to the career services office; after an initial consultation, referrals can start within a week. With the increase of mature students continuing their education, or re-careering, tapping into career services as a recruitment resource makes increasing sense for recruitment at all but the highest levels.

Of course, there are challenges for both sides in this kind of endeavor. Students sometimes don't want to put off graduation by doing full-time internships unless they fully grasp how their commitment will give them a fast-track start in the professional world, and companies may experience short-term scheduling and management problems while breaking the young professionals in to the realities of professional responsibility. But adjustments can be made, and the potential benefits far outweigh the challenges.

There is no point in initiating co-op or internship programs if you treat the students like slave labor; if this is the prevailing attitude, you will defeat the undertaking's purpose. Your interns need to feel useful, accepted, and appreciated. There is no point in bringing them onboard to make the coffee and empty the trash cans, because they will simply reject your offers of full-time employment and spread ill will to other students and to the career services office. If, on the other hand, you offer challenging work and a learning experience, equitable pay (career services will help you here), and a good measure of professional respect, you will establish firm foundations for an ongoing college recruitment program.

Interview potential interns just as you would other job candidates, against a carefully developed job description, and with an intelligently conceived roster of behavior-based questions. We'll talk about behavioral interviewing later in the book, and you'll also find a whole section of questions that are useful when interviewing candidates who don't have much experience or a track record.

The Local Department of Labor as a Recruitment Source

Early in the chapter, we discussed not making the mistake of overlooking the U.S. Department of Labor's excellent Web site, America's Job Bank. You can also do yourself a grave injustice if you overlook your local department of labor as a recruitment resource. No matter what sort of employee you are looking for, contact with your local department will give you someone assigned to your needs, who will actively search for registered workers who match those requirements.

To tap into this resource effectively, you have to do more than make contact and register your needs; you have to apply a little psychology. You will be assigned a caseworker responsible for monitoring and helping you fill needs as they come along. Although this person is a government worker, he or she still has performance quotas and a boss to please, and therefore will usually be as eager as the next person to prove productivity to management. Help your contact to perform well, and you can get yourself a sincere and motivated extension to your recruitment efforts.

Important to your success in developing a win-win relationship is an understanding of what demotivates government workers. Heading the list is the awful feeling that all of one's good efforts *have always gone and will always go unnoticed*. When convinced that their work will make a difference to the people they refer and the employers they refer them to, these contacts will exhibit the attention, motivation, and persistence you associate with the private sector.

While your local department of labor and America's Job Bank can help you with positions at all levels and in most professions, they can be especially helpful with multiple hiring needs for skilled, semiskilled, and unskilled workers. Consider the following story:

A major computer memory company in Silicon Valley was faced with a problem: serious labor shortfalls in unskilled and semiskilled labor. Turnover approached 40 percent, even though double minimum wage was the starting point for the company's unskilled workers, and even though the benefits and surroundings were among the best in the area. Advertising hadn't worked; job fairs hadn't, either. There wasn't a headhunter to be found who would consider a search for workers in the categories in question.

What was left to do? The only option left was the local department of labor's unemployment office, which was long felt by the company to be irrelevant to its needs. In desperation, the manager made a call and explained the problem in a straightforward way. No one had any right to expect that it would work out as well as it did—thirty-five good hires—or as fast as it did: the company went from shortfall to waiting-list status in a matter of months. The kicker is that in hiring this way, the firm actually built up tax credits that reached six figures by the end of a twelve-month period! So hires in this area end up making money and solving the staffing shortfall. This resource might not be right for every need, but it is worth the time of your investigative phone call.

Employment Services

Corporations choose their lawyers, their accountants, their advertising agencies, and their public relations firms with care and prudence. All of these outside professionals are important to the success of the company. Yet when it comes time to choose an outside employment service—vendors who supply the employees who are the lifeblood of an organization—the attitude is often downright cavalier, and this needs to change.

There are distinctly different types of employment services. Here is the basic breakdown:

- Permanent employment agencies to which the candidate pays the fee

- Permanent employment agencies to which the employer pays the fee

- Retained/executive search firms, to which the company pays a retainer for the firm to work on the assignment and picks up search expenses

- Contingency search firms, to which the company pays the fee if and when a suitable candidate is hired (though expenses are occasionally charged)

The vast majority of employment service companies work under an arrangement whereby the company pays the fees. Each of the major employer-paid categories performs a slightly different service.

Employment agencies provide services similar to companies in the other two categories, but for the most part the employment agencies restrict their activities to the local job market. A traditional employment agency will not only actively recruit on your assignments, but will also do extensive advertising both in newspapers and on the Internet at its own Web site and on the major job boards.

These firms are market oriented, and will frequently present the same candidate to you that they present to other interested parties. To avoid a bidding war for the best talent, move fast, refuse to get involved in salary-escalating games, and develop a good relationship with key players at the agencies of your choice. You may eventually win a measure of exclusivity when it comes to the best candidates.

The retained/executive search firm charges a retainer based on the first-year remuneration package, typically one-third on signing, one-third on presentation of the short list, and one-third on completion. Expenses are often prorated; there is no refund if the search is unsuccessful. Only you can determine when to say the search hasn't succeeded, however; the search firm can be counted on to continue the assignment for a considerable period of time. Firms in this category will only present candidates to fill a special assignment or opening, which means that you won't hear about someone who may be right for you somewhere down the line.

These firms are most effective for those positions that pay over $100,000 yearly. A number of the better ones are members of the National Association of Executive Recruiters.

The contingency search firm provides essentially the same services as the retained variety, but a fee is only paid by the employer upon successful completion of a search, and there is only occasionally an attempt to charge expenses. Clients frequently use more than one such firm at a time. Many of the companies in this category will present you with the opportunity to see candidates outside of the specific area you've requested if they feel you might have an interest in those people. Contingency search firms are most effective for positions that range from $25,000 to $150,000.

This category makes up the single largest sector of the employment services community. With more than 21,000 such companies out there, the quality, as you might imagine, can vary dramatically from company to company.

Choosing an Employment Services Company

So which type of employment services company is best for you? The one that will get you the right employees in the most professional and hassle-free manner. Every manager has different needs, and often at different levels and in different disciplines, so it might take some experimenting before you identify the recruitment resource that is right for you. With that in mind, let's examine a few myths that surround the employment industry.

First of all, a retained/executive search firm is not necessarily any better or more professional than any other employment firm. Each category has its exemplary practitioners and its charlatans. Your goal should be to establish good relations with a handful of firms within each of these categories. You should also try to avoid antagonizing employment services people, unless you want your staff targeted as a recruitment resource!

Ask plenty of questions in your efforts to separate the employment services wheat from the chaff. How long has the firm been in business? What are the professional qualifications of both principal and individual consultants? A company's involvement in professional associations is always a good sign. It demonstrates commitment and, since these associations usually offer extensive professional training programs, can indicate a greater degree of competence than you will find in other companies.

In the employment services industry, the National Association of Personnel Services is the premier professional organization, with state associations in all fifty states. Reputable retained and contingency firms and employment agencies are represented in the members of this organization, which provides extensive training programs and maintains a strict code of ethics.

You should also ask if your contact has CPC designation, which stands for Certified Personnel Consultant. The international equivalent is the Certified International Personnel Consultant, or CIPC. CPC and CIPC designations, which represent the only professional accreditations in the field, are recognized as standards of excellence and commitment, and are only achieved after rigorous training and study. Even the newest holders of CPC designation will have approximately five years of experience, with the average running between seven and ten years for all holders. It is to your advantage to find a CPC with experience in the particular field you are hoping to hire in. Not only will the communication be easier than with someone outside your field, but also the contacts at your disposal will be better.

Qualified CPCs can be relied upon to have superior knowledge of the legalities and ethics of the recruitment and hiring process, as well as the expertise that only comes from years of hands-on experience. Needless to say, these are advantages that you will want to have on your side during a search. A listing of all current CPC designates who are also members of the National Association of Personnel Services *(www.recruitinglife.com)* is available at the association Web site. Look for links to third-party recruitment resources in Appendix B and at knockemdead.com.

Working with Employment Services

In working with any outside employment services provider, first find out whether there is company policy that governs your relationships with these vendors. Your company may wish you to work with certain companies, or may give you a complete free rein. Even when you have to work with approved vendors, your success will come down to the individual headhunters you choose and the way you manage the ensuing relationship. Here are some sensible guidelines for nurturing a productive relationship:

▶ You can't work with everyone, so ask for current client references from everyone who pitches you. If you're working with employment agencies and contingency headhunters, establish relationships with two to six individuals; more than six will swamp you with calls.

▶ Establish written agreements on fees and guarantees, the percentage of annual salary you will pay as a fee, due dates of such fees, and the length of time the placement of the worker is guaranteed.

This guarantee period varies depending on the size of the fee, often ranging from ninety days to up to a year for higher levels.

- At senior levels, where fees based on annual salary can get stratospheric, it is possible to negotiate a fee cap.

- Establish written agreements about who will actually do the work. Don't automatically assume that the people you meet will be the ones doing the work.

- Check references on the individual headhunter/employment counselor as well as the company, because your relationship can only be as good as the person working on your search needs.

- If you wish to encourage diversity within your department, you should mention this to your headhunter(s).

- If you expect resumes and plan on telephone screening interviews, establish this at the outset.

- Ask for a contract stipulating that the headhunter's company will not recruit from your firm for a specific period. Whether you can swing this will depend on how much business is going their way, but it doesn't hurt to make the request.

In a retained search, for which you pay significant monies up-front that will not be returned in the event of an unsuccessful outcome, you can expect and should ask for more:

- Obtain a written list of companies with whom they have exclusive recruitment agreements (forbidding them to use those companies as recruitment resources), and from whom you cannot expect to see candidates; remember to do this *before* you sign contracts.

- Establish before the search starts that you will receive and approve written job descriptions, including all necessary competencies and the work experiences in which these competencies will have blossomed.

- Because people respect what you inspect, require a weekly briefing on the status of the search.

- Require reference checks, including any specific areas you feel are important. This does not mean that you will fail to make the time to check final references.

Above and beyond these basic requirements, you need to play your part in nurturing the relationship. With a retained search, in which you and the headhunter are tied together financially from the outset, there is already a shared interest and the expectation of a successful outcome. When working with contingency recruiters and employment agencies this is not the case; in this latter instance you will need to do your share to encourage a productive relationship. In a contingency relationship, the headhunter will put most effort into those relationships in which the client is honest, to the point, courteous, and who either takes telephone calls or returns those calls promptly.

Executive Search Research Companies

Some headhunters do their own sourcing (especially contingency recruiters), but when you get into the more senior levels of search, dominated by the retained search companies, you usually find that they either have dedicated sourcing departments, or they outsource the research to a third-party company specializing in locating potential candidates.

These companies, which are known as search research companies, typically work on a billable-hours basis, generating a candidate list based on the headhunter's specifications. In most instances they will be capable of handling other aspects of the recruitment process, such as initial candidate qualification and reference checking. These researchers work from their own databases and contact lists, and they also rely heavily on data-mining software, which allows "spiders" to crawl the Web seeking resumes using keywords from your job description. There is nothing to stop you using either of these approaches, and in doing so you would be cutting out the middleman (the headhunter) and perhaps containing your costs a little more efficiently. This approach is not for everyone, however, especially the harried line manager filling just a few positions a year. It is perhaps of more interest to the small and overworked Human Resources department that has some dedicated resources to manage the product. Sifting through the results of data mining can be a Herculean task.

A good resource for search research companies is *The Executive Research Directory*, published by Ken Cole, who also publishes *The Executive Search Directory*. These books are available directly from the publisher: Ken Cole Publications, Box 9433, Panama City Beach, FL 32417. Alternatively, your IT department would be the best place to gather information about the wisdom and costs of doing your own data mining for resumes via data-mining software.

Non-Permanent Recruitment Solutions

Temporary-help services have long been an integral part of the corporate world for job titles from light industrial to interim CEOs. Your company almost certainly has established relationships with local providers, usually managed through your Human Resources department.

Prior to hiring temporary workers, you may find it helpful to analyze how you are using your own current employees. Where practical, you may want to consider assigning less desirable tasks to temps, thereby freeing permanent staff for more rewarding work. Define which tasks are best performed by permanent staff and which you can allocate to interim people.

Bear in mind that the temporary staffing business has two separate arms: the salespeople (whom you see, and who promise the moon), and the production people (whose job it is to make good on those promises). Always ask such firms for references—then check the references, particularly those in businesses similar to yours. Such references will be more relevant, and you will expand your own professional networks.

How does the temp company recruit and retain employees and thereby ensure that it provides a qualified work force? Ask to see the organization's recruitment package; benefits and training offered to temporary workers can go a long way toward determining a temp's productivity once inside your place of business. You'll want to know how the temporary-help company assesses the capabilities of the workers it places. Temporary employees need to know enough about your business to be able to test for the work that needs to be done; don't be shy about asking for a detailed rundown on the screening and selection procedure, and don't let the firm fob off nonspecific answers.

Can you approve the selection before the person starts work? Any reputable company will send you qualifications summaries or resumes of the temps they have in mind. These days, temps do a lot more than fill in while you hire that permanent employee, and so there is an increasing necessity to interview the potential temps yourself before you hire them—especially if you are considering using the temporary assignment as a way to audition future permanent hires.

Does the temporary-help company offer a service guarantee? If the interim person doesn't work out, you won't want to wait around forever for someone new. The company should be able to send you a replacement quickly and with no fuss.

Many professional associations, including the National Association of Temporary and Staffing Services and the National Staff Leasing Association, require adherence to strict codes of ethics and performance standards for membership. I am a strong advocate of dealing with members of recognized professional associations; the practice gives you increased levels of confidence in your people and channels of recourse if there are problems.

Temporary-to-Permanent

You also have the option to hire a temporary worker on a full-time basis. Increasingly, the temporary-help option is seen as a viable means of evaluating potential full-time employees on the job without risk or obligation. In Europe, this "temp-to-perm conversion" (as you will hear it referred to when you want to hire a temp on a full-time basis) accounts for 35 percent of all hires. Just as we followed Europe in our initial use of temporary help, we seem likely to follow in this trend as well; in America the ratio is running about 25 percent and growing. The approach is a fiscally prudent and professionally savvy way to maintain company flexibility and minimize the liabilities associated with employee termination, especially during turbulent economic times.

Using this option to "try before you buy" has become increasingly popular, and with outsourcing and automation creating an increasingly dislocated professional work force, the chances of finding a temporary worker suitable for your permanent position are better than ever.

You will be charged a conversion fee if you decide to hire a temporary employee on a permanent basis, and because all temp companies expect this to happen, a temp-to-perm cost schedule is usually available.

If you intend to use temporary help as part of your approach to full-time recruitment, your relationship with the individual service provider is very important to your success in finding a temporary employee suitable for conversion. Explain that you are looking to fill a full-time slot and get a clear understanding of the conversion costs. Because the skills and motivation of an ideal permanent employee will differ from those of an acceptable temp worker, you improve your odds by clearly explaining your recruitment needs, just as you would to a headhunter. With a clear picture of your needs, the temporary services consultant (who will get part of the additional fee from the temp-to-perm conversion) will be far better equipped, and more motivated, to send you the very best of the firm's available people. You might suggest their cycling through different temps every two or three weeks to give you a selection of candidates, with you retaining the option to cycle someone out just as soon as you are sure that the person is not suitable for the full-time position.

The temp-to-perm approach will, at the very least, get you the best possible help on a temporary basis, and the opportunity to "test-drive" a selection of candidates for your permanent position, without obligation.

Independent Contractors and Consulting Companies

Independent contractors/consultants are also accustomed to coming up to speed quickly—and they can make it their business to learn your organization and methods in short order. In some circumstances they can offer an alternative to a hasty permanent hire in a position that is difficult to fill.

Follow the same standards for securing consultants as you would for selecting a full-time employee or a temporary services firm. Check references and interview people carefully, examining their capabilities to ensure that they can meet your needs of ability, motivation, and manageability.

Whether you hire a solo practitioner or a 500-person consulting firm, rehiring people for future projects offers some distinct advantages. During the first project, the contractor will gain an in-depth understanding of your company, your industry, and your market. Consequently, that education and orientation won't need to be paid for twice. Prior training can be just as important for independent contractors as it is for temporary help. Contractors or consultants who make an ongoing effort to upgrade their expertise, whether through continuing education, professional affiliations, or knowledge of new technologies, demonstrate a commitment and professionalism that they are likely to carry into your business. The same can be said if they maintain certifications, licensures, and membership in professional organizations. You can inquire into all of these areas during the interview cycle.

Staff Leasing

Staff leasing, while often lumped into the contingency work force category, does not actually meet the usual definition: "contingent upon the need of the employer." But the option is worth examining. Usually, under this arrangement, a company fires employees, who are then hired by an employee-leasing firm. The employees continue to work at the original workplace, but it is the leasing company that is responsible for meeting all government reporting and regulatory requirements, providing benefits, executing the details of any hiring and firings necessary, and paying salaries. In many cases, because the leasing company has the leverage of many more employees, insurance becomes more affordable and provides better coverage. (The original employer generally retains some degree of say in matters of hiring, evaluation, promotion, and termination.)

Most employers contract for these services because they want to retain their full-time employees minus the administrative burden and cost, not because the work is sporadic, short-term, or incompatible with a permanent work force. Prudent operations of all sizes, but especially smaller companies, are now looking closely at the staff leasing option.

Widening the Candidate Pool

So far in this section we have discussed ways to reach candidates. Now we'll talk about ways to widen the pool of qualified applicants.

Flex Hours and Job Sharing

Most people, when asked to think of the typical American family, still envision a working father, a mother who is the homemaker, and perhaps two children. In fact, this picture hasn't truly reflected life in America since the 1960s. Today, only 5 percent of all American families fit this description.

There is no average household anymore: It is estimated that the majority of the people entering the work force through the coming years will be women and minorities. Nowadays most married couples work and try to raise a family; single parents, by some estimates, constitute more than 30 percent of the work force; and elder care is becoming an increasing reality for a plurality of Americans. For these reasons, many of today's workers will provide anything but a "traditional" profile. As an employer you need to be open to the opportunities these realities provide.

Flexible work schedules are perhaps the most effective of the alternative recruitment ideas that have arisen in recent years. The last time the nation was surveyed (2001), we learned that 29 million full-time wage earners worked some kind of flexible work schedule. Given that this was double the number from ten years earlier, it seems that this is a trend that is likely to continue.

For example, companies in the health-care field simply couldn't get along without flexible work schedules. Consider for a moment the remarkable record of your own local hospital. In all likelihood, it has not shut its doors since the day it opened. This means continuous operation, 24 hours a day, 365 days a year, on into the foreseeable future. Flextime is simply the approach of stepping away from the traditional 9-to-5 concept in recognition of the increasingly complex time demands of our employees. The idea is often intertwined with that of job sharing, the system whereby people assume joint responsibility for the completion of work normally allotted to one full-time employee, or whereby two full-time workers on different shifts must provide 24/7 service and/or care to the same customers.

Permit me to share a story that illustrates how important these ideas are today. There is a street in San Jose, California, known as Steven Creek Boulevard. It is one of the two or three highest volume areas for automobile sales in the world. As you might expect, competition for good sales reps on this street is fierce. At one dealership worked a single parent—a father—who was the highest producing sales rep in his organization. After his divorce, he had found it literally impossible to get his daughter to day care and make it to work by 8:30 in the morning. He tried to talk about this problem with his manager, but heard something along the lines of, "Sounds like a personal problem; around here, everyone starts at 8:30. Always have, always will."

The father was left with no choice, so he started looking for another job. He contacted the manager of a competitive dealership, who could hardly believe his luck. "It was like manna from heaven," the competing manager remembers. "Here I had the choice of letting one of the best salesmen on the boulevard slip through my fingers, or letting him come in to work fifteen minutes late and make the time up at the end of the shift. It was no contest." The employee broke all of his previous personal sales records on joining the company. His manager said, "I'm convinced the performance I'm getting is the result of our showing just a little decency and concern for his circumstances."

While not as common as flex hours, job sharing can open up totally new and untapped labor markets, and might be worth considering if you are having difficulty filling certain types of position, or problems with turnover in those positions. Apart from helping in these situations, you can also save money on health care because the job sharers work fewer hours.

To understand job sharing, look at jobs as hours, not as positions in which one person does one job forty hours a week. With job sharing there might be two people combining hours to do that same job. The division can be made in whatever way attracts the most reliable and best workers. Job sharing is appropriate for virtually all non-management positions. It is a superior way to attract those who are returning to the work force after (or while) raising a family, and those who, perhaps because of elder-care responsibilities or other considerations, find full-time employment difficult. These people represent a growing pool of talent that is going largely untapped.

Make no mistake: there is top-notch professional talent, not simply support workers, within the ranks of the job-sharers. By 1988, almost 35 percent of the female MBAs of 1977 had already left the work force, and as the years pass the numbers grow, meaning that you have a pool of very savvy potential job sharers for almost any job you have to fill. Many of these women left the work force to have children. Increasingly, however, women want to return to the work force after childbirth and regain a productive position in the business community, even if responsibilities to their children make returning full-time impractical.

Job sharing does carry its own special challenges. For example, paper trails become extremely important. There also is the fear of waking up one morning and learning of one team member's departure. Fortunately, retention among job-sharing teams is proving to be well above average, and when one person does leave, the job-sharing network invariably has ready replacements.

Scheduling the teams can be difficult. In effect, the manager must abandon the idea of "having a staff" of ten people beavering away for forty hours a week, and must begin thinking instead of being responsible for the management of 400 hours. The adjustment, for most, is well worth the effort, and the end result can be cheaper, motivated workers who will stay with the company longer.

Getting away from the one job, 9-to-5, forty-hours-a-week template to look for alternatives isn't going to take you out into left field. In 2000, Hewitt Associates, a well-respected HR consulting firm, found the following: "Flexible scheduling continues to increase in the workplace, with 57 percent of employers offering flextime, and 47 percent offering part-time employment."

The New Realities of Work-Force Makeup

Women today plan to stay in the work force over the long term, perhaps taking time off for child rearing, but increasingly returning to the professional workplace, either on a full-time basis or in one of the part-time/job sharing/flextime scenarios we have discussed. Women compose the majority in university and college freshman classes, and women account for approximately half of the enrollment in law, medicine, and business schools. These trends are supported by U.S. Department of Labor statistics that indicate that women will soon make up over 60 percent of the work force.

Economic demands dictate that the number of two-income couples will continue to increase, and these couples will, increasingly, decide to raise families while both pursue professional careers. This will lead to scheduling problems as partners try to balance their personal commitments for child raising and elder care with their professional lives, and these personal concerns are likewise going to be part of the modern manager's awareness. A working mother will no longer tolerate being relegated to lower-level jobs. Also, women at all levels are going to constitute the mainstay of our work force.

Even if, historically, women have dropped out of the labor market upon reaching childbearing age, we must now accept the fact that we are faced with a different set of women—and a different set of principles by which they can be expected to live their lives. Seventy-six percent of mothers are in the work force, and 40 percent of this total put in forty hours a week or more. These women all are working out of economic necessity and can be assumed to treat their careers with appropriate seriousness.

The changes facing the world of work are no less stark when we turn to the role of minority workers (statistically defined as Latin, African-American, and Asian) in the labor pool. In 2005, it was estimated that the proportion of our work force made up of minority workers was approaching 30 percent, and that the growth of these groups in the work force will dramatically eclipse that of Caucasians. The U.S. Bureau of Labor Statistics stated in a 2004 study that "between 2002 and 2012, for example, the labor force growth rate for Asians is projected to be 51 percent, compared with about 3 percent for whites." A related consideration is that the economic growth of the last twenty years, coupled with record levels of educational attainment for minority groups, has brought a uniquely diverse population into the middle and professional classes of America. In the process, those groups are changing, in no small degree, the customer base for every company's products and services.

On the one hand, this means that there is more at stake than simple corporate altruism when organizations fail to recruit minorities, women, single parents, and the physically challenged. It becomes not a matter of fashionable community relations work, but rather one of survival to reach out to these new workers. Companies that do not heed the demographic writing on the wall will only place themselves at a significant competitive disadvantage by striving to remain white and male-dominated.

There's a very smart adage that says the best way to best penetrate your particular market is to understand it from the intimate perspective of your customer. From a personal point of view, this means that whatever your sex and ethnicity, you are best advised to have an ever-increasing sensitivity and sympathy to the melting pot that makes up working America. Such awareness is likely to improve your productivity and your ability to climb in the ranks of management.

Military Personnel

The military offers another wonderful resource for recruiting motivated and disciplined workers from a cross section of cultures, races, and both sexes. When you tap into this resource you are directly recruiting young men and women from all walks of life who have already made Herculean and admirable efforts to improve themselves, and they are just awaiting new challenges.

If you don't know where to start, visit the Web site of the Destiny Group, a company that specializes in connecting corporate America with soon-to-be ex-military job seekers *(www.destinygrp.com)*. This is a well-trafficked site for military personnel cycling into the corporate world. You can post jobs on the site and/or search any one of its ten specialized resume databases.

If you work in a high-turnover field, in which employees rarely last the year—fast food, for example—catching military recruits after they have passed their physicals but before they are inducted can pay real dividends; recruits in a delayed-entry program can sometimes wait up to nine months before induction. The Department of Defense (DOD) actually developed a program to support this very initiative, which was a smart idea; however, the DOD being the DOD, you can't find out anything about it! You are on your own with this one. Forging a relationship with local recruiting offices, and mentioning the suitability in your recruitment advertising, such as "great opportunity for delayed-entry recruits," are options worth consideration.

Disabled Workers

Employers invariably find that hiring the disabled pays off handsomely in terms of greater productivity, less absenteeism, and an enhanced spirit of teamwork and sensitivity to the needs of a significant portion of your customer base. Despite laws protecting the rights of all American workers, the disabled are consistently discriminated against, leading you to workers who are exceptionally motivated and loyal when they do receive the opportunity to make a contribution and to compete in the workplace.

An open-minded manager can learn that there's no substitute for giving people the opportunity to reach their full potential; employees with disabilities gain equal or higher job performance ratings, and have higher rates of retention and lower rates of absenteeism than do other workers. It's a powerful message that reaches everyone in the organization, many of whom will know a disabled person. You will find plenty of resources in the Appendix that can help you tap into this deep talent pool.

Diversifying your department by recruiting a more balanced work force that reflects the makeup of your community and customer base will create a more flexible, entrepreneurial, productive, socially charged, and motivated team. After all, the more your work force reflects your customer base, the better your workers will understand, capture, and service that base.

The 1990 Americans with Disabilities Act, signed into law by President George H. W. Bush, brings equal rights to America's largest minority, which *any of us could join on the way home from work today.*

A purely pragmatic viewpoint demands that you consider not only the strictures of the law but also the many benefits of embracing the idea that underlies it. See Chapter 14 for all of the legal ramifications of noncompliance, plus the tax benefits and other incentives for complying.

Older Workers

We live in a youth-oriented culture, and one where age discrimination (despite laws to the contrary) is rampant. Once people hit their fifties and get displaced, it becomes increasingly difficult for them to get back into the ball game (pay attention; this unpleasant reality is in your future and should be anticipated). Add to this that we are all living longer and remaining more active, and you have another overlooked talent pool. If you have the interview skills to sort the wheat from the chaff and the self-confidence to manage someone who may have greater experience than you do yourself, you'll get two things:

- ▶ Someone who has made most of his or her mistakes on someone else's payroll

- ▶ Someone who is happy to be back in the saddle and who will loyally stand at your back

- ▶ Someone who can bring balance and stability to a younger team

Outsourcing

More and more businesses are farming out whole departments—including such areas as customer service, accounting, human resources, and information systems. Almost any job is susceptible to outsourcing.

It all began with the emergence of the temporary-help industry, but the idea of reducing corporate commitment with just-in-time temporary local staffing is now entirely separated from shipping whole functions to other parts of the globe. The Human Resources department is the most likely to initiate an outsourcing program, as a way to staff company needs in an efficient and cost-effective fashion. However, a basic understanding of the elements of the process will help you take a more responsible part in any discussions, and perhaps give you a heads-up that even your job might be headed out on a slow boat to China.

Outsourcing, or offshoring, is a hot topic in all of corporate America, all made possible by technology and high-quality communications links. It is an approach to staffing that will not be going away. It started in earnest with NAFTA (North American Free Trade Agreement), which encouraged the export of manufacturing jobs—auto plants to Mexico, and garment manufacturing to China and the Dominican Republic; in addition, aircraft manufacturing, including a substantial part of the engineering, is likely soon to begin in China. Now there are call centers in Ireland, the Philippines, and India for customer care, airline reservations, and insurance claims. Likewise, computer programming, engineering, and medical and legal services are all being outsourced. By 2003, Hewlett-Packard already had 10,000 technology workers in India. You can expect that within the next five years, companies of all sizes, but especially our larger employers, will routinely be exporting functions throughout IT, customer relations, manufacturing, supply chain management, HR, finance, accounting, and health care.

Whether or not this trend to outsource American know-how is to the long-term benefit of the American economy or our morale as a nation is not within the purview of this book. It is perhaps just enough to know that Gartner Research estimated that between 2003 and 2004, up to 5 percent of all IT jobs could move overseas—and, as we know, technology has a way of impacting all of our lives. Any function that does not require face-to-face interaction with the customer, or for which output and performance can be easily quantified or service can be measured and audited, is a candidate for outsourcing in an increasingly educated global work force. In the near term, the success of any particular outsourcing endeavor is likely to depend on how closely they conform to these considerations.

The obsession with outsourcing is obviously tied to profits. The goal is to reduce overall costs, most especially by getting employees off in-house payroll, thereby gaining access to capital locked up with the most expensive work force in the world.

If your area of professional and management expertise falls into any of the areas discussed here, you will want to quietly study the impact of potential outsourcing on your company and your career. You will also want to pursue your development of professional, management, and multicultural skills to differentiate yourself from other managers. Should outsourcing rear its head in your future, you might have an ace up your sleeve with an awareness of the Americans with Disabilities Act and the benefits (cost, performance, tax incentives, and community PR) that can accrue to companies that embrace the spirit of its intentions. There is a vast, underutilized, and highly motivated pool of qualified disabled workers capable of doing almost all jobs that are being sent overseas. By employing them, you might just save your job and become a star in the bargain.

Roundup of the Recruitment Process

As the hiring manager, you determine, perhaps along with the involvement of HR, the position to be filled; at this time, if appropriate, you'll consider internships as a way to fill the position, and perhaps the use of temporary services as both an interim measure and perhaps as a temp-to-perm hiring solution. You follow the approved requisition procedures, and start the recruitment process only after all necessary approvals have been gained.

Your job analysis clearly identifies appropriate skill sets, educational and professional background, and work experience; you are also careful to identify the behavioral profile that successful candidates will possess. At this point, when you have a clear picture of what the successful candidate will look like, you begin recruitment. Initially, you concentrate on using all the different networking tools that give you introductions to candidates at little or no cost, and ensure that the position is posted on the company Web site. If an employee referral program is in place within your company, you promote it to encourage referrals.

Then, as urgency for filling the position dictates, you implement the more costly approaches of print and online recruitment advertising, job fairs, and headhunters.

Acceptance of the importance of a diverse, well-trained work force is one of the most basic preconditions for your success in the coming years. Financial plans, sales targets, and long-term projections are all moot unless they are anchored in a solid understanding of the labor supply and knowledge of what it will take to attract and keep good people over time. If you don't have the horses to pull the wagon, you won't make the grade.

To paraphrase Bob Boschert, founder of Boschert Associates and one of Silicon Valley's forefathers of the "knowledge era," recruitment in the twenty-first century will be a little like running around in front of a steamroller: "You can outrun the steamroller easily at any given moment, but if you ever sit down, you are going to get squashed." I offer this as a gentle reminder that there are no recruitment shortcuts in the career of a successful manager—only a comprehensive personal recruitment program will put you at a competitive advantage. This is your life and your career, and if you think that recruitment is the role of the HR department, you will be putting the trajectory of that career in the hands of others. Yes, HR is there, among other things to support the recruitment process, but the more you understand the whats, hows, and whys of recruitment, the more effectively you can interact with HR (and thereby get the best that department has to offer), and the more effective you can be in your own ongoing recruitment efforts. When it comes to management and recruitment, who you know and how you are connected can be a very important ingredient in the recipe for your success.

Putting this in context, as you proceed through this tumultuous first decade of the new century, with its downsizings, rightsizings, and outsourcings, you will experience both worker surpluses—largely of workers you can't use—and worker droughts of the very workers you need. You need to understand recruitment, and to be connected to your profession in ways that give you access to skilled and motivated professionals in your field.

As your recruitment program gathers momentum, the trickle of print and electronic resumes turns into a flood and you are faced with the next task: creating a short list of viable candidates to interview from the mass of flotsam and jetsam that comes with the flood. Short-list development is the topic we'll handle next.

How to Read a Resume 4

From your side of the desk, as a hiring manager, resumes are a practical, timesaving device. Without them, you would have no choice but to interview everyone who applied for a job, and all your other activities would grind to a halt. To get the best out of resumes as a screening tool, you should look at them first from the job hunter's perspective. If you understand why particular resumes are structured the way they are, you get a clearer picture of each candidate.

Some resumes are nothing more than a recitation of work history. With others you will be looking at a document that was written to focus on a specific target job, or perhaps hide a problem. Resumes get longer and more complex as there is more experience to draw on, and at the same time their very structure varies to accommodate the twists and turns that happen in every person's half-century-long work life.

If you want to avoid getting fooled, it is useful to understand the cracks that different resume types are designed to hide. It is not accidental that resumes follow different formats; depending on an applicant's circumstances, one style will demonstrate the same track record in a far better light than will another. There are three resume formats in common use, and one common resume alternative, with each having abilities to highlight certain strengths and leave the skeletons, or weaknesses, hidden in the closet. Let's open the door and have a look.

The Chronological Resume

Here is an example of a simple chronological resume, which is probably the most common and needs the least explanation. Its setup is exactly as it sounds: a chronological record of employment history. People who have a steady work history and a logical progression from job to job frequently use this format. It works well when there are no employment gaps, or when those gaps can be hidden.

However, just because this format is the most simple and most common doesn't mean that it represents a preferable candidate, or that it cannot contain its fair share of distortions. The chronological format is the most common because it is the easiest to create and requires the least thought by the writer. Sometimes these resumes come entirely without focus and are simply a recitation of a series of jobs; as such they can represent someone who in turn is not very focused.

CHRONOLOGICAL RESUME

Jane Swift, 9 Central Avenue, Quincy, MA 02169
(617) 555-1212 • *jswift@careerbrain.com*

SUMMARY: Ten years of increasing responsibilities in the employment services industry. Concentration in the high-technology markets.

EXPERIENCE: **Howard Systems International, Inc.**   **2003–Present**
Management Consulting Firm
Personnel Manager
Responsible for recruiting and managing consulting staff of five. Set up office and organized the recruitment, selection, and hiring of consultants. Recruited all levels of MIS staff from financial to manufacturing markets.

Additional responsibilities:
- Coordinated with outside advertising agencies.
- Developed PR with industry periodicals—placement with more than 20 magazines and newsletters.
- Developed effective referral programs—referrals increased 32%.

EXPERIENCE: **Technical Aid Corporation**   **1993–2003**
National Consulting Firm, MICRO/TEMPS Division
Division Manager   *1998–2003*
Area Manager   *1995–1998*
Branch Manager   *1993–1995*
As Division Manager, opened additional West Coast offices. Staffed and trained all offices with appropriate personnel. Created and implemented all divisional operational policies responsible for P & L. Sales increased to $20 million, from $0 in 1987.

- Achieved and maintained 30% annual growth over 7-year period.
- Maintained sales staff turnover at 14%.

As Area Manager, opened additional offices, hiring staff, setting up office policies, and training sales and recruiting personnel.

Additional responsibilities:
- Supervised offices in two states.
- Developed business relationships with accounts—75% of clients were regular customers.
- Client base increased 28% per year.
- Generated more than $200,000 worth of free trade-journal publicity.

As Branch Manager, hired to establish the new MICRO/TEMPS operation. Recruited and managed consultants. Hired internal staff. Sold service to clients.

EDUCATION: Boston University
BS Public Relations, 1992

The Functional Resume and Broadcast Letter

This format has the most flexibility for users from a wide variety of backgrounds, from the highly qualified financial pro with just a couple of jobs to list and no secrets to hide to a different highly qualified financial pro with just a couple of jobs to list plus a few years in the pokey to hide. Identifying features of this format include an ability to focus attention on skills and accomplishments, while de-emphasizing job titles, employers, and dates.

A wide selection of workers will use this format at some time in their lives. An entry-level worker with some relevant experience cobbled together from a series of short-term and part-time jobs will use this format, as will the trailing spouse from a corporate relocation who spent a year getting the house organized and the kids settled in new schools, and who wants to de-emphasize the employment gap and include the achievements from interim activities. You can also find people with outstanding work history and no employment gaps using this format, because the layout encourages a strong focus on skills and achievements in an accessible format. It's a format that requires focus on a specific job, and as such might tell you something about how well the writer understands the job in question.

High-powered, heavily experienced, and mature workers who get laid off in their late forties and fifties typically experience longer job hunts because of incipient age discrimination. Often such professionals are encouraged to use a functional format, allowing focus on the depth of experience while de-emphasizing the chronology.

We live in a youth culture, in which the cream of our work force—pros in their forties, fifties, and sixties—are being chucked onto the slag heap at the height of their productive powers. Remember that these are people who have seen the problems before, who have extensive frames of reference for projection and anticipation, and who are more likely to have developed the habit of doing things right the first time rather than doing them over again. These professionals can be eminently desirable, and this choice of format coupled with heavy relevant experience could give you a heads-up on such a person. By the same token, however, you will want to take their relative manageability carefully into account at the interview.

Candidates with military, government, and educational backgrounds will also sometimes use a functional resume or a broadcast letter. While such people probably have nothing to hide, the format allows the writer to focus on what he or she brings to the table rather than the diverse titles held while gaining that experience. Each one of these professional

FUNCTIONAL RESUME

Jane Swift
9 Central Avenue
Quincy, MA 02169
(617) 555-1212
jswift@careerbrain.com

OBJECTIVE: A position in Employment Services where my management, sales, and recruiting talents can be effectively utilized to improve operations and contribute to company profits.

SUMMARY: More than ten years of Human Resources experience. Extensive responsibility for multiple branch offices and an internal staff of 40+ employees and 250 consultants.

SALES: Sold high-technology consulting services with consistently profitable margins throughout the United States. Grew sales from $0 to over $20 million a year.

Created training programs and trained salespeople in six metropolitan markets.

RECRUITING: Developed recruiting sourcing methods for multiple branch offices.

Recruited more than 25,000 internal and external consultants in the high-technology professions.

MANAGEMENT: Managed up to 40 people in sales, customer service, recruiting, and administration. Turnover maintained at 14% in a "turnover business."

FINANCIAL: Prepared quarterly and yearly forecasts. Presented, reviewed, and defended these forecasts to the Board of Directors. Responsible for P & L of $20 million sales operation.

PRODUCTION: Responsible for opening multiple offices and accountable for growth and profitability. 100% success, and maintained 30% growth over seven-year period in 10 offices.

WORK EXPERIENCE:

2003 to Present HOWARD SYSTEMS INTERNATIONAL, INC. Boston, MA
National Consulting Firm
Personnel Manager

1993–2003 TECHNICAL AID CORPORATION, Needham, MA
National Consulting & Search Firm
Division Manager

EDUCATION: BS, 1992, Boston University

REFERENCES: Available upon request.

types can be of real benefit to you. Once they adjust to civilian life again, ex-military personnel, of all ranks, can be an asset to any department or company; they can bring a great sense of organization and cooperation to the workplace. In fact, you will find that leading companies, such as GE, lean heavily on military experience throughout the management organization. Professionals from government and academia are used to working in political environments, and their degree of comfort with duality and a strong sense of diplomacy will be helpful in a highly structured yet dynamic company.

Career changers and those with unusual employment backgrounds are also fond of the functional and broadcast formats, again because they can avoid tying their background to seemingly irrelevant jobs. With these styles, they can concentrate on the skills and achievements they bring to the job, rather than where, when, and under which job title they exercised those skills. The question you ask yourself in these situations is whether the achievements, rather than the employment history, will indicate a person of high drive and intelligence, to compensate for, say, a lack of relevant industry experience. Here is an example of an exceptional professional in the fine arts world. Look at the resume, and afterward I'll give you the story.

COMBINATION RESUME USED IN CAREER SHIFT

Christian Barkley
458 East 57th Street
Charleston, NC 72933
(479) 232-8296 • *curator@earthlink.com*

CAREER SUMMARY & OBJECTIVE

My professional life is focused on art in all it embraces: drawing, painting, sculpture, photography, cinema, video, audio, performance and digital art, art history and criticism; my personal life is similarly committed. Having recently relocated to the area, I hope to make a contribution within the Charleston Arts community that harnesses my knowledge, enthusiasm, and sensibilities.

RESUME FOR SENIOR CURATOR

Art History

Thorough knowledge of art history from cave of Lascaux through current artists such as Bruce Nauman, Jessica Stockholder, and Luc Tuymans. Film history from Lumiere Brothers to Almodovar. Current with key critical art and film theory. Ongoing workshops and lectures with the likes of Matthew Barney, Louise Bourgeois, and Andy Goldsworthy.

Research New Artists

Connected to cutting-edge art and artists through involvement with the art communities and galleries of New York and Boston and the faculty, student, and alumni networks of RISD, Columbia, Boston Museum School, New England School of Art and Design, and now MassArt. Twenty years of Manhattan gallery openings and networking with artists at MOMA, PS1, Guggenheim, Whitney, Metropolitan, Film Forum, International Center for Photography workshops and lectures.

Gathering Art Work

Through local artists, regional and global artist networks, intercultural artist exchanges, alumni groups, first-rank private collectors, personal and family networks, and Internet calls for submissions.

Art and the Community

Conception and launch of themed, resourced, and sequenced shows that invigorate campus and community involvement. Reconfigure existing art spaces to create dynamic dialogue with visitors. Education and outreach programs.

Installation of Art

Maintain fluidity of gallery space in preparing exhibitions with recognition of size/time considerations for the art, to ensure a sympathetic environment for the presented works. Hang, light, and label shows in sequences that create dialogue between the works.

Page 1 of 2

79

PR Materials

Energizing invitations, comprehensive press kits, illustrated press releases, and artist binder materials. Sensitive to placing art in historical/cultural context. Adobe Photoshop.

Management Experience

Fourteen years art staff management experience, including curriculum development. Responsible for art instructors, art handlers, maintenance crews, and working with printers, catering, and graphic arts staff.

EMPLOYMENT

1993–2005 **Chair of Visual Arts,** The Sentinel School

Duties: Curriculum development, portfolio preparation, internal and external monthly shows, theater sets, monthly video news show, taught art history and all the studio arts, managed staff of three.

1989–2004 **President** Art Workshops

Duties: Private art studio and art history curriculums, staff of four. Private groups to DC and Atlanta museums and gallery tours.

1980–1989 **Freelance artist, photographer, and editor**

Highlights from the *sublime* to the *ridiculous* include: Taught photography at Trinity School, Manhattan; photographer for the Ramones; editor of Pioneer, insurance industry trade magazine; assistant to Claudia Weill, documentary filmmaker, director of *Girlfriends*.

EDUCATION

MFA, Magna cum laude, Columbia University, 1982

Awards: Andre Bazin Prize for film criticism

Taught undergraduate Intro to Film, under Andrew Sarris and Milos Forman.

Subscriptions

Art in America, ARTnews, Artforum, New York Times, Parkett, Sight and Sound, Film Comment, Modern Painters.

Memberships

MOMA/PS1, Whitney Museum of American Art, Guggenheim, Metropolitan Museum of Art, DIA.

What we see with this resume is an obviously qualified art gallery or museum curator, with a world of relevant experience. The focus is legitimately on the skills and understanding brought to the target job, not on the writer's most recent job title, Chair of Visual Arts at a prestigious prep school. This doesn't take away from the person's credibility; it is merely an illustration of why one format might be chosen over another.

Broadcast Letters

It is possible to say that a broadcast letter is similar to a functional resume, only with less chronological detail. It typically features three to five achievement-packed paragraphs, and is designed to knock you off your feet with relevant achievements and depth of experience.

Seasoned professionals, who are also using a traditional resume in one format or another, most frequently use broadcast letters as a marketing device. You will also find broadcast letters used as alternative marketing devices by professionals in industries badly hit by outsourcing, because the format puts the focus on goal orientation and productivity. Typically, the writer of a broadcast letter will also have a resume. Here is an example of a broadcast letter from a professional caught in the heavy outsourcing of the apparel industry to China.

BROADCAST E-MAIL (OPERATIONS)

From: Jonathan Johnson [operationspro@hotmail.com]
To: *fordh@msn.com*
Cc:
Subject: Operations Management

Dear Harry Ford:

Perhaps your organization is seeking a take-charge individual to manage multifaceted apparel production and distribution operations with direct responsibility for overseeing all aspects of yarn purchasing, delivery schedules, staff management, and vendor relations, along with many other areas too extensive to mention on one page. If this is the case, then you will want to consider me as a viable candidate.

I bring with me fourteen years of solid experience, a bachelor's degree, and a lot of common sense, which goes a long way in this industry. Currently in my eighth year of dedication with Weave 'N Wear, Inc. in the capacity of Yarn Manager, I continue to prove myself as a professional highly capable of wearing many hats in a fast-paced manufacturing environment.

In addition to my ability to manage a broad scope of daily operations, I have played an instrumental role in the development and implementation of a multimillion-dollar computerized system that has greatly improved productivity levels, reduced unnecessary spending, and improved overall communication in the workplace. That, combined with my ability to lead, motivate, and train direct reports; multilingual communication skills that include fluency in Spanish and German; and a talent for making sure the job gets done right, make me confident that I would be an asset to your management team.

I would appreciate an opportunity to interview with you at a convenient time. Thank you for your time and consideration. I look forward to hearing from you soon.

Sincerely,

Jonathan Johnson
(516) 555-1212
operationspro@hotmail.com

Though job-hoppers and others with employment problems often use functional resumes and broadcast letters, the range of desirable, competent professionals who also can effectively use this format means that you must not reject them out of hand. Rather, your awareness of who is *likely* to use these formats allows you to ask yourself the appropriate questions as you evaluate the resume and in your screening telephone interview. We'll cover that topic in the very next chapter.

The Combination Resume

The combination resume comes from combining the functional and chronological resume styles. It is the most comprehensive and revealing format, clearly showing both employment history and significant skill and accomplishment detail, *as they relate to a specific target job*. It is clearly the most useful to any hiring manager, and often speaks of an experienced professional, with relevant experience and steadily increasing responsibilities.

COMBINATION RESUME

Jane Swift
9 Central Avenue
Quincy, MA 02169
(617) 555-1212
jswift@careerbrain.com

OBJECTIVE: Employment Services Management

SUMMARY: Ten years of increasing responsibilities in the employment services marketplace. Concentration in the high-technology markets.

SALES: Sold high-technology consulting services with consistently profitable margins throughout the United States. Grew sales from $0 to more than $20 million a year.

PRODUCTION: Responsible for opening multiple offices and accountable for growth and profitability. 100% success and maintained 30% growth over seven-year period in 10 offices.

MANAGEMENT: Managed up to 40 people in sales, customer service, recruiting, and administration. Turnover maintained at 14% in a "turnover business." Hired branch managers and sales and recruiting staff throughout the United States.

FINANCIAL: Prepared quarterly and yearly forecasts. Presented, reviewed, and defended these forecasts to the Board of Directors. Responsible for P & L of $20 million sales operation.

MARKETING: Performed numerous market studies for multiple-branch opening. Resolved feasibility of combining two different sales offices. Study resulted in savings of more than $5,000 per month in operating expenses.

EXPERIENCE: **Howard Systems International, Inc.** 2003–Present
Management Consulting Firm
Personnel Manager
Responsible for recruiting and managing consulting staff of five. Set up office and organized the recruitment, selection, and hiring of consultants. Recruited all levels of MIS staff from financial to manufacturing markets.

Additional responsibilities:

- Developed PR with industry periodicals—placement with more than 20 magazines and newsletters
- Developed effective referral programs—referrals increased 320%

COMBINATION RESUME page 2

Jane Swift, (617) 555-1212

Technical Aid Corporation   1993–2003
National Consulting Firm, MICRO/TEMPS Division
Division Manager   1998–2003
Area Manager   1995–1998
Branch Manager   1993–1995

As Division Manager, opened additional West Coast offices. Staffed and trained all offices with appropriate personnel. Created and implemented all divisional operational policies. Responsibilities for P & L. Sales increased to $20 million, from $0 in 1987.

- Achieved and maintained 30% annual growth over seven-year period.
- Maintained sales staff turnover at 14%.

As Area Manager, opened additional offices, hiring staff, setting up office policies, and training sales and recruiting personnel.
Additional responsibilities:

- Supervised offices in two states.
- Developed business relationships with accounts—75% of clients were regular customers.
- Client base increased 28% per year.
- Generated more than $200,000 worth of free trade-journal publicity.

As Branch Manager, hired to establish the new MICRO/TEMPS operation. Recruited and managed consultants. Hired internal staff. Sold service to clients.

EDUCATION: BS, 1992, Boston University

Analyzing Achievement Claims

No matter which resume style is used, all job hunters are told to list their achievements as a way of demonstrating how well they performed for previous employers. Sometimes these statements of achievement are true; at other times, they can be exaggerations of a more modest truth; sometimes, they are outright lies. Your task is to consistently separate the fact from the fiction. Statements of achievement almost always relate to productivity: earning money, saving money, and saving time. Because examination into claims of achievement will be an important part of any interview, you'll want to make a habit of reading resumes with a fluorescent yellow highlighter in your hand to spotlight any claims like those that follow for further examination. When you read of achievements that seem just too good to be true, they probably are.

> *Money Earned for the Company:* This junior salesman not only sold more peanut butter than anyone else, but he also got the entire population of Maine to stand on their heads and gargle it. He would like to do the same for your company.

> *Money Saved for the Company:* This accountant saved her company from certain ruin by inventing the modern computer and reducing staffing needs in her department by 98%.

> *Time Saved:* This computer programmer designed a new program that reduced processing time by half, and that time savings is valued at $1.5 million so far this year.

The root of such claims has long been wittily referred to as the Apollo Syndrome, after a low-level functionary at Cape Kennedy who claimed the success of the first Apollo mission because he served coffee to the scientists, who, he claimed, would not otherwise have stayed awake long enough to get the ship launched successfully. He claimed he "provided key support to top scientists."

Such misrepresentation of job responsibility is a substantial form of resume embellishment. This "painting with broad brush strokes" is done both with claims of skills and responsibilities and by the words used to describe the person using those skills. Such words are commonly referred to as action verbs: *achieved, streamlined, managed, implemented,* and so on. Just because such words are in front of you on 22-pound rag paper does not make them true. It is not always so much that the writer is lying to you, but that you cannot be certain of the objectivity of those claims.

It is easy for you, the manager, to misinterpret them. Take "conceived" and "designed" and "implemented," for example: "conceived, designed, and implemented facility reorganization with resultant 22% space saving. Avoided moving to larger facility for one year." Now maybe you work at a 20,000-square-foot facility and say, "Wow, this guy must have saved his company a ton of money in rent!" On the other hand, the resume writer might work in a four-person 800-square-foot office and this could be a rather grand way of saying, "I helped shift some desks around one slow Thursday afternoon." Now while you won't automatically project your situation onto the resume, or assume that the candidate walks on water, you will examine the claims and give credit where credit is due. In this context, if the claims were defensible, even though the achievement was perhaps in a smaller context than your situation, the candidate still showed initiative, used his analytical skills, and made a difference with his presence.

When you come across action verbs, flag them with your highlighter for further examination. You will either learn good things about the behavioral profile of your candidate, or save yourself a management headache. Consider the word "managed." Whenever you see it in a resume, immediately highlight it and start asking yourself questions: How would this person define management: management of a process, a project, or people? How does the candidate see the difference between management and supervision? How long has he or she been in management, at what level, and how many people were managed? Did this person hire, fire, and perform salary and performance reviews? The questions that don't answer themselves in your examination of the resume are the ones for which you will frame questions at the interview, thus ensuring that you get a firm understanding of the candidate's real-world capabilities.

Educational Attainment

Of any item on a resume, educational claims are the most prone to exaggeration. It's been said in the reference checking and credential verification communities that upward of 30 percent of all educational claims are exaggerated.

Unfortunately, apart from using your native savvy, there is little you can do about this, unless you and/or your company make a habit of credential verification. We'll talk about reference checking later; you'll also find a selection of credential verification companies in the Background and Reference Check Companies section of Appendix B.

So given the likelihood that three out of every ten candidates you evaluate aren't being entirely truthful about their educational attainment, and also knowing that people reach the professional heights and do good work *despite* having lied about their educational attainments, what do you do? You verify credentials if practical and deemed important by you and the company. Beyond this you recognize that over time, professional experience gradually replaces educational attainment in degree of importance in your evaluations, and you are careful not to confuse credentials with accomplishments. They are an indicator of a certain level of awareness and analytical skills, and they promise potential, but even when verified they are not proof of superior performance.

Use a Matching Sheet

Employee selection is all about prioritization. Applying carefully analyzed priorities throughout the selection process will always save you time and deliver better hires. You prioritize in the recruiting approaches you apply, beginning with the cheapest and most effective (both in terms of delivery time and longevity of hire), logically applying more expensive, labor intensive, and time-consuming options as needs demand. The selection process adds hours to your work week, so anything you can do to streamline the selection process pays dividends.

Though candidates have the right to show themselves in their best light, you still have to decide which ones you might want to see, which ones you wouldn't hire on a bet (like the one who claims excellent written communication skills but whose resume is filled with typos), and those not right for this situation but worth keeping in mind for future reference.

A matching sheet can simplify the resume evaluation process, helping rule candidates in or out, and it can also provide a formulating tool for interview question development. Creating a matching sheet is not a complicated process:

- ▶ Open a new document on your computer, or take a sheet of paper and draw a line down the center.

- ▶ Consider the most important facets of the job and list them bullet style, down the left-hand side.

▶ Save the document with a job title heading; say, Physical Therapist Matching Sheet.

▶ Print out copies as needed.

To use matching sheets, just read through a resume and jot down the person's relevant experience in the right-hand column opposite the appropriate line. Because this technique makes the matches so obvious, it saves considerable time in sorting the long list of potentials into a short list of must-talk-to candidates.

How to Recognize Employment Gaps

Armed with the most viable candidates from your matching sheets, you need to return to the resume and establish employment history and experience continuity. With each of the different resume styles, watch out for employment gaps. *Last-Chance Electronics 1998–2001*, then *Fly-By-Night Software 2001–Present* seems like a fair progression at first glance. But what if the candidate had left one company in January of 2001 and not joined the next one until December 2001? You could have an employment gap of up to a year.

This could mean that deception is being employed; there is one less year of experience than at first assumed, and a similar amount of time has been spent doing work not relevant to the position. However, in this day and age, taking months to find a new job after getting laid off is no longer unusual, and it can be defensible from the job hunter's viewpoint: he or she didn't lie about employment dates, he or she simply didn't include between-jobs downtime. Nevertheless, annual employment dates are worthy of a flash of the yellow highlighter as a topic for possible investigation.

Unless you are wary about employment dates in the very beginning, your tendency will be to accept them on second reading as given fact. *This tendency results in asking questions that merely confirm resume content, rather than examining and questioning it.* As mentioned, people respect what you inspect, not what you expect, so a habit of inspection now will help you set a tone for truthfulness during the selection cycle and for honest performance once the chosen candidate is on the job.

Along with start and termination dates for successive jobs, you will want to learn about salary progression through starting and leaving salaries. Often on a resume you will find no specific comments about salary; at best, you are only likely to come across current earnings or desired earnings for the upcoming job mentioned in a cover letter. However, learning about a candidate's salary progression can reflect his or her general industriousness and motivation, and give you some idea of the kind of offer this person will be happy to accept. Your highlighted employment dates now remind you to confirm salary progression as well as employment continuity at an appropriate time during the interview cycle.

Because questions about the past are less threatening and therefore more likely to get you truthful answers, get in the habit of asking these questions about earlier jobs.

When you ask yourself these job-progression questions about each job, you will become sensitive to the professional growth achieved in each successive job, and it all comes from screening those resumes intelligently (and with a highlighter) the first time through.

Last Thoughts on the Resume Screening Process

Evaluating resumes isn't anyone's idea of a good time. After a dozen, even the strongest minds gradually turn to mush. When you are faced with a daunting stack, work through them in batches, using the task as a break from your major duties or perhaps when sitting in a conference room waiting for a meeting to begin.

While it is best to screen resumes yourself, it may well happen that HR also delivers screened resumes to you. It is important to have good relations with HR, working with them to define needs and showing appreciation for their efforts. If you have a good working relationship with HR, you can trot over once in a while to examine the ones that have been rejected. Doing this not only shows that you are involved and paying attention; every now and then you might find some interesting fish that was about to be thrown back into the swim. When you do this with a collegial spirit, you will help the HR recruiters gain a better understanding of your needs and enable them to perform better in their jobs. Everyone wins and everyone forges useful alliances for the future.

Once you decide that a particular candidate is worth seeing, read through the resume again and jot down questions for any areas that you feel need clarification or probing. Do it now, while your analysis is still fresh and still objective, unaffected by personality impact. You'll be able to use these first impressions to formulate knockout questions to ask during the screening interview, which we'll move on to next.

Telephone Interviews: 5
The Great Timesavers

*T*here are three major mistakes that managers make in their approach to interviewing job candidates. The biggest mistake is hiring in their own image: "Only someone who looks like me, talks like me, walks like me, and went to the same schools I did—in other words, someone with whom I would immediately be socially at ease—can possibly do this job."

The second-biggest mistake managers make is in hiring someone 100 percent capable of the job. Doing so gives you a fast start, but leaves you with a new employee who may be quickly bored with the lack of challenge.

In the majority of situations, in which significant raises and promotions are not immediately probable, you are better advised to look for someone who can do the job but still has room for growth in the position, as the resulting "learning curve" provides challenge and enrichment to keep your new employee motivated.

The third-biggest mistake is in moving from resume evaluation straight to in-person interviews, skipping the telephone interview. Avoiding that mistake is what this chapter is all about.

From Phoner to Short List

If you don't use telephone interviews to screen your long list of candidates into a more manageable short list, you will be wasting much of your valuable time. With a face-to-face meeting, it takes about five minutes to get the person into your office, seated, and over the normal pleasantries. Then you have to get into the Q&A, and then (when you realize the mismatch) it takes another five minutes to get the candidate out of your office. Very few in-person interviews ever take up less than thirty minutes of your busy day. On the other hand, screening someone on the telephone allows you to move through the pleasantries in under a minute and to cut to the chase more quickly. You can refer to your notes and make further notes without concern for the niceties of body language, and when the time comes to get off the phone, you can be done in under a minute. Very few well-structured phone interviews need run thirty minutes; most can be done in half the time and gather the same amount of information. In short, telephone interviews make great time management tools.

Your goal with a phone interview is not to decide whether or not to hire the person; rather, it is to decide whether he or she has the essential capabilities for your job that justify an in-person meeting. Once you know that the candidate in question is worth seeing, schedule an interview. If you determine that a candidate is not suitable for the position, say so, in a courteous and professional manner, and get off the phone.

The interview strategies in this chapter will help you make fast and prudent decisions about in-person interviews. Your only goal should be to determine the essentials; you shouldn't try to probe all the niceties of ability, motivation, manageability, or the intangibles of personal chemistry over the telephone, if for no other reason than that it isn't possible to do.

Using the telephone as the next step of your screening process is also sensible when relocation is a factor and the cost of flying in any but the strongest candidates is prohibitive.

Scheduling Telephone Interviews

Arrange your telephone interviews in a manner convenient to both parties. This is especially important when dealing with employed candidates, because a phone call during business hours can cause some embarrassment. With an employed candidate you might consider an e-mail suggesting a time and date to talk on the phone for a few minutes, and you must be prepared to conduct such meetings outside of business hours or perhaps at lunchtime, when he or she has more options for privacy. When the interview is scheduled during working hours, allow the candidate the flexibility of choosing the time of day and also of initiating the call. Bear in mind that the candidate may suddenly be limited to yes or no responses, or request that you pick up the conversation later. At that point, it is best to suggest an evening hour convenient to you.

Questions and Techniques for Phone Interviews

Phone interviews require a little preparation if they are to gather the right information and work as a time management tool. A little organization now will ensure that your evaluations are objective and your decisions logical.

Fortunately, you did the work necessary to ease the flow of your telephone interviews when you developed your job description and matching sheet. Go back to these documents and identify the "must-have" skills and behaviors, and prioritize them. While all your "must-haves" should already be prioritized on your matching sheet, going back and matching them again against the job description allows you to add any additional "must -haves" to your matching sheet template.

As the interviewer, you will guide the conversation, but if you say too much, the candidate will have the time and necessary information to tell you just what you want to hear. The 80/20 rule applies to interviewing, in that you should be asking questions 20 percent of the time and listening to answers 80 percent of the time. By sharing adequate information about the deliverables of the job without going into detail, you allow the candidate to have a clear focus but not enough information to overly tailor responses to your questions.

Use the question examples in this section to help plan specific questions ahead of time. You'll start the conversation with a few pleasant words to set the relaxed atmosphere of a conversation between professionals (you learn more when people are relaxed). Then, after a skeletal review of the deliverables, ask the candidate to give you a brief recap, not of his or her entire work history, but just of the current job. You might identify a potential mismatch immediately; if so, share your concern with the candidate and ask about anything in prior work history that might change the picture. If there is a mismatch, bail out. (I'll show you how to bail gracefully a little later in the chapter.)

If the current job responsibilities are in line with your needs, you can proceed with questions more specific to skill and behavior. Focus your questions around the special skills, knowledge, and professional behaviors necessary to deliver on each of the major functions of the job.

The following questions follow a logical flow, but nevertheless might not match your specific needs exactly as they are worded, or in the sequence they follow. Use them as a touchstone for your needs, and phrase them and locate them in the interview according to your purposes. You will see that the questions start off very general in tone and gradually get more specific and detailed as the interview progresses.

"What would you say are the broad responsibilities of a [computer programmer]?"
This question is carefully geared to be nonspecific. As the interview cycle progresses, such a question will become increasingly detail specific, but at this point in the proceedings, you are simply trying to focus on the big picture. The answer you receive provides a clear indication of the candidate's understanding of the general functions and responsibilities of someone in this job. Additionally, the candidate will tell you what his or her perceived limits of responsibility are and also how he or she thinks the position relates and interacts with other positions and departments.

Remember that your phone interview is, at heart, a time management tool. You only need enough of these skill/deliverables questions to rule the candidate in or out of consideration for the face-to-face interview.

"Tell me about your experience with _____."
You can ask for a series of these explanations, addressing each of your critical deliverables/skill sets in an orderly and somewhat more detailed fashion. This is more effective than "How much experience do you have?" which may allow you to bamboozle yourself with quantity rather than with quality of experience. More than one manager over the years has discovered that ten years of experience is not always ten *progressive* years, but perhaps in effect just the first two years repeated five times. Asking specifics gives you a qualitative rather than a quantitative answer. You will also notice that the phrasing of the question requires a response that can tell you a great deal more than does a statement such as) "I have six years' experience," which, on consideration, tells you very little.

"What aspects of your work do you consider most crucial?"
The answer to this will show the interviewee's grasp of functional responsibilities and perhaps to what degree that person understands the overarching goals of the department. The candidate may well highlight how he or she prefers to spend time at work, and you can expect to learn something about motivation and professional behaviors. In the answer, you are naturally alert for a potential mismatch. One obvious example: the personal

assistant who does not regard the smoothing of your daily path to be a crucial function.

"Of all the work you have done, where have you been most successful?"
The answer to this question will demonstrate the candidate's ability to contribute in your areas of most crucial need, or might display inappropriate focus on less important aspects of the job. You might follow up this question with one that examines how the candidate has been successful in this area: "Why do you think you have been able to achieve success in this area?" The answer to this question should address the learned professional behaviors brought into play to help achieve that success.

"What would you say are the major qualities this job demands?" or *"What would you say are the traits a competent _____ would possess?"*
These two questions have the same intent but slightly different wording. Behind them both is an awareness that every job has its good and bad points, and that every job demands certain professional behaviors to assure success. For instance, oversensitive salespeople rarely make the grade—and we have yet (to our collective chagrin) to find an IRS auditor heavy with the milk of human kindness. In developing the job description, as we discussed earlier, you will have already identified the specific traits necessary to be successful in this position, so an answer that is way off base will naturally raise a red flag.

"Describe to me how your job relates to the overall goals of your department and company."
Everyone should know that a company is in business to make a profit, and not running a social club to keep the feebleminded off the streets. Consequently, the candidate who is alert to how his or her individual efforts fit into the big picture is liable to be more productive and conscientious than one who hasn't a clue. Specifically, this is because this awareness allows a person to take some ownership in the company's success. Additionally, when you have a worker who understands how his or her awareness and best efforts affect everyone else's ability to do their work, you will usually find someone willing to work as a team player.

Likes and Dislikes

Having started with a broad determination of functional capabilities, and having examined the candidate's grasp of his or her role in the great scheme of departmental and corporate affairs, you can now bring the questioning into sharp focus, concentrating on the candidate's likes and dislikes. These questions focus on an individual's ability to take the rough that goes with the smooth in every job. Carol and Sheldon may have great voices and good telephone personalities, but if they have short tempers or are easily ruffled, you would not want to hire them as customer service staff dealing with customer complaints.

You will see that these questions gather valuable information without guiding the candidate toward desirable answers, and while they have been traditionally asked at the face-to-face interview, they are so effective in unmasking mismatches early in the selection process that they can be used effectively during the telephone interview.

"What aspects of your job do you like best?" and *"What would you change about your current job?"*
These two questions can be most effective when asked in sequence, getting an answer to the first before proceeding to the second. The first question connects the dots in the like/dislike area. It might reveal that what a potential employee likes most is the "busywork" connected with the job. We have all seen individuals who seem to work like Trojans all day but never seem to get anything done; they are task oriented rather than goal-completion oriented. So, the question helps reveal good potential matches with your candidates when the most favored areas closely match your defined needs.

The second question in the sequence becomes a potential knockout if the "changes" or "least likes" are in conflict with your most critical functions and "must-haves." And no matter how qualified, someone who has problems with one of your "must-haves" is obviously not suitable for your job and should be rejected now; job distraction can lead only to fast turnover.

"What are the most repetitive tasks in your job?"
This is the first part of a two-part question. With this setup, you will gain knowledge of a candidate's real understanding of the job and whether his or her work ethic matches your requirements. It will also reveal those areas the candidate may find boring. The second part of the question is, "How do you handle them?" You inquire in two parts to avoid giving the candidate any guidance toward the type of response desired. In this second part of the question sequence, you are looking for clues as to how the candidate handles the necessary but repetitive tasks that come with every job.

"What are you looking for in your next job?"
This question fits in comfortably here or, alternatively, could find its way into the conversation while you are verifying employment and salary history. In the candidate's answer, you will be alert for a match between the candidate's needs for the future and what your opening can genuinely provide. A match will give the candidate job satisfaction and provide you with a motivated employee. The farther apart the candidate's desires are from your ability to satisfy them, the smaller your chances of maintaining a long-term working relationship.

"What kind of things bother you most about your job?"
You must remember to compare the answer to this question honestly with the job's realities. Just imagine hiring a receptionist who hated being rushed, or loathed the sound of ringing bells. Again, we are looking for matches to move forward, and mismatches to give you opportunities to bail out.

Money

Money makes for good specific questions. It is also a topic that should always be addressed first on the telephone, because it is foolhardy to waste time and money conducting a face-to-face meeting when there is a serious fiscal imbalance. At the same time, you should be aware that neither of you are in a position to negotiate money at this point. There are a number of questions that you can ask here, but probably just one will suffice, just as long as it puts the candidate in the ballpark.

"How much money are you making?"
You might expect a little fudging on earnings: everyone has done it at one time or another. Consequently, you might find it advisable to add a little preamble along the lines of, "I've lost really good people because they felt it necessary to fudge, so I make it a point to tell everyone two things: We always do our best to make fair offers, and we always check references and salary history." If the candidate is making more than the top of your salary range, and you have no control over changing the position's approved parameters, you might as well end the conversation here, and keep that good candidate in mind for a more senior opportunity.

"How much money do you want?"
I really recommend you stay away from this question, unless the answer to the prior one has put this person at or very near the top of your approved salary range for the job. You may get this response: "That depends on the job. How much are you paying?" If this happens, I've always found it best to be quite straightforward: "I'm not trying to negotiate with you now, John; it is just that you are already quite close to the top of my approved salary range, and I wouldn't want to waste your time or mine."

"What else should I know about your qualifications for this job?" or *"What else should I know about you?"* or *"Is there anything else you want to tell me?"*
Such questions are clear signals to the interviewee that the conversation is drawing to a close, and that it is the last opportunity for the candidate to bring forth or emphasize any strengths or relevant experience. You may even discover hidden talents that the course of the interview has not revealed. At least, you will reassure yourself that nothing valuable has been missed.

At this point, and with a selection of questions like these, you should probably have adequate information to determine whether or not a particular candidate is worth meeting in person.

The Verdict

By the end of the interview, you will have reached one of three conclusions:

The candidate is not able to do the job. If this is the case, you will terminate the interview as soon as you make the determination; you do not have to continue with the interview once you have determined there is a mismatch. Instead, let the candidate down gently. For one thing, it is common courtesy, and though he or she is inappropriate for today's opening, this same person could be right for tomorrow's urgent need. You can say, "Joan, a lot of people are interested in this job, and I feel that you may not make the short list for this particular position. However, you have some unique skills, and I would like to keep you in mind for the future." Or "Mark, it sounds like you have some interesting skills, but I have already spoken to a couple of people who seem a little better qualified for this particular position. We never know how our needs are going to change, and I'd like to keep your resume in my database for future reference."

You are still not sure. Tell the person how you feel (we can all handle the truth) and suggest that while you are considering the matter, the applicant may want to write you a letter emphasizing his or her relevant strengths.

You might say, "Competition is keen, and I have others to talk to. I'm not sure at this point whether you will make the short list, but I have to give it further consideration. If you are interested in the job, I'd like you to write me a letter detailing your strengths, and how you would overcome your weaknesses. It could help." This additional test might also help you evaluate professional behaviors such as determination, motivation, and written communication skills.

The candidate is able and motivated. This is someone you will want to talk to; it is now time to invite the candidate in for a face-to-face meeting and also time to set the ground rules:

▶ Agree on a mutually convenient date, time, and location to meet.

▶ Explain that you will treat any and all information shared with you as confidential.

▶ Explain that you expect application forms (where relevant) to be filled out accurately and completely.

▶ Explain that if all goes well, you intend to check references.

People always respect what you inspect. These statements (especially the one about checking references) will encourage honesty throughout the selection process.

As much as the pressures of the real world allow, schedule interviews with all the short-list job candidates as close together as is practical, so that you are able to objectively compare them against one another.

Delegating the Phone Interview

Once your telephone interviews have helped you confirm a short list of candidates, you will want to prepare for each conversation, and that is where we are headed in the next chapter. Before that, though, let's look at a way phone interviews can become a further time management tool for you and a skill development tool for some of your better people.

Once you are comfortable with the phone interview procedure, you can delegate the process to one or more of your trusted people. Because the phoner is a straightforward fact-finding mission, you can assign the task to competent individuals on your staff, provide some initial interview training, and with clear instructions have those people conduct the telephone interview as outlined in this chapter.

Or, between this interview and the face-to-face meeting, you could have one of your employees conduct a fact-finding interview based on the questions you have from the resume. You would instruct your employee to verify all of the flagged areas from the resume, paying attention to employment dates, salary progressions, and reasons for leaving different employers.

Your only concern here is having a staff member at or near the same level engaged in salary discussions of any type, because this is a matter for serious consideration.

The quickest way to prepare staff members to become part of your selection team might be to have them read these sections in *Hiring the Best*, then walk them through how it applies to your current job openings, showing them your matching sheets and what you've marked on the resumes, the areas you want them to address, and maybe a list of sample questions that you use yourself. It wouldn't be a bad idea to have them role-play the entire process on the telephone with you a couple of times, with you playing the interviewer and subsequently the candidate.

This delegation might take some additional time initially, but you are ultimately freeing management time while building the skills of your people and motivating them through the opportunity for further professional growth. As you know, to climb the ladder you have to have someone to fill the gap behind you.

Backstage Passes: The Art and Science of Interviewing 6

*T*here are two terrible places to be during an interview: Sitting in front of the desk, as the candidate, wondering what is going to happen next; and sitting behind the desk, wondering the same damn thing. If you feel that way as an interviewer, don't panic. When learning any new skill, everyone starts as an unconscious incompetent; in this case, that's the interviewer who doesn't know that he or she doesn't know how to interview, and who looks at a face-to-face meeting as a chance "to get to know" the person. Unconscious incompetence is the first of four stages necessary for skill development.

Next, when we start to pay attention—"Omigosh, I don't know what I'm doing, and I'd better take action!"—we progress to the second stage of enlightenment, which is that of conscious incompetence. At this stage, the interviewer knows that there is more to interviewing than at first realized, and commits to increasing his or her knowledge. The third step, and the one you are taking by reading *Hiring the Best,* will take you to the level of the conscious competent: the interviewer who knows what he or she is doing every step of the way, who does not wear the mask of self-deception, and who consciously plans each action for the results it will yield. That fourth step of learning? That of the unconscious competent. This happens when conscious competence has become second nature, and you no longer remember what it was like to stumble along wondering what question you should ask next and what you would do with the information if you got it anyway.

F. Lee Bailey, perhaps the greatest courtroom performer of recent times, has talked of going into court with fifty rabbits in his hat, but never knowing which he will need to use; consequently, he has to be ready with multiple approaches and questioning techniques. F. Lee Bailey is attentive to detail, and he usually wins.

You too have your day in court, whenever you interview a potential new employee. In each instance you are defending your livelihood and your standing as a competent manager, with your metaphorical top hat full o' tricks. In this chapter we will talk about how to structure an interview. We'll also give you an array of different approaches to the art of polite interrogation, along with a comprehensive selection of questioning and conversational control techniques and a primer on organizing sequential multiple interviews and getting the best out of second opinions.

Interview Structure

For your interviews to be productive when you are evaluating one candidate against another, they must be based on objective criteria. You need to evaluate the same criteria in the same way, with each candidate, to assure that objectivity. You can achieve this by creating a structure, or template, for your interviews and following that structure when you conduct them.

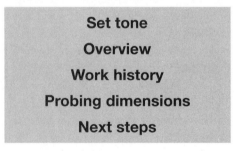

Set tone

Overview

Work history

Probing dimensions

Next steps

Setting the Tone

It all begins with setting the right tone for your interviews, so that the candidate will feel respected and as relaxed as possible. You want this tone because a relaxed candidate will give you more information, and a candidate who experiences an atmosphere of professional respect is most likely to accept a job offer. You need maximum cooperation from the candidate to gain the most insight, and rejected offers represent an embarrassing waste of your time.

While the need for your offers to be accepted dictates that you must have the ammunition ready to sell the job—the educational and professional growth opportunities, and the desirability of your company as a place to work—that does not mean you must use it with every candidate who comes through the door. In fact, selling the company too early in the process, and therefore to too many candidates, wastes your time both while doing it and later in dodging anxious follow-up calls from congenital imbeciles you probably wouldn't hire on a bet.

Getting in the habit of setting the right tone also saves you the necessity of "selling" the company so strongly during the interview process. A job interview is an uncomfortable affair for you, and worse for the poor devil who's sweating in the lobby. The candidate's tension is created by the very nature of the decision about to be made. Every job candidate feels at some level that the acceptance/rejection decision soon to be handed down is based on his or her validity as a person. To understand how to treat the job candidate respectfully without overtly "selling" the company, just turn the tables and think of the atmosphere that would encourage you, as a candidate, to open up during a job interview.

First and foremost, make the candidate comfortable and relaxed as easily and as quickly as you can. It's not so much part of wooing as it is part of not getting fooled: a person treated in a warm and friendly manner from the start will respond to questioning in a more open and honest manner than will someone whose defenses are raised.

First impressions are indelible, and you can make a positive or negative impression before you ever meet your short list of candidates. Does the front desk know that you are expecting someone? How are interviewees normally treated on arrival at your company? The tension a candidate feels at these times can be blown all out of proportion by a poor reception: "Oh, yeah, another lamb to the slaughter, seats for the abattoir are over there, take a number." Creating the right impression in the lobby means that your candidate immediately gets a picture of your company as a good place to be, if the receptionist says, "Good morning, Ms. Jones; Martin Yate told me to expect you. May I offer you some refreshment?" Every staff member who comes in contact with potential employees should be trained to treat them as welcome guests. It is usually easy to get people on the same page once they understand that they have an important role in the process.

The same concept applies when meeting a candidate for the first time. It is conceivable that you could impress someone with your importance by sending a minion to lead the way to your castle—it is done all the time—but setting the right tone takes no more effort than using the same good manners you exercise when welcoming a visitor to your home. Meet the candidate in the lobby yourself if you possibly can, and offer a sincere welcome.

Look the candidate in the eye. Give a firm handshake and say, "Hi, I'm pleased to meet you, Ms. Jones, and I'm looking forward to getting to know you better." If it hasn't been done yet, offer something to sip—coffee, tea, or water. Between interview nerves and cotton mouth, your gesture will be greatly appreciated.

Much has been written about the interview environment, including tripe like this: "Set a relaxed atmosphere. Don't interview across a desk. It sets a barrier. Instead, sit in easy chairs across a low coffee table." I say "tripe," because for most of us it is impractical; we mostly live in cubicles so small you have to step outside to change your mind.

Easy chairs, a coffee table, and good service would be nice, of course, but if you can't snatch a plush office for your interview, privacy is the main thing. You need a room with a door that can be closed, and both your staff and the front desk need to know that you are not to be disturbed with telephone calls or unexpected intrusions. Very little can happen in your department during the twenty minutes to an hour needed for a typical interview that cannot wait until its end for your attention.

In preparation, make sure that you have all the relevant information about the job and the company in one master file (HR can help you set up something with all the right documentation). In the candidate's file, which you will sensibly have set up, of course, will be the resume and any notes from telephone conversations.

The Benefit Statement and Interview Outline

Your interviews should always begin with a little small talk to relax the candidate: "How was the journey; did you find the place easily?" This shouldn't take more than a minute.

Proceed with a nonspecific outline and benefit statement. "We are looking for a _____ ," and I want to learn about your experience and the strengths you can bring to our team. We can get the best out of this by turning it into a conversation between a couple of pros, sharing information and specific examples from your work experience. You'll talk about your work experiences, and I'll explain a little about what we do here. I want you to know that you wouldn't be here unless I already have a feeling that you have what it takes."

Tell the candidate that his or her background looks interesting, you were impressed by the way the telephone interview progressed, and "I have lots of topics to talk with you about." If you intend to take notes, say so! If note taking is too distracting for you, take ten minutes immediately after the interview to create a written review of the interview; do it before you get back into the daily swing of emergency, catastrophe, and mayhem.

If there will only be one interview, you might want to briefly explain the process: that you have a number of people to interview, and that with a final candidate you intend to check references and salary history prior to an offer, or that an offer will be dependent on subsequent checking of both. Making that announcement early helps to create an atmosphere of honesty; again, people respect what you inspect, not what you expect.

Job History

A job interview is a situation in which every moment you spend talking is lost evaluation time, so your next step is to get the candidate talking and you listening. Any candidate is going to be nervous, so you start with nonthreatening questions about work history.

It will get you both on the same page, and the candidate's vocal cords working, if you have him or her walk you through the work history on the resume: "I'd like to get an idea of how you got where you are today, so why don't we take just a couple of minutes for you to walk me through your resume?" For the most part, restrict yourself to easy-to-ask, easy-to-answer questions that allow the candidate to get used to talking and to the idea that you are thorough in your analysis. Ask basic questions about the type of tasks and projects; what the candidate liked and disliked about certain jobs (only those most closely resembling your opening are relevant) and certain managers; how past managers have gotten the best out of him or her; the reason for leaving the last job; and the reason for leaving the current position.

This is as far as most interviews go, but if the candidate warrants deeper consideration, it is where your interview is just getting serious. If that isn't the case, your candidate will be quite happy with what feels like a typical interview, and you can bail out in one of two ways:

- You can say that there are other candidates to consider, and that you will be in touch. You can either call with the news or develop a polite rejection letter that you can use on a regular basis.

- You can reject the candidate in person: "I've enjoyed meeting you, Carla; however, I have already interviewed someone who has a little more suitability for the job. This has by no means been a waste of time. I have enjoyed meeting you and I'll definitely keep your resume on file."

Performance/Deliverables/Skill Set/Behavioral Profile Examination

When you have a candidate who looks promising, you will move forward into the meat of the interview by examining the candidate's skills, accomplishments, and supportive behaviors as they apply to each of your critical, "must have" competencies.

Because you performed a proper job analysis and used a telephone interview for initial screening, you have already isolated these critical components of the job. Your task will now be to examine candidates' abilities to perform each of these duties, their possession of the professional behaviors that allow them to execute the duties with efficiency, their motivation to do the job well, and their overall manageability at work. The hundreds of interview questions in the following chapters will help you frame the questions you need to gather the right information, and the following interview strategies will ensure that you get the truth and maintain control of the process.

For some positions there will be a number of carefully structured interviews, in which case the first interview in the cycle will logically restrict itself to the "must have" critical performance skills of the job, with subsequent meetings looking into the presence of "nice to have" skills. If there is to be only one interview, you will want to add another level of performance evaluation to cover any of the "nice to have" skills and attributes you identified in your job analysis.

The Science of Interviewing Styles

Beyond asking a carefully sequenced series of questions to determine competency and skill levels, there are four fairly distinct approaches to interviewing, each of which can add depth and substance to the information you gather with your questions. They are *situational*, *professional behavior profiling*, *stress*, and *behavioral*. Each style has its strengths and weaknesses, but none of them stands entirely alone as a sole approach to selection. There are really useful techniques to be learned from each of these approaches, so let's look at them individually, and then adopt facets of each into a comprehensive interviewing template that is customized to fit your specific needs.

Situational

Situational interviewing is based on the theory that the closer you can get a candidate to the real work situation, the better your evaluation will be. You take a candidate on a tour of the workplace as an integral part of the proceedings, but not just to fill in time. You will also get the prospective employee to actually perform some aspect of the job. You stand by the computer with a programmer and discuss applications, then have the candidate use that application on a prepared exercise; you ask an accountant to analyze a balance sheet with procedural mistakes built in; you put a telemarketer on the phone in another office and role-play a few typical marketing calls.

As a corporate management trainer by trade, I was once surprised by being submitted to situational interviewing techniques myself. At an interview for a management-training job, I was shown around the corporate training center, and the tour finished with my interviewer and me standing by the flip charts, overhead projector, and other presentation paraphernalia. "How do you think you'd like training here?" asked the interviewer innocently. "Fine," I said, unaware of what was to follow. "Great. Then to get a feel for what it will be like, why don't you teach me something? I'll take a seat over here. Take five minutes and teach me anything you want." Afterward, I reviewed what had happened. There I was, a top trainer, being put through my paces. No amount of probing and reference-checking could give the interviewer quite the same taste for my platform skills as seeing those skills in action. It also allowed the interviewer to see whether I had a style compatible with the fabric of the corporation. As an interviewer, situational ploys can get you closer to the real job than can almost any other technique. Take a few minutes to consider aspects of a job you will be filling that could be adapted to a role-play or other situational interviewing approach.

Professional Behavior Profile

We discussed a number of universally desirable, learned professional behaviors earlier in the book, when we addressed defining a position's specific needs: analytical skills, determination, communication skills, time management, and organization, to name a few. The relative presence of desirable professional behaviors becomes important at this point; for example, many core competencies require the application of time management and organization for any employee to be successful in his or her work.

As another example, salespeople (given knowledge of the product or service) still need good communication skills to succeed, and even then they will not be successful unless they have a determination profile that enables them to experience rejection of their product or service without getting emotionally destroyed. Though such behaviors are paramount to success, you cannot search for them in a vacuum, because they have most relevance when we examine them in the context of their application. Consequently, you will need to identify the professional behaviors that each of your critical skills demands for successful completion, and search for the presence of those behaviors as you evaluate that particular competency: "David, I'd be interested to hear which aspects of your personality help you succeed when you are doing an off-site audit."

Understanding the professional behavioral profile of a candidate will also help you to determine his motivators, and whether he is likely to be manageable and a team player. Consciously looking for certain behaviors in your candidates is a useful approach that, when blended with all these other techniques, will give you an accurate picture of the whole person.

Stress

Every manager can regretfully tell a story of an ex-employee who "looked good on paper," but who just couldn't handle the rigors of the work. Often the problem was an inability to handle the stress that was an integral part of the job. If there is stress on the job you are filling, an employee who has all of the skills in place still will not be successful if he or she cannot function under normal workday stressful conditions—in other words, cannot remain calm while at the same time having listening and analytical processes in high gear.

Depending on the demands of a job, this can be a valuable approach at some point during the selection procedure. In speaking with the manager of a Washington, DC, television talk show, I heard a revealing story about just such a stress dimension. The story is especially valuable because it puts the stress in context: it comes at us unexpectedly. A TV anchor position is a very stressful job; a million things can go wrong and often do, and it is the anchor's task to remain calm and collected under fire. The interviewer in the illustration would end each interview with a promising candidate by saying, "We really are not sure you are suitable for the job." One young woman, who up to that point was a sure top contender, revealed her true colors by getting up and saying, "Well, I'm not sure I want to work here anyway." She showed herself to be someone who couldn't handle the pressure the job called for. She didn't remain calm, her analytical skills jammed, and she didn't listen, and so heard a personal insult rather than an opportunity to set the record straight.

If stress is a real part of the job you are filling, by all means add a stress dimension to the interview, but do be aware that your interviewees are already in a highly stressed situation. Look at some of the stress questions in the coming chapters and adapt them to your needs. You might even involve the stress when applying a situational interview technique: imagine the pressure that the young HR trainer experienced on being told to "Get up there and teach me something."

Behavioral Interviewing

Behavioral interviewing, or past-performance interviewing, applies the leopard-never-changes-its-spots philosophy. It bases all questions in the past, and it requires the candidate to give specific examples from work history. The belief that an individual will do at least as well on the new job as he or she has done in the past is often a reasonable assumption. Past behavior can and does predict future actions, so by asking candidates to talk about specific work experiences, they will recall the details and then get into the habit of answering your questions with details of on-the-job experiences. This is a very effective approach that should be woven into your own customized interview template. We'll go into the techniques of application in a few pages.

With these interviewing approaches, it isn't a matter of choosing either one or another; they probably all have something applicable to your needs. It is a smart idea to have a wide selection of information-gathering techniques at your disposal, because if you rely too heavily on any one selection technique, candidates rapidly become acclimated to that particular approach. Throw nothing but negatively phrased stress questions at a candidate, and the questions soon lose their bite; consistently ask questions about a person's past performance, and the average candidate quickly learns the rules of the game. The same applies to the situational and professional behavior profiling approaches. The sensible approach is to take the best aspects of each style and combine them to produce a comprehensive strategy, a sum greater than its parts. Your template may allow time for the inclusion of situational techniques and the opportunity to test poise with some dastardly stress questions. You will adopt a little from here and a little from there, until you have an approach that is entirely unique to your personality and your needs.

The Art of the Question

Gathering information is the key to competent interviewing, and nothing is going to be more helpful in gathering information than a certain flexibility in your questioning techniques. Here are eleven questioning techniques that will help you vary the structure of individual questions as the situation demands and ensure that you strike the right note every time. You will also be able to apply these conversational techniques in many other areas of your professional life.

#1: The Closed-Ended Question

This is the most frequently abused questioning technique. How often have you heard an interviewer, maybe even yourself, ask a closed-ended question such as, "Can you work under pressure?" Only "yes" and "no" are the possible answers (and who answers "no"?). The result is little or no information, and no way of evaluating any one candidate against another. But while a closed-ended question is inappropriate most of the time, it does have its uses.

The closed-ended question is a useful technique when you are looking for commitment—"Can you start on Monday?"—or when you are refreshing your memory or verifying information from earlier in the interviewing sequence: "You were with Xerox for ten years?" You can also use it to get the ball rolling with a series of questions on the same subject, following with, "And what was your starting title?"

#2: The Open-Ended Question

This is the opposite of a closed-ended question. With an open-ended question, the candidate cannot get by with a monosyllabic answer; instead, the question demands an explanation in response. For example, "How do you respond to pressure at work?" is an open-ended question that asks the interviewee to answer in detail. As a rule of thumb, this style of question is preferable to closed-ended questions, and is more likely to keep the candidate talking and you gathering information.

Open-ended questions can begin in many ways: "I'm interested in hearing about . . . ," "I'm curious to learn . . . ," or "Would you share with me . . ." They also include questions that begin with how, what, where, why, and when, such as, "What typically happened on your job the last time there was an urgent deadline?"

#3: The Past-Performance, or Behaviorally Based Question

Past-performance, or behavioral, questions are based on the premise that patterns of past actions accurately predict future behavior, and that anyone can be expected to do at least as well or as badly with a task on the new job as he or she did with that task in the past. These types of questions help you look at examples of past behavior, and in the process they:

▶ Enable you to learn about the professional behaviors (or lack of them) that a particular candidate has developed to effectively execute his or her duties.

▶ Get the candidate used to illustrating claims and statements. Past-performance questions are open-ended by nature, yet focus on requesting specific details of past events. They are usually prefaced with, "Tell me about a time when . . . ," "Share with me an experience where you had to . . . ," or "Give me an example of a situation that . . ." Ask past-performance questions early in the interview, so that a candidate recognizes early on that he or she is expected to give detailed examples about the past. Showing early in the interview cycle that a pattern of openness and honesty is expected will help establish a foundation of honesty in the candidate's mind.

#4: The Negative-Balance Question

Interviewing isn't anyone's idea of fun, and as a manager you just want to fill the position and get back to business, so it is all too easy to believe that a candidate strong in one area is equally impressive in all areas of your needs. This is not always the case, so when an eerie light appears around a candidate's head, and hymns from a choir of heavenly angels replace the background noise of your office printers, it is time to get a grip and look for negative balance. Try, "That's very impressive. Was there ever an occasion when things didn't work out quite so well?" or the simple, "Now can you give me an example of something in this area of which you are not so proud?"

There will be times when it is obvious that your candidate has all-around strength in this particular area, and you will be comfortable that you exercised due diligence. Also, when you have sought and found negative balance in a skill or behavioral area, you may feel content that you are maintaining your objectivity, and move on.

#5: *The Negative Confirmation Question*

On the other hand, the answer you receive may be disturbing enough to warrant negative confirmation. Let's say the interviewee told you about a time she found it necessary to go around or behind her supervisor to achieve a goal. As a manager, you will be given considerable pause: If such behavior were a common behavioral trait with this individual, you would be unwise to invite her onto your team. Consequently, you will seek negative confirmation with, "You know, that's very interesting. Let's talk about another time when you had to . . ." Successive examples will help you confirm negative traits and perhaps save you from a poor hire. On the other hand, you might find that particular negative situation to be a one-time aberration, and that perhaps there were reasons for the course of action. In all instances, it is a smart idea to ask, "And what did you learn from this experience?"

You can exercise negative confirmation questions at the time, or make a point to use them later during the interview in search of other examples of the unsettling behavior at work. Learn to trust your instinct. If you feel uncomfortable with a candidate in any area, you should always make a point to examine that area further, from different angles, using different techniques and perhaps second opinions.

#6: *The Reflexive Question*

Reflexive questions are great topic-closers and conversation-forwarders. They help you to calmly maintain control of the conversation and, with an overly talkative candidate, your valuable time. If, for instance, your interviewee starts to ramble, it is easy to interrupt with a reflexive question, one that is essentially closed-ended and encourages agreement, and that will allow you to proceed with other topics. This is done by adding to the end of a statement such phrases as: *Don't you? Couldn't you? Wouldn't you? Didn't you? Can't you? Aren't you?* For example: "With time so short, I think it would be valuable to move on to another area, don't you?" The candidate's reflex is to agree, and the conversation progresses in your intended direction. You will of course be careful not to carelessly misuse reflexive questions by asking, "You can work under pressure, can't you?"

#7: The Mirror Statement and Silence

Remember the last cocktail party you attended, when the silence lasted just a couple of seconds and was terminated by two or three people talking at once? This human frailty can be used to your advantage during the interview.

Using mirror statements and silence is a subtle way to ask a candidate to expand on an answer to your question. It says, "Carry on, tell me more." The technique is to mirror or paraphrase a key statement from that answer, and follow it by closing your mouth, nodding, and looking interested.

You can use mirror statements to capture the essence of a candidate's answer and to get more detail. Repeat the substance of key comments: "So, whenever you are two hours late for work, you take off two hours early to make up for it." Then sit and wait for the candidate to expand on the mirrored statement.

You can also just use silence as a signal that you are still interested and listening, to encourage the candidate to continue talking.

#8: The Loaded Question

Loaded questions require a candidate to decide between options that are tough, and sometimes impossible: "Which do you think is the lesser evil, embezzlement or forgery?" There is, however, a very fine line between absurd loaded questions and carefully balanced judgment-call questions. For most interviewers, loaded questions are most commonly used when analytical and ethical behaviors are at a premium and you want to probe the candidate's decision-making processes. The easiest and most effective way to apply a loaded question is to recall a real-life situation in which two divergent approaches were both carefully considered. Then frame the situation as a question starting with "I'm curious to know how you would decide between two approaches where . . ." or, "What would be your approach to a situation in which . . ."

#9: The Leading Question

Leading questions, which are different from loaded questions, allow you to lead the listener toward a specific type of answer, sometimes to reach agreement and then move on to the next topic, and sometimes to begin a series of follow-up questions on the topic.

You have to be careful not to misuse leading questions. This could happen in your explaining what type of company the candidate will be joining. You might proudly explain, "We're a fast-growing outfit here, and there is constant pressure to meet deadlines and satisfy your ever-increasing list of customers. What's your stress threshold?" Any interviewee will know that to retain a chance of landing an offer, he or she must answer a certain way and consequently does so. This is not to say that leading questions are inadvisable, but like closed-ended questions, they must be used appropriately.

Their best use is as information verifiers, to get the candidate to expand on a particular topic. For example: "We are a company that believes the customer is always right. How do you feel about that?" The answer will naturally be in agreement with your question, so you then follow up with other questions on the topic: "So tell me about a time when a customer . . ." "What would you do with a customer who was clearly . . . ?"

#10: The Layered Question

As you can see, we are already taking simple questioning techniques and beginning to blend them together. While a good question poorly phrased will lose its bite and give you incomplete or misleading information, question layering can probe an answer thoroughly and on many different levels. Let's start with the classic example of wanting to know whether a potential employee can work under pressure. Many interviewers would simply ask, "Can you work under pressure?" While the intent is good, the question style is wrong, as it requires only a "yes" or "no" answer, and it leads the interviewee toward a clearly "desirable" answer. The result of misusing a questioning technique is that you learn nothing with which to evaluate this particular candidate against others.

Instead, you can take a leaf out of a good reporter's notebook and layer your questions. The reporter uses *all* the styles we have discussed, peeling layers of truth until a topic has been examined from every angle. The reporter asks who, what, why, when, where, and how. In this instance, you do the same thing by using a closed-ended question to open a behavioral examination that uses a number of questioning techniques.

"Can you work under pressure?"

"Tell me about a time when you had to work under pressure."

"So, it was tough to meet the deadline?"

"How did this pressure situation arise?"

"How would you avoid this situation in the future?"

"Who was responsible?"

"What did you do?"

"What have you learned from the experience?"

"Why do you think these situations occur?"

"Where did the problem originate?"

"Where do you go for advice in these situations?"

With question layering you have different angles of approach to the topic, each revealing a little more about the skills, the personality, the performance, and the professional behavioral profile of your candidate. Nearly every one of the hundreds of interview questions in this book can be given the layering treatment. The technique makes the possibilities for questions theoretically endless; it just depends on how thorough you want to be on a given topic.

Underlying all questioning techniques, and this one in particular, is the understanding that you are not obliged to accept a candidate's first answer to any of your questions; it is, after all, your job that's on the line here. You have a right to look closer and to dig deeper. If you feel that something is lacking in an answer, pursue it by layering your questions. You'll never know unless you ask.

#11: The "Hamburger Helper" Question

Just as people will sometimes use a little Hamburger Helper to make the ground beef go a little farther, so you can use these three questioning techniques to stretch a question. We have touched lightly on each of them already, but they are worth repeating because you will also find them useful from another practical perspective. It sometimes will happen that time constraints force you to conduct one interview after another, and during these mammoth interview sessions you will find yourself comparing one candidate against another as you are asking questions (bad idea, but it happens), and sometimes (from sheer exhaustion) completely forgetting who you are, what you are doing, and what this stranger in front of you is talking about. In all instances, you'll be thankful for knowing about "Hamburger Helper" questions:

1. If you are either dissatisfied with the first answer and want more data, or are so fascinated with the answer that you also want to hear more, say, "Give me some more detail on that. It's very interesting." Or, "Can you give me another example?"

2. You may hear an answer and add after it, "What did you learn from that experience?" This is an excellent layering technique that can give you a handle on analytical skills, judgment, and emotional maturity.

3. Perhaps the best technique for gathering more information is simply to sit quietly, looking at the interviewee and saying nothing. Most people are pressured by a conversational lull.

The Art of Conversation

A wise person once said that people never really listen, but merely wait for their turn to speak. This universal truth can be used to your advantage during the interview. Once you learn the handful of techniques that keep the candidate talking and you evaluating, your interviewing style will begin to take on the feel of a conversation.

Live by the 80/20 Rule

People like to talk, and given the encouragement, most of all they like to talk about themselves to an appreciative audience. At the same time, for each moment you talk during an interview, you lose valuable evaluation time, and the predictable outcome is that you don't have enough information on which to base your decision. Whenever you interview, strive to live by the 80/20 rule: Ask questions 20 percent of the time and you will be able to listen 80 percent of the time. Plan the questions you will ask to gather the information you need to make a decision, and you will be able to dedicate the greater part of your time to listening.

Many interviewers eat up valuable time by commenting on a candidate's answers. Not only does this editorializing take up time; it can also show the candidate where your priorities lie and encourage answers that reflect your values, not the candidate's. While a little conversation as the interview gets going is necessary to set everyone at ease, try not to show signs of agreement or disagreement. In fact, don't comment on answers at all, unless it specifically serves your purpose. Just plug along pleasantly with another question that shows you are deeply interested in the conversation.

Framing Questions

The candidate needs to concentrate on answering your questions, not deciphering them, so use easily understood words and keep the questions simply framed. Don't string too many questions or themes together in one breath. Sloppily framed questions can sound like this: "Tell me about what kind of people you like to work with, what kind of people you don't like to work with, and how you get along with them." On the one hand, this is confusing, and on the other, it also leads candidates toward a "desirable" answer: "I never met a person I didn't enjoy working with."

Sequencing Themes

Try to ask your questions in themes. Address performance and behaviors in critical skill areas one at a time, and then move from one topic to the next, offering clear signposts so that the candidate knows what is happening. For example: "Good, now that we have established that you are a graduate of the Genghis Khan School of Business Management, let's talk about employee turnover." Or, perhaps more seriously, "I have a good feel for your code writing now. I'd like to move on and discuss dealing with in-house clients."

Keeping the Candidate on Track

The person asking the questions in any conversation controls and directs its flow. As the interviewer and the candidate's possible future manager, you should establish that control now. Otherwise, the candidate may find ways to hide vital information you need or to direct the conversation away from your aims. If you ask a chemical engineer what personal qualities he or she thinks are necessary for success in the field, and get an answer like, "Well, you need at least three years' experience and an up-to-date knowledge of recent chemical patents," then you've received an evasive answer, or you are facing an engineer whose ears apparently don't work. Put the interviewee back on track by being gently persistent: "Perhaps I didn't make myself clear; I meant what personal qualities are necessary for success, not what kind of experience."

Handling the Flustered Candidate

Sometimes during a job interview, your candidate will be stumped on a question, either from not knowing the answer, or from that mind-numbing nervous adrenaline rush we have all experienced at one time or another. Then you, as the interviewer, perhaps from a mixture of embarrassment, awkwardness, and common fellow feeling, will let the candidate off the hook with, "That's all right, let's move on." This is the wrong approach. You never want to let a candidate off the hook if he or she is experiencing difficulty in answering your questions; it sets a bad precedent for the interview and for your future management of this person. At the same time, you do want to calm the interviewee down, rather than exacerbating the situation, so whenever this difficulty arises, look the candidate in the eye and say, "That's all right. Take your time to answer. I'm sure something will come." And sure enough, it will. Just sitting quietly and looking at the candidate will encourage more talking.

Don't be a blank wall, though; use silence judiciously. And be careful not to nail a candidate early on with this technique. He or she may become too nervous to proceed. If you face a candidate who is severely stumped for an answer, back off before the trauma gets intense and the interview becomes an exercise in futility. Sometimes it is advisable to move on to another topic to maintain the flow of the interview, but whenever you do this, make a mental note to come back to the topic later when the candidate is more settled: "That's okay, Jodie, everyone gets flustered at an interview. Let's move on to another topic right now, and we'll come back to this later."

Control and the Overly Talkative Candidate

When confronted with a candidate who is inebriated with his own verbosity, your challenge is not so much keeping the conversation going as it is guiding its flow to gather the information you need to make a hiring decision. Difficult as this problem has appeared over the years, it can be easily handled with either of these techniques:

1. Jump into the conversation with, "You know, that's very interesting. It makes me want to ask you about . . ." and then move on to the topic of your choice.

2. Start talking along with the candidate and redirect the conversation to a new area. Keep talking until the candidate shuts up, which should be in the first few seconds.

Do ask yourself, however, that if you have difficulty controlling the candidate now, when he is arguably on his best behavior, what will things be like once he is on payroll and no longer on that "best" behavior?

Some people just need to talk, and they will latch on to any topic at any time to assuage that need. So, for instance, when things go wrong in your department (as they do at times in every department), you will have a prime candidate for stirring the pot of contention rather than putting out the flames. Think carefully about such candidates.

Master these conversational gambits, and your interviews will proceed in the direction you want and deliver the information you need to make objective decisions about any job candidate. This might seem an exhaustive procedure to begin with, so look at it in the context of how this developing skill will help your career over the long run. As we mentioned, mastering these conversational techniques should have professional applications outside of the interview arena.

Next Steps

Once you have completed your carefully considered agenda of topics and questions, it is time to wind down the interview. You do this by saying, "This has been a very interesting meeting; is there anything you would like to add?" This gives the candidate the opportunity to add additional information that she thinks might serve her cause. It is also better than asking, "Do you have any questions?" This invariably leads to queries about salary, vacation, and benefits. You are not obliged to disclose the salary, and you can cover the other matters in a minute or two. What you want to avoid is selling the company to a candidate you do not want to hire, and your evaluation on this issue will guide the detail and enthusiasm you employ in answering such questions.

At this point you need to identify the next steps. If you want to see the candidate again, or have her meet with other staff members, either do it now, or schedule the next meeting (we'll address multiple interviews next).

If you do not wish to proceed further, bail out now, using the phrases we discussed earlier. Alternatively, you can have HR send a polite rejection letter (be sure to understand and follow HR procedures where they exist), or you can send the letter yourself.

Multiple Interviews, Multiple Interviewers

With more complex jobs, additional interviews, and often interviewers, may be required to make a sound decision. Interviews running more than two hours (at the outside) become counterproductive, owing to everyone's exhaustion. If you can't cover all the bases in this time period, it is better to break the one mega-interview into a series of shorter interviews. However, all too often these multiple interviews and second opinions are so poorly orchestrated that they produce little in the way of additional insight.

Just how many interviews and interviewers does it take to make a good hire? It all depends on your planning. Time and again, you hear that familiar request: "Will you spend a few minutes with this candidate for me and tell me what you think?" These additional opinions (and therefore interviews) are sought at least in part because everyone is reluctant to make a wrong decision, and second opinions allow the spread of blame. It doesn't have to be this way.

Let's freeze the actors for a moment during a typical "multiple" interview, walk onto the stage among them, and see what is really going on. To request that colleagues give you merely a second opinion is usually a waste of time. Frequently, the colleague has been given no warning, his or her mind is on other things, you probably forgot to furnish a detailed job description and resume, and there is no preparation time. Like most every other manager, he or she will rely on the same trusty six or eight questions that you already used. You know it's true.

If more than one interview is necessary, decide who should do it, and why. If you still have a lot of uncharted territory to cover because of the complexity of the job, you should be conducting the interviews. A team member could also conduct the interview, if you are doing succession grooming, or more likely another manager with whom you have a reciprocal arrangement could do it, or your boss, when you just want a second opinion.

To make second opinions effective, there has to be clear communication about the determined job requirements as well as a commentary on what has been covered so far, and to what result. It will pay dividends to clearly outline what *you* hope will be covered (you can supply some useful questions), and the insights you expect to glean as a result of the interviews. When people have clear expectations and the tools to deliver on them, you are more likely to get what you seek.

It's more productive if you build an interviewing team that you can use for all your department's hires, and always give participating colleagues adequate notice for interviews and confirm that they can commit the time necessary to gather the information you require. It's a given that you will conduct a briefing with each interviewer; this will include providing *copies* of your personalized job description, the matching sheet, resumes, application forms, and notes about areas covered to date. You will get best results when each interviewer has specific areas to cover; you can even go so far as to provide some suggested questions to accomplish your set task. Of course, this has to be done diplomatically.

When you assign specific and different topic areas to interview team members, everyone will cover different ground, and provide you with a three-dimensional view of your candidates. Your aim is not to get a view of the candidate that merely confirms a hunch, but to get different photographs from different angles, and through different lenses. This is the best way to see the candidate as a whole and to make a considered judgment.

There will be times when you will want your team to repeat certain questions, to see whether you are all getting the same answer. Examples of such an integrity check might be consistency in reasons for leaving jobs, or to re-examine an area where you were uncomfortable with the answers given.

When a candidate's potential peers are involved in the selection process, clearly delineate areas you want addressed and be clear about which areas you do not want them to discuss. Whereas management traditionally sticks to the same six or eight questions, peers restrict themselves to three if left to their own devices: "What's your greatest weakness?" "How much are you making?" "How much do you want?" Questions like these can be harmful to your team-building efforts if you make the hire. With direct reports, you can feel comfortable being specific about the questions you want them to ask and the information you expect to receive.

The Three-Act Play

How many candidates should you interview for one position? As many as it takes to ensure the long-term success of both your department and your career. And how many interviews should you arrange with one candidate? Again, as many as it takes ... but let's be realistic. For lower-level employees, one interview with one interviewer is usually sufficient. As your positions move higher up the ladder, the judgment calls become more complex. You may want to arrange two or three interviews, and perhaps use different interviewers in the process. Let's look at a schematic of what might be addressed in such a sequence of interviews, recognizing that such a schematic is intended merely as a "straw dog"; something that allows you to say, "No, this and this won't do for me; instead I'll organize it this way."

The First Interview

With complex jobs, or when you have a lot of candidates to plow through at lower levels, you might restrict the first interview to dealing with ability in critical functional areas: Are the "must have" competencies present? Do they collectively mean that the candidate can do the job? Does the employment history withstand scrutiny? You will want to feel comfortable about relative strengths and weaknesses in these critical areas, along with the extent of the individual's current responsibilities.

Concentrate on ability questions—leave the "nice to have" aspects of the job, the motivation and manageability issues, to subsequent meetings. If meaningful verbal or written communication is part of the job, now is the time to evaluate and make the necessary decisions. If you decide to use any federally approved skill or aptitude tests, now is the time to do it.

Make sure you get answers to all of your personal knockout questions and find out why the person wants to leave the current job, what the candidate knows about you, and why you are perceived as a suitable potential employer.

The first interview in a sequence becomes a major part of your winnowing process. It should be short, never more than an hour—and when you are organized, it can usually be accomplished in half that time.

The Second Interview

A second interview will continue to examine ability and capability in critical areas, double-check items from earlier discussions, and proceed to look at motivational and manageability factors. If the first interview was performed by HR or delegated to a trusted team leader, you come in at the second level to requalify any area you feel is worthy of your attention. In addition to other factors already mentioned, you might want to address self-esteem, maturity of business comprehension, and degrees of energy and stamina.

When candidates make it to the second round of interviews, they should be real contenders, and as such you begin to pay a little more attention to courtship. Now could be the time for a tour of the facility, as opposed to a walk about the immediate workplace. If permission to check references (required under the 1970 Fair Credit Reporting Act) has not been obtained, get it now. Normally, the permission is included in the application and granted by the candidate's signature, but you should inspect your company's forms to make sure. The end of the second round of interviews should result in only one or two final contenders coming back for a third and final interview.

The Third Interview

Although this final meeting should re-examine sensitive and open areas, and tie up the loose ends, it is also the opportunity to talk about responsibilities and expectations in terms of the projects with which the candidate will immediately be involved. It is the time for any "rubber-stamp" meetings with higher-ups (be sure to prep them succinctly and accurately beforehand; it's an opportunity for you to gain a little bit of credibility and visibility). This is also the time to parade the corporate colors and dazzle the candidate with the company's eminent desirability. During the third interview there are some definite musts. Be sure that all of your remaining short-list candidates understand how your company makes money, and their would-be role in the process. Explain what will be expected of the future employee during this interview, which is when candidates are likely to be most receptive. Take the time to outline the department's mission; these goals and objectives form the umbrella for the future employee's responsibilities. Your clear statement of expectations at this time will build the candidate's confidence in your leadership, the job, and the company.

Multiple interviews can take place over a day, a few days, or a few weeks. While there may be enough time to do it in one day, it is rarely practical, except at the lower levels. Such a scenario restricts the ability of your interviewing team to give each other critical leads and feedback on interesting areas to examine further. In addition, a whole-day session is likely to turn that bright young thing into a basket case. Whenever marathon sessions are necessary, give the candidate time to regroup every now and then in a private office, with a cup of tea or coffee and a telephone. You can use this time to caucus with your team and plan strategy based on the direction the interview is taking.

If you have to drag the hiring process out over an extended period, keep your short list of candidates fully informed. Otherwise that ideal body will be long gone when you are ready to extend an offer. Perhaps your particular situation requires fewer than three interviews and interviewers to make a prudent decision on the short-list contenders; it is, however, unlikely that it will require more than three, if you engage in effective planning.

The Power Luncheon

It may be desirable (social graces are an important determinant of success) or necessary (you gotta eat sometime) that one of the interviews take place in a public setting. Using a luncheon or similar quasi-social meeting as the third interview setting can be a good opportunity to gain additional information that would be difficult to obtain in the more formal office setting. You can learn much of value and gain insight into the candidate's personality while to all appearances indulging in the simple delights of the table.

Eating in front of others can make job candidates nervous. Throw a question-and-answer dimension in, and you have a stress interview situation thrown in as an added benefit. Even without the questioning, these occasions give you the opportunity to see signs of poor self-discipline, exemplified by over-ordering food and drink. You can observe an inherent insensitivity to others, which could affect team building, in the way your guest behaves toward waiters and buspersons. Aspects of doubtful judgment and emotional immaturity can be detected in the way your guest orders the most expensive and exotic foods on the menu. What does one think about a person who is profligate with company money before even reaching the formality of being on the payroll? What is your travel and entertainment budget going to look like? You might also note insecurity and free-floating hostility when your guest starts returning the ice water.

The candidate is there primarily to talk and be judged, which is another reason for remembering the 80/20 rule on these occasions. With it firmly in mind, you can eat quite decently as you listen to answers to your questions.

For a power luncheon, you should choose a restaurant you know and where you are known in turn. Book a secluded table, ideally in a corner, and explain the importance of this when you make the reservation. Allow your candidate the privilege of sitting with his or her back to the wall, which can make a person feel more secure. You might also ask whether the candidate is comfortable with the choice of restaurant. You want the candidate to bare the innermost reaches of the soul, which won't happen if he or she feels nervous about current employers appearing.

In vino veritas, so offer drinks; you may well have made prior arrangements for your gin and tonic to be absent the gin. To increase privacy and avoid interruptions, order all your food at the beginning of the meal. With these simple matters in mind, you can get down to the questions you had planned.

Competent Interviewers

Managers who build teams that can conquer any problem or bounce back from any setback are, first and foremost, competent interviewers. As you can see, becoming a competent interviewer takes time and effort, but the lessons you have to learn are logical and common sense: to make good hiring decisions, you need a plan of attack, and a structure that offers a flexible approach to understanding skills, supportive behaviors, experience, credentials, motivation, and manageability. Such a structure ensures that you cover all the necessary bases all the time, thus encouraging objectivity in your evaluations.

It is now time to look at the questions you will place within your structure to ensure that you live by that 80/20 rule.

Ability and Suitability

*I*t is a fallacy to think that all you need to make a good hire is finding someone whose resume says he or she can do the job. Ability, as expressed by experience with each of the required skill sets, is obviously important, but you are also looking for someone who has a clear understanding of the job's deliverables: what it must produce, the problems it is there to solve, and the problems it is there to avoid. Beyond these considerations, you also need to determine the presence of all the relevant learned professional behaviors that enable an employee to execute the required duties in a responsible and timely fashion.

Industry sensibilities can play an important consideration. It isn't mandatory to always hire someone with experience in your particular industry, but it can shorten the start-up time. For example, a computer programmer working in a bank has certain technical and professional skills; that is, the ability to write code for an application. That same programmer also has certain knowledge of how things get done *in the industry in which he or she operates*; in this case, understanding why the banking industry operates the way it does. Such professional or industry knowledge speaks to another level of awareness and *suitability*.

So when you ask questions to determine "ability," you are looking for information on a number of levels: ability to do the job, with an awareness of the professional context in which the job exists, as well as ability to anticipate problems and solve them when they do occur. All the information that you gather about a person's ability to do the job will be supported by the presence of desirable professional behaviors. Let's review the areas that help you evaluate ability and suitability for the job.

Can the Applicant Do the Job?

Hiring the candidate who says "Hey, I can do this job—give me a shot and I'll prove it to you" is not enough anymore. You want to hire the candidate who can *prove* it by demonstrating a combination of all of the attributes that define an ability to do the job. How well the candidate programs that computer, services that client, or sews up that appendix is part of the picture: knowing the steps involved well enough *to be able to explain them clearly and simply to others*, and understanding how and why things are done in a certain way in the profession or industry, is a further consideration.

Review your analysis of the technical/professional duties as they parallel the job requirements. Then analyze the processes and skills that are needed to effectively discharge each of those duties. Recall real-world situations that illustrate an employee handling a particular task both exceptionally well and exceptionally poorly. This can help you structure questions around the realities of work in your department and generate questions that ask, "What would you do in a situation when/where . . . ?" "Tell me about a time that required you to . . ."

When you recall real challenges that occur on the job, you will be better able to break down the component parts of the job, and devise questions whose answers will reveal a candidate's analytical skills and problem-solving abilities. Additionally, the answers to your questions will reveal whether or not a candidate has adopted the behaviors that will help him or her be successful in the timely execution of duties.

Determining ability, problem-solving skills, learned professional behaviors, motivation, teamwork, and manageability is important, but you need to proceed in an orderly manner. For example, you need not take the time to evaluate a candidate's manageability and team orientation until you know that a person can do the job. Likewise, that key attribute of motivation only becomes important once ability is determined.

With this in mind, the focus of this chapter will be how to determine a candidate's ability to do the job, supported by his or her problem-solving skills and professional behavioral profile. In the next chapter, we will look at questions that help us determine motivation. Motivation is critical, of course, but there's no need to determine the "will do" until you have established the presence of "can do."

Without the ability to do the job, motivation is irrelevant, and without ability and the motivation to take the rough with the smooth, who cares if a candidate is manageable? You should bear this in mind when sequencing your questions, so that you won't waste time determining a candidate's relative manageability when that person simply isn't capable of doing the job. At the same time, as you work through the hundreds of interview questions in the coming pages, you will see that a question specific to ability, for example, will also begin to deliver insights into motivation, teamwork, and manageability.

You Start with Questions about Ability

The meat of an interview starts with getting a reading of employment history, and then carefully examining specific competencies and behaviors as they apply to your job opening. What was the person's functional responsibility and ability in each of those positions? Is the candidate therefore functionally suitable for the job you have in mind? When you start off with questions that are easy to answer, it helps the candidate to relax, and helps you to hit your interviewing stride. Remember the 80/20 rule, which requires you to ask questions 20 percent of the time and then listen for 80 percent. Only when the candidate is comparatively relaxed should you start throwing the curve-ball questions. If you start in with tough questions too soon, your candidate's defenses will never come down and she or he will never open up to you in a way that will give you the greatest insight.

The past is less threatening for the candidate than is the present, so begin with questions about earlier jobs. That way, you will be more likely to get truthful, straightforward answers. Then, as your questions gradually approach the present, your candidate will have established a pattern of honesty, a habit that is hard to break and easy for you to identify when it is broken.

Each manager's situation is unique, so there is no proper sequence to follow, no single revealing, streamlined set of questions to ask. You will naturally customize the questions to suit your particular needs for a specific opening, and you should take the time to put any question into your own voice. The written word varies dramatically from the spoken word, and on top of that, no two people have the same speech rhythms or vocabulary. The way you phrase a question, and the tone of voice you use in asking it, will give your questions range and depth.

The question sequences in this and all of the following chapters have been organized to proceed logically, but they are only intended as a template that you can adapt to your specific needs and to the information-gathering style that is comfortable for your personality.

Basic Responsibilities

This first sequence of questions examines areas of a candidate's functional responsibilities. These questions may help you gain insight into skills, special knowledge, and relative strengths and weaknesses. You can repeat this particular sequence as required through every job the candidate has held. The cumulative result will be a clear picture of the candidate's essential "can do" abilities. You may have asked some of these questions during the telephone interview, but it doesn't hurt to go over them again in greater detail, especially as they concern the candidate's current job.

When you have walked the candidate through his or her work history, you reach the first decision-making, or bail-out, point. If the candidate can't do the job, or you have already seen four more who are better qualified, bail out now using the words and phrases you employed for this purpose during the telephone interview. If the candidate passes this first hurdle, you can move on.

"What would you say were the most important responsibilities in that job?"
This is a simple information-gathering question that is also the start of a sequence that helps you delve deeper. Jot down the answers and then examine each of these responsibilities in turn: *"Tell me about your duties in [specific area]."* Then follow it with, *"What special skills or knowledge did you need to perform [this duty]?"* If the candidate responds in terms of education, look out especially for any courses or seminars to which a prior employer may have sent the person. This kind of information is useful to you in a couple of ways: First, it tells you that a prior employer felt that the candidate was a good investment of time and money, which is an endorsement in itself; second, it tells you that such an investment won't have to be made on your budget. Then ask, *"What, if any, were the personal behaviors you applied to get the job done?"* Combined, these questions will not only tell you about functional experience, but will begin to give you an insight into the depth of understanding that the candidate has for his or her work.

In most instances, the most valuable and relevant information will come from the last seven to ten years or last three jobs, whichever comes first. This is because the pace of technology is such that if you go much farther back you are peering into the mists of antiquity. Apart from establishing depth of experience, any information from the more distant past has less practical value regarding the ability to execute the tasks at hand. Of course, with a management hire, you will be searching for the progression that led to management, the growth and presence of hands-on skills, and that candidate's ability to get work done through others.

The following questions can be asked about major duties on any job, but will be most valuable when the duties under examination relate directly to your critical needs.

"What decisions or judgment calls did you have to make in these areas?"
The answer to this question defines the individual's level of responsibility, or at least what he or she sees as the extent of that responsibility. For instance, it could be useful to know that a candidate routinely makes decisions alone that in your department would require consultation with a superior. It can be helpful to follow up this question with, *"That's interesting. Tell me how you approach decision-making in an area like this."* You can add a situational follow-up question here: "*Can you give me a real-world example of your making a judgment call like this?*" In the answer you will hope to hear about the analytical skills of problem identification and solution, coupled with an awareness of systems and procedures.

"What achievements are you most proud of in this particular area?"
People are always happy to talk about their achievements, and you are happy to listen for what the answers can tell you about the individual: Were the achievements something that truly benefited the company and the department, or not? Be especially alert for exaggerated claims, and if you sense possible exaggeration, ask about the role of others in this achievement. This question can also be positioned as the first part of a two-part probe, the second part being, *"Tell me about a problem you experienced in this area, something you found difficult to handle."* This is an example of consciously introducing a negative-balance dimension. Whenever you give a candidate the chance to dazzle you with excellence, give yourself the chance to balance the view. The mettle of a man or woman can often be best judged by how he or she handles adversity, and while your question is primarily examining ability, the answer will also tell you something about motivation.

"What was the most difficult project you tackled at [that job]?"
With this question, you are looking for parallels to your situation, as well as analytical skills. Undoubtedly, you are hiring a new staff member to solve problems of some kind, so it would be interesting to discover how your candidate's success with a difficult project could be brought to bear on some of your upcoming challenges.

"How did you feel about your workload at that company?" and *"How did you divide your time among your major areas of responsibility?"* and *"With all of your responsibilities, how do you plan and organize your workload?"*
These are questions that examine a candidate's time management and attitude toward the workload. While you may well decide to probe time management more closely later in the interviewing cycle, these questions will logically fit into the conversational flow at this point and neatly end the question sequence.

"What was more important on your job, written or oral communication?"
You will receive input on verbal communication skills throughout the interview. Though the quality of verbal skills can be a predictor of writing skills, written communication still is more of a challenge. The higher up the professional ladder, the more important written communication becomes. The resume, cover letter, and subsequent communications that the candidate sends can give you insight here. Your needs may dictate that you request some examples of written communication, or that you ask the candidate to send you a follow-up letter about his or her interest in the job. You might also examine comprehension of business practices and analytical skills (and utilize a little situational interviewing technique) by having the candidate encapsulate a long report, or tell you which of two reports is the best, and why. Nothing's better than seeing communication in action.

When written skills are important, you can ask, *"What was the most complex report you ever had to write?"*

And follow up with, *"What made this report so difficult? How did you handle it?"* Follow with, *"Looking back, how would you have improved it, made it easier to understand?"*

All of the questions in this section, when tailored to your individual circumstances, will help you determine ability, and of course, you'll find many more in the balance of the book. As the interviewer, however, it is unwise to leave this topic without throwing in one catchall question: *"What other functional, day-to-day activities were you involved with that we haven't discussed?"* Here the candidate has the opportunity to bring up skills and attributes that may not have surfaced so far in your conversation.

How Long Will the New Employee Stay?

Hiring is usually done in the hope that you will land the perfect employee, someone who will serve faithfully down through the years as your star rises in the corporate heavens. Sometimes this dream is shattered when a valued employee unexpectedly pulls up stakes and moves on. With that in mind, it is a good idea to examine all of the candidate's attitudes and reasons for leaving jobs in the past. That knowledge of the past can help us predict, and therefore avoid, unpleasant problems in the future. The answers you receive will also help give you a handle on motivation and manageability issues, because you'll learn what it will take to get the best out of this person.

"If you went to your boss for a raise, why would you be doing it?"
This may seem like a strange place to start, but closer examination of the reasoning will settle your mind. Anyone initiating an approach for salary or performance review feels a real or perceived lack of recognition and appreciation, and as someone once said, loyalty is a function of appreciation.

Watch out for answers such as, "I deserve it." What you want to hear are citations of solid contributions that demonstrate how the individual has the company's interests at heart. Often, the response will lead the two of you naturally into a discussion about the reasons behind a candidate's desire to make a job change.

"What will your boss say when you go in to resign?"
This question can be helpful in determining how serious the person is about making a move. Sometimes, an employed candidate uses your job offer as leverage with a current employer, and has no real intention of leaving the present situation.

"What was the date you joined that company?"
This question will be followed by, *"What was your title when you joined?"* and *"What was your starting salary?"* Together, these three questions help to set a tone for the meeting. They show that you intend to get specific answers. Immediately, the candidate will realize that you are someone who expects, and has the inspection tools to get, the facts. The salary questions

asked for each job—*"What was your starting salary?" "How much were you making when you left?"*—show you the type of raises this person is likely to be satisfied with and the level of salary increase he or she is in the habit of accepting when making a job change. Sudden jumps in earnings can alert you to potential untruths. For example, when a person with a history of 5 percent increases suddenly makes a 20 percent jump, one of two things has happened: Either the individual is fudging the truth or has started to achieve way above prior performance levels, perhaps making a major contribution to an employer. Whatever the case, you will want to know.

However, because just about everyone has fudged on earnings every now and then, you may want to limit the number of black marks you award; it is up to you. Many managers use the exercise just to establish a truthful pattern in the candidate's answers, and when they come across a fudge of this nature prefer simply to let the candidate off the hook with some dignity by saying, "That is such a big increase that perhaps I should have made myself more clear. I am just looking for salary, not the value of your benefit package as well."

"Why did you leave[the company]?" or "Why did you leave that/this job?"
This is one of the world's most popular—and usually least effective—interview questions. On its own, it has become ineffective through overuse; almost every job interviewee has a pat and acceptable answer ready. That's okay, because here you use this question as the first of two parts. The second part is less common and more likely to get you an honest answer:

"In what ways did your boss contribute to your desire to leave?"
Now, while this question fits very neatly in the procedure of establishing work history and general ability to do a job, it also sheds light on potential manageability and emotional maturity.

If a candidate tells you that he or she was laid off, it bears further examination. There are only two ways to leave a job: You either quit or get terminated. That termination might be for cause (burning down the company cafeteria) or, increasingly, because of company downsizing and offshoring; it might just be that the candidate was in the wrong place at the wrong time. Whichever it is, inquiring minds want to know.

Whatever the explanation, you will want to verify it when you check references. If the candidate explains that he or she was fired, you'll ask, *"Why were you fired?"* and listen very carefully to the answer. Watch for the pointing finger of blame. When we point the finger of blame we often ignore the three fingers pointing back at ourselves. Firing an employee is usually one of the most unpleasant jobs a manager will ever have to do, and because of legal ramifications it is not a decision that is ever taken lightly. If there has been a termination with cause and the candidate has taken responsibility and made changes as a result, you shouldn't necessarily rule that person out; we all make mistakes, and we can all learn from them.

If you discover gaps in the work history, probe the reasons for them and their duration with a question such as, *"Why were you out of work for so long/so often?"*

More than one manager has confided in me that they sometimes find that these reason-for-leaving questions throw a candidate off balance, and they want to know how best to get the interviewee back on track. This problem is neatly solved by asking, *"How did you get your last job?"* Answering this question relaxes the candidate after the difficulty of talking about unemployment or job changing. The answer can also profile the candidate's determination, creativity, and analytical approaches to problem solving, which are three character traits common to many successful professionals.

"Why have you changed jobs so frequently?"
It costs money to hire and bring someone up to speed on a new job, so unless there are solid reasons for a candidate's job-hopping—and in today's workplace there often are—you won't want to invest valuable time in a person who is likely to stay with you only a short while.

On the other end of the spectrum you might find that a candidate has been with one company for many years. In this case you might ask, *"Why, after all these years, are you changing jobs now?"*

If stress is a dimension of the job you are filling, this might be an opportunity to introduce some when least expected: *"Some people feel that spending so much time on one job demonstrates a lack of initiative. How do you feel about that?"*

The question will come as such a shock that it will give a good reading on fast thinking and poise. You can, of course, temper the question to suit the situation, the job, and your personality.

"What have you learned from jobs you have held?" or *"In what ways has your job prepared you to take on greater responsibilities?"*
This is a wide-open question that provides absolutely no guidance toward a right answer for the candidate, but it can provide you with considerable insight. You will look for increased skills, professional awareness, industry

sensibilities, knowledge of human nature, and an increasing awareness of what it takes to be successful.

Early Decision Time

If you focus first on ability questions, you can end an interview whenever you determine that a particular candidate is unsuitable for the job; there is no point in wasting your valuable time. This basic sequence of questions (and the customized sequence you build for yourself) will enable you to make a decision to terminate the interview, or to invest more time with a promising candidate.

This is a judgment call on your part, so if you are not sure, ask some more questions about the areas of your concern. As we have already discussed, you are not necessarily looking for people who can do this job in their sleep. All that will do is give you a fast start and an employee rapidly demotivated through lack of challenge. You are looking for someone who has a good grasp of the essentials, but who will still be motivated and given room for professional growth as dictated by the challenges of the job.

Once you can say that a candidate fits this profile, your next step is to continue your examination of ability and suitability with an examination of motivation—that willingness to take the rough with the smooth that goes with any job. Your candidates' answers to the questions in this section probably shed a little light on motivation, teamwork, and manageability. In the same way, the questions from the following chapters, which focus on those very topics, will continue to enlighten you about a candidate's ability, analytical skills, and professional behavioral profile.

Motivation

On any day, in any town, in every company and every department, you'll find the clock-watchers. Year in and year out, they expend just enough effort to keep their jobs, but no more. They are the same people who were telling you to slow down and take it easy when you were on the way up. They are the ones long on complaints and short on solutions. They are never happy and never challenged, yet always endowed with perfect 20/20 hindsight.

The problem is that these folks are difficult to spot when you first meet them in the artificial atmosphere of the interview room. Most of the time, they are professionally competent, they *can* actually do the work, and, after all, this is where most interviewers stop: "Hey, she can do the job, and the money is right? Fine, hire her, and let's get on with business."

This is wrong. "Can do" accompanied by "won't do" or "will only do when wind is from the south" makes for a bad hire. Don't fool yourself into thinking that your magic touch will shift someone's low-gear career into interstellar overdrive. People are largely who they want to be, and you cannot change them, so your task is to separate the clock-watchers from the candidates who intend to make a difference with their presence.

The questions and techniques in this chapter will help you look beyond basic ability and find candidates who come to work with the intention of making a contribution, and who want to spend the day engaged with

focused activity. We are going to look at questions that will help you identify the candidates who are motivated to do a good job, no matter what
that job, or what the circumstances.

Understanding What It Takes

This first sequence of questions is based around self-esteem and self-
knowledge, understanding of the job, and what it takes to get that job
done. You will learn to tell whether or not the candidate is going to spend
time on the critical aspects of the work or whether the unpleasant but
necessary work will be avoided with more amenable tasks.

"What personal qualities do you think are necessary to make a success of this job?"
During your job description development process earlier in the book, you
considered the professional behaviors that would complement the "must
have" core competencies of the job. With this question you begin to see
how close each candidate comes to possessing those behaviors. You continue the sequence with a follow-up question: *"How many of those qualities
do you possess?"* Then you may choose to ask the candidate which of these
traits is his or her greatest asset, and which traits need further development. Once you have this qualifying information, you can continue by
asking past-performance questions that seek specific examples of those
professional behaviors at work. For instance: *"You say that persistence is
important in your job. Give me an example from your current job that demonstrates your persistence at work."*

Though you will want to get examples of all of the candidate's professional behaviors at work, you might not want to bundle all six or seven
of them together in one place. If you get into the habit of following a
sequence like this to begin with, you will remember to lard the interview
with questions about other behaviors as you address topics that require
them. For instance, in talking about client visits, you would follow up with
a question about getting the paperwork done: *"What's your procedure for
keeping track of client visits and activity?"* This question then leads you to
examine time management and organization.

"How do you feel about your progress to date?"
This will tell you about a person's self-esteem. It will also sometimes
unmask an overinflated ego, though with younger workers you should
write off some of that as enthusiasm. Having offered the candidate an

opportunity to sing her own praises, you'll follow it with the opportunity for a little objectivity: *"In hindsight, in what ways could you have improved your progress?"* This second question looks at the candidate's understanding of what it takes to be successful in the profession, and will tell you about judgment, objectivity, and emotional maturity. Most important to remember with these self-esteem questions is that you are looking for people who feel good about themselves, and have confidence in their ability to perform.

"Do you consider yourself successful?"
This will probably get you only a yes/no answer, which is okay, because you planned it as the first part of a two-part question. Follow up with the wonderful catchall, *"Why?"* or *"What professional behaviors do you think contribute to your success?"* Look for self-motivation, organization, tenacity, and resilience in the answers you receive. It is acceptable to hear that part of the reason for changing jobs is to gain the opportunity for more visibility; you just have to exercise judgment when lack of success is consistently attributed to a third party. It's that "finger of blame" consideration again.

"How do you rank among your peers?"
This variation on a theme is also designed to examine self-esteem, so expect a degree of subjectivity. On the other hand, the candidate could interpret the question as a request for a factual answer, such as, "I'm number two in the nation." In most instances, it is salespeople who will interpret your question in the latter fashion, in which case you will remember to verify that ranking with other questions (see Chapter 11 for more on "The Sales Hire"), and when checking references. However this particular probe is answered, your follow-up question need not change: *"How do you plan to improve your professional performance?"* This question requires more objectivity, and will speak to the candidate's understanding of ongoing self-improvement in the profession.

"What have you done that you are proud of?"
This is a seemingly innocuous question for the candidate, but the answer will tell you a great deal about his or her vision of work and which areas are seen as important. Are they the same areas that you know are important to the work at hand? If there are no accomplishments to be proud of, your candidate is either excessively modest or limited in abilities and motivation, either of which could pose a problem.

"What do you consider your greatest strength?"

It isn't a particular achievement that is most interesting here; it is the professional behaviors that make such achievements possible. The answer you get may say in part, "my communication skills." This can be a launch pad for a specific evaluation of past performance: *"Tell me about a time when your communication skills played an important role in getting a difficult job accomplished."*

This question about strengths has been used so frequently, along with its partner—*"What do you consider your greatest weakness?"*—that they are both beginning to lose their potency. But by all means ask the question, because you never know what you'll turn up. Listen carefully to the answers you receive to both of these questions, and if they sound a little too smooth, it would be a good opportunity to practice your layering techniques with a series of questions examining the what, why, how, where, and when of the candidate's greatest strengths and weaknesses. In most cases, however, you are likely to learn more about candidate strengths and weaknesses from your whole body of questions rather than from just the answers to these two.

"Tell me about a responsibility/project/task you have enjoyed."

Here you learn how a person likes to spend time. Is it in the area of the job's critical functions, or is it in the area of busywork? You might also follow up this question by asking, *"And what did you do to meet that responsibility?"* You could also ask, *"Can you tell me about a project that really got you excited?"* This is another way of probing the candidate's motivational focus. It can be tied to follow-up questions that examine what happened to the project, how it turned out, what problems arose, how they were handled, and perhaps most important, whether the candidate's obvious enthusiasm led to any oversights or miscalculations.

It would be a wise decision to follow this sequence of questions with, *"Now tell me about a responsibility/project/task you didn't enjoy."* Learning about candidates' demotivators will also enlighten you about their motivation, and how they respond to challenging situations.

Problem Analysis and Decision-Making

We have already looked at some ways to examine a candidate's problem-solving abilities. However, for a candidate to have a problem-solving frame of mind, he or she must have the motivation to be challenged by difficult situations. You can learn about analytical abilities, determination, motivation, teamwork, and manageability when you ask questions about problematic situations.

"How do you deal with complex problems in your job?"
Every job has its complexities; even the fast-food server has to deal with irritable customers, long lines, and the absence of the fry cook. It can be an eye-opener in itself when the candidate in front of you is unaware of the particular complexities and subtle nuances of his or her current job. You can then proceed with, *"Tell me about a complex problem you had to deal with."* Remember to give the candidate all the time he or she needs to come up with an answer.

"What are some of the things you find difficult to do?"
This is a question that sets the scene for the layering technique as you examine the problem-solving and analytical skills from all angles. *"Why do you find this difficult?"* *"How do you overcome the problem?"* *"Where/to whom do you turn for help?"* *"Where/when does this situation most commonly arise?"*

"What kinds of decisions are most difficult for you?"
Here you want to learn about why such decisions are difficult, and also about the analytical processes that lead your candidate to the right decision. In addition, the answer can identify the areas in which an indecisive candidate will spend most time dithering rather than doing. Follow up with the layering technique if the answer you receive doesn't include an explanation of why such decisions are difficult and how they are reached. Staying with this theme, you could continue with, *"Tell me about a time when a difficult decision had to be made quickly."* This is a behavioral question focused on past performance to provide you with a specific real-world example. Weigh the steps the candidate took in coming to the decision more than the decision itself. You are not so much interested in the example of a right decision being made (you can't possibly expect to obtain all the extenuating factors anyway), but rather the analytical process that led up to it. Find a candidate who has a logical approach to problem solving and decision-making, and you have an employee who doesn't need to be watched every moment of the day.

Organizational Abilities, Time Management, and Energy Levels

Next, we come to the aspects of planning, organization, time management, and energy levels. These intangibles are difficult to judge, yet vital in hiring someone who is not only capable of doing the job but has the motivation to get out there and actually do it. Such behaviors are to motivation what a guidance system is to a missile. These questions will help you decide whether a candidate is able to plan projects and budget the available time in a fashion most likely to lead to a successful completion.

"How do you plan your day?"
This is a straightforward time management and organization question that also has an analytical skills dimension. Look for individuals who have at least a basic understanding of the essential principles of time management. These include three essential building blocks. The first is the habit of having a set time every day, either first thing in the morning or last thing in the afternoon, to review the previous day's activities and, based on that analysis, plan the coming day's activities. The second principle is the habit of prioritizing all the planned activities; the third is the steadfast adherence to those priorities as the day's activities are conducted, to ensure that the important work, rather than the busywork, gets done. These three principles collectively are commonly known as the Plan, Do, Review cycle. No one, especially a manager, will be successful over the long haul without it.

"How do you organize and plan for major projects?" Follow this question with "Tell me about an important project you worked on. How did you organize and plan for it?"
A blank look, accompanied by a slack jaw, bodes ill for your future peace of mind, because candidates without a firm grasp of planning and organization are not likely to be goal oriented. Instead, they are likely to be people who simply let tasks expand to fill the time allotted to them. Logic and good training in time management, organization, gap analysis, and project planning should show themselves in the answers here. The logical approach to planning and executing major projects includes establishing the project deadline, then working backward to identify key turnaround points in the project. The good planner will explain how he or she builds a milestone schedule with commencement and completion dates for every component part; each stage will include a breakdown of human resource utilization. For good measure, there also will be an awareness of the need for contingency planning.

You might then follow up with a question about any formal training in the many approaches to managing time, and organizing and managing projects.

"Tell me about a job or project for which you had to gather information from many different sources and then create something with the information."
The answers to this question can be diverse, allowing you to learn about written and verbal skills as well as creativity, planning, and energy levels. Overall, though, you will look not so much at the project itself (apart from its applicability to your job), but at the logical and orderly approach that the person took to face the challenge successfully.

"Do you set goals for yourself?"
This is a simple closed-ended question that comprises the first part of a three-part sequence. It is followed by, *"Tell me about an important goal you set recently,"* or *"Tell me about a goal you are currently engaged in reaching."* Then, if necessary, ask *"What have you done to reach it?"* These questions will tell you about the candidate's professional priorities, determination, and willingness to stretch for something that's important. Obviously, you also will learn about how the candidate is handling such challenges today.

This sequence can be continued with a question that examines a candidate's get-up-and-go quotient: *"Do you always reach your goals?"* Watch out for people who claim they always reach their goals. Such claims may once in a while be true, but just as often they signify someone who sets low goals because he or she is afraid to fail, or who is not telling the truth. Every true professional knows that going for the ring and missing it once in a while is part of what makes business and businesspeople successful.

We usually learn more from our failures than we do from our successes, and most motivated professionals are aware of this, so you might ask, *"Tell me about a time when you failed to reach a goal."* You want to take a peek at how the individual handles failure; how resilient his or her character makeup is. The ability to achieve success is based on a person's ability to accept the constructive criticism of failure, and then learn and move forward. Does this candidate learn from negative experiences and bounce back all the smarter for the experience, or merely wallow in the depths of despondency, not knowing what happened, or why?

"What do/did you like about your last/current job?" and *"What do/did you dislike about your last/current job?"*
Here are two more common questions that have lost some of their potency through overuse. If you insert them in a sequence of questions like the current one, however, you can give them new life. Instead of timeworn answers, you will now receive meaningful replies that can tell you how a candidate feels about corporate systems and procedures, as

well as planning and reporting procedures. With answers to the "dislike" dimension of this sequence, be sure to follow up with a question about how the candidate handled those disliked aspects of a job. There are unpleasant aspects to all jobs, and that's okay as long as we recognize it and do our jobs just the same.

"How many projects can you handle at a time?"
The ability to multitask, to juggle sometimes conflicting priorities, is necessary in most modern jobs. This question will tell you whether a candidate prefers to ride a horse with blinders until one job is finished, or whether he or she can change mounts in midstream. You can naturally follow this with, *"At what point do multiple projects reach the point of overload?"*

"Describe your typical day for me. What problems do you normally experience in getting things done?"
Better to ask this question rather than the common *"What is your energy level like?"* which is asking for a reply that would put a triathlete to shame. The description of the day will tell you something about planning, time management and, of course, energy . . . which, without efficient use of time, ain't a whole lot of good to anyone.

"Describe a project that required a high amount of energy over an extended period of time."
This question, followed after its answer with, *"What did you do to keep your enthusiasm up?"* continues the themes of time management and energy, and adds the dimension of resiliency or determination. All professions are an endurance race, and not everyone has the same degree of stamina; you would prefer a team composed of marathon runners. An alternate question is, *"When you've a great deal of work to do that requires extra effort and time, where does your energy come from?"* This examines the same areas and can help you evaluate a candidate's approach to work and problems under pressure. Will she stay calm and get the job done? Will he fall apart and waste valuable time confirming an escape route?

"How do you organize yourself for day-to-day activities?"
This is an organization and time management question that can quickly reveal a clock-watcher or other undirected soul. This theme can continue with, *"How many hours a week do you find it necessary to work to get your job done?"* Together, they might just help you identify a task-oriented person when you want a goal-oriented one.

"Is it ever necessary to go above and beyond the call of duty in terms of effort or time to get your job done?"

The answers to this one are always wide open, and while current corporate culture encourages burning the midnight oil, beware of the people who portray themselves as martyrs, coming into the office at 3:00 A.M. on Sunday to get the job done. This claim may in fact be true, but such an individual might be putting in long hours as a result of poor work habits. Look for a sense of balance, wise use of time management and planning skills, and energy level.

"Tell me about a system of working that you have used, and what it was like." Follow up with *"What did/didn't you like about it?"* and *"Tell me about a method you've developed for accomplishing a job. What were its strengths and weaknesses?"*

These three questions all address creativity and objectivity within the context of planning. Additionally, you can learn about the determination someone will call on to create new, workable approaches. Listen carefully. You can sometimes pick up a useful trick or two here for yourself, whether or not you hire the person.

Coolness under Fire

It is now time to look at stress, pressure, and composure under fire a little more closely. If you feel that there are never tight deadlines in your department, that everything in your company always goes according to plan, that there is never sickness or employee turnover, that all of your people always pull their weight and never run for cover, then you can skip this section. It is intended for those of us who are awake between nine and five every day.

"Tell me about a time when an emergency caused you to reschedule your workload/projects."

This question will reveal flexibility, willingness to work extra hours when really necessary, and, you hope, the ability to change course without nervous breakdowns. You can tag on a follow-up question—*"How did rescheduling your workload affect you/make you feel?"*—to learn about the stress a candidate experiences in such usually common occurrences. As a manager, this instantaneous realignment is probably second nature, but that isn't necessarily the case with everyone, and you have to be careful not to project your attributes onto others.

"Think of a crisis situation in which things got out of control. Why did it happen, and what was your role in the chain of events and their resolution?" You can also ask, "What was the most difficult situation you have faced?" After you receive an answer, follow with "What stress did you feel?" and "How did you react?"

In a mining disaster, there are always those who will scream against the darkness and those who will light the candles and look for a way out. You probably know your preference.

In the candidate's answers, look for parallels to your situation and the crises that happen in your world. You could even take a real-world example of a time when things got out of control, and pose it as a hypothetical *"What would you do in a situation in which . . . ?"*

"Tell me about a directive that really challenged you."
You will be looking at the nature of the challenge and how it relates to your needs, how the challenge was analyzed, and the solution subsequently implemented. You can make a secondary probe for originality and drive by asking, *"How was your approach different from that of others?"*

"What do you do when you have a great deal of work to accomplish in a short time span? How have you reacted?"
With this question, you are looking for emotional maturity, for calm under fire, for someone whose analytical processes go into high gear, or at least stay functional, and someone who utilizes a degree of planning even at such harried times. You should also, of course, look for evidence to the contrary: "When in trouble, fear, or doubt, I run in circles, scream, and shout."

"When you have been in difficult and crisis situations, which areas of your professional skills did you vow to work on further?"
This will reveal the candidate's perceived areas of weakness far better than will asking "What's your greatest weakness?" You also can tag on these zingers: *"Tell me about self-improvement efforts you are currently making in this area." "Tell me about a task you started but just couldn't seem to get finished." "I'd be interested to hear of a time when you couldn't complete a task due to lack of support or information."* The answers will throw light on determination and willingness to accept responsibility for actions.

"Tell me about an occasion when your performance didn't live up to your own expectations."
This is a tough one to answer. Give the candidate points for poise and honesty, and be sure to see whether anything was learned from the situation. A person who takes a concrete lesson away from a troubling experience is likely to retain the knowledge, and you will benefit from that life lesson.

"Can you recall a time when you went back to a failed project to give it another shot? Why did you do it, and what happened?"
There's a famous piece of corporate graffiti that profiles the six stages of a failed project:

1. Enthusiasm

2. Disillusionment

3. Panic

4. Search for the guilty

5. Punishment of the innocent

6. Praise and honor for the survivors

Sad commentary, but often a true course of action for many people, especially those struggling along in the more mature and institutionalized corporations. Someone who has not only experienced association with failed projects but then went back to give it another shot, on whatever terms, is certainly worth looking at more closely.

Some Final Questions about Motivation

Here are some final questions to help you examine motivation.

"What have you done to become more effective in your position?"
Here you learn how important the candidates regard their careers to be, and what steps they have taken to forward them. Look for candidates who have gone out of their way to form mentor relationships; who read books, listen to audio CDs, and watch DVDs related to the profession/industry; who are members of professional associations; and who are engaged in ongoing education related to their professional lives.

You might proceed with this line of questioning about professional development by asking, *"What books have had the greatest effect on your business life?"* You may be met with a blank stare (which tells you a lot) or given a specific answer. Whatever the answer, remember that reading is nearly always done on personal time and therefore demonstrates a commitment to a career. Follow this up with, *"Why did this particular book have such an effect on you, and how has it changed you?"* You might go on to determine the depth of study by asking for other examples.

"How long will it take you to make a contribution?"
For once, the candidate has a wide-open opportunity to sell all of his or her good points. That's okay, as long as you keep your ears open for danger signals such as, "Well, I could get started with overhauling your credit and collection procedures as soon as my coat was off." No matter how competent the individual, a practical professional knows that it takes a while to understand the fabric of any company, and that usually a method exists in the seeming madness of first impressions.

"What do you think it takes to have a successful career?"
The question seeks to understand how realistic a candidate is about the commitment, focus, and sacrifice necessary for professional achievement. So the answer to this one can help you find out whether this particular candidate will give your job the effort you'd like. Along the same lines you can also ask, *"Why is this the type of career you want for yourself?"* which might shed a little light on how long the candidate will be happy in the job.

Once you feel comfortable with the degree of motivation emanating from each candidate, or the lack of it (and this can happen at any point), it is time to make another formal decision. Perhaps a candidate is able, but lacks the degree of motivation to be a really outstanding employee when compared to other candidates, in which case you will politely bail out.

When your evaluation tells you that a candidate is able to do the job and is motivated to take the rough with the smooth that goes with every job, it becomes relevant to examine whether he or she will also be a team player and manageable once on board.

The Teamwork and
Manageability Quotient

9

"Something should have told me it wouldn't work out," said a manager at a Hiring the Best workshop. "He could do the work and seemed enthusiastic enough, but there was something there I couldn't put my finger on. After the usual honeymoon, though, I began to notice the problem. Things didn't get done, and it was always some other employee's fault. Whenever I was away, he'd be sick and take time off, or go behind my back to another manager. I tried talking about it to him, but my efforts to solve the problem were always taken as personal affronts. Morale seemed to slide, my people started playing CYA rather than focusing on their deliverables. Finally, I fired him, but it took the best part of nine months before I really localized the problem. My question is, how could I have avoided the mistake in the first place?"

A situation like this is one you want to avoid, and you can learn how to do so by asking a selection of questions from the following pages. Of course, you will want to confirm your evaluation of final candidates with reference checks.

To be a successful manager, you should build a three-dimensional picture of the short-list candidates, establishing an acceptable level of ability coupled with a high degree of motivation, then go on to determine manageability and whether the candidate will be a team player or team destroyer. Customize the questions in this chapter to your needs, and you will learn both what it would be like to manage each of the candidates on your short list, and how each person is likely to perform as a member of the work group. Though the chapter is broken into two sets of questions, one for the manageability factor and one addressing teamwork, you will learn that a conscientious team player will invariably be manageable, and that a manageable employee will usually be a reliable team player.

While these questions will help you understand whether or not the potential behaviors and motivations of a candidate will be a cohesive influence, they cannot help you to get an honest understanding of yourself as a manager; that is up to you. Very few of us fit the profile of the manager we read about in management books, so there is little point in hiring candidates who can only be managed by such an ethereal creature. It's important to hire only those people you can manage, and that takes self-knowledge.

As a manager, you may be the let-'em-alone-type, in which case you shouldn't hire candidates whose answers fairly scream that they need constant supervision and encouragement. If, on the other end of the spectrum, you are an autocratic manager, you are unlikely to have a happy relationship with creative self-starters. You know yourself like no one else, and that knowledge must color the suitability of all answers to the questions in this chapter.

Though these questions are phrased with the current or last job in mind, there is nothing to stop you from asking similar questions as they relate to past employers. Most of the answers to these questions will not be earth-shattering on their own. Rather, the cumulative information and patterns that appear in the answers will give you the key to manageability.

Now let's look at a whole smorgasbord of questions, from which you can choose a selection that will help you determine manageability and team player orientation.

Manageability Questions

"Whom did/do you report to?"
This first question of the sequence gives you the name and title of the individual who will (when you check references) verify salient facts about the candidate. It is normal to follow these questions with inquiries about worker-manager relationships. *"What was your boss like?"* is a good follow-up question that offers you a lead in to any of the following questions.

"How did your boss get the best out of you?"
Surprisingly, this question is very rarely asked, yet it can provide you with a wealth of information. All candidates, you'll find, will be only too happy to tell you how they like to be managed. Consequently, you will learn whether you can provide the kind of management under which the person functions best. The answer to this question gives you tangible advice on how to manage the individual effectively, should he or she become your chosen and appointed. A neat twist to give to this particular question is to follow it up with, *"How did you get the best out of your boss?"* This answer will show manageability from a different perspective: How likely you are to be supported and/or manipulated by the candidate. You can also ask, *"What increased responsibilities or promotions were you given on that job?"* The answer to this question will confirm or disprove the answers given to the two prior questions in your sequence.

"What do you think of your current/last boss?"
This is another chance for the candidate to praise or complain. While common sense tells even the meanest intelligence that it is unwise to criticize former employers, always ask the question, because some people just cannot resist the temptation to complain. An answer that states, "I would have liked more direction" is acceptable and gives you usable input when applied to your particular management style. On the other hand, if the answer comprises a rant of invective, you might consider that the same might be applied to you one day in the not-too-distant future. Other questions you can ask to gather input in this area include the following:

"Describe the best manager you ever had," followed by, "What made him or her stand out?" "How did you interact with this manager?" "How did you react to feedback, instructions, and criticism he/she gave you?"
Then repeat the sequence in its entirety with this small change: *"Describe the worst manager you ever had."* Both of these question sequences will tell you a great deal about what constitutes a good work environment for the candidate. Then you can evaluate whether you are able to provide a productive work environment for this person. The responses can also be a valuable tool for your own development, and can contribute to your effective management of the individual. From a self-development perspective, you might find an unpleasant truth, which could help you learn to manage more effectively.

"What are some of the things your boss did that you disliked?"
This is a variation on the previous question. One of the two is usually enough, unless the first gets you a really intriguing or disconcerting answer. In that case, offer the second as a further opportunity to expand on the same subject. Of course, you can also keep the candidate talking by adding, *"That's interesting. Tell me more,"* or using a mirror statement.

"In what areas could your boss have done a better job?"
This is another case in which the answer will tell you how the candidate likes to be managed as much as how he or she *doesn't* like to be managed.

"How well do you feel that your boss rated your performance?"
While you might think that this one is by nature too subjective to gauge self-respect and self-image, you will be surprised at how truthful the answers sometimes turn out, especially concerning those areas in which the candidate feels underrated.

"If you could make one constructive suggestion to management, what would it be?"
Here you are looking for the constructive content of the answer, and the tone in which it is delivered. You could interpret "I don't know" as a response from someone who lacks initiative, intelligence, and motivation. On the other hand, you could interpret "They should have . . ." as a warning bell alerting you to a problem employee. Over time, and from a number of different answers to this question, you might add a little more to your store of knowledge about employee motivation.

"How do you take direction?"
There are two kinds of direction: the kind you give when you have all the time in the world, and the kind you give when you are under the gun. If you get a pat answer, follow it with, *"Tell me about a time when your manager was in a rush and didn't have time for the niceties."* Underlying both of these questions is the desire to get a grasp on the candidate's emotional maturity.

"Would you like to have your boss's job?"
Listen closely! It might be your job that you're talking about. If the answer is yes, ask whether the candidate feels qualified for it, and why. Such an answer is acceptable if the candidate is many years behind you in experience, and it's perhaps okay to have someone to groom so that you can

move upward, but someone snapping at your professional heels is perhaps not such a good idea.

"Tell me about a time when you came up with a new method or idea. How did you get it approved and implemented?"
While hoping for creativity but also alert for attention to systems and procedures and a sense of ethical process, you want to see a history that not only demonstrates an understanding of the development process, but also for following the chain of command.

"Tell me about an occasion when there were objections to your ideas. What did you do to convince management of your point of view?"
Following along with the sequence, this question can give you insight into how far and how hard this candidate will push a thought after initial rejection. This may also be a good opportunity for a little situational interviewing. For example, after listening carefully to the answer, you could say, *"I might find it easier to grasp if you could demonstrate that point for me. If I said your solution was too expensive, what would you say?"*

The question clearly examines manageability in connection with determination, but it can reveal other disturbing information. When I asked this question on one occasion, I gained tremendous insight into the true character of the individual when he replied that he had finally sold an idea to upper management by waiting until his boss was out of town and going above his head. If you get the same answer, the trick is not to fall off your chair in astonishment, but to store this valuable piece of negative information and to go for negative confirmation: You want to establish whether this person will habitually destroy your established systems and procedures.

"Can you think of a time when another idea or project was rejected? Why was it rejected, and what did you do about it?"
This provides good negative balance to the previous question, and can give you insight about how the candidate handles rejection and criticism. Watch out for misplaced anger—that finger of blame pointing outward. In some professions, you will want the employee to accept rejection and move on; in others (such as sales) you'll be looking for the tenacity of a bulldog.

"For what have you been most frequently criticized?" Better still, *"I would be interested to hear about an occasion when your work or an idea was criticized."* In this instance, you want to look at the cause of criticism, how the candidate accepted the input, and how it is reported to you. If the candidate seems determined to prove the past manager wrong (be alert for voice tone and smoldering anger), beware. You can do without people who bear grudges down through the ages.

"Tell me about a situation when people were making emotional decisions about your project. What happened, and how did you handle it?"
This is a neat emotional maturity question. If you examine the question in the context of the real world of business, you see that it is really asking, "How did you behave, when for pragmatic reasons and in the best interests of the company, a project of yours was canned or criticized? Did you act like a professional or like a spoiled brat?"

"What are some of the things about which you and your boss disagreed?"
While you listen to the answer, you will remember not to comment on it, no matter how much you want to defend a fellow manager. You gain no benefit from engaging in discussion about manager/employee relations. Rather, you should listen, absorb, and evaluate: Could the disagreements cited in the answer cause problems for you? For example, if you are the type of manager who does not believe in keeping your employees advised of every corporate decision, you would well have concern with the candidate who complains that a past manager always kept him in the dark, and who found it frustrating to work in a vacuum. No judgment on either part is intended here, yet the dictum "know thyself" is important; it is one of the cornerstones of getting work done through others.

"How necessary is it for you to be creative on your job?"
The appropriate response naturally depends on the position you are filling. Where the job requires strict adherence to policies and procedures, high degrees of creativity are often not desirable. Creativity in copywriters is desirable; in typists, it is not. The answer might also give you some idea of the candidate's adherence to systems and procedures. If you want to examine this further, you might ask, *"When there are procedural roadblocks to your ideas, what do you do to get around them?"*

154

"What do you do when there is a decision to be made and no procedure exists?"
This question is a natural follow-up to any of the last four. In the answer, you want to analyze the following: Will the individual come to you? Will he or she, in developing an appropriate procedure, stick to the rules or devise new systems that fit the whim of the moment?

"Have you ever been in a situation in which people overruled you or wouldn't let you get a word in edgewise?"
Depending on the job, this question can give you many different insights. For example, some jobs require someone who can defend his or her opinions; in customer service you need someone who can be conciliatory; and in sales you will want a candidate to be assertive.

"Give me an example of a time when you were told no. What did you do in response?" or *"Describe a time when you didn't get an immediate yes from someone. What did you find necessary to do?"* or *"What have you done that required you to ask for something you weren't going to receive right away? How did you react?"* or *"Tell me about an idea that was rejected. What did you say and do subsequently? What was the outcome?"*
Emotionally immature people seek instant gratification of their desires, immediate acceptance of their ideas, and universal recognition of their talent. As a group, these folks are notorious for their inability to handle even temporary rejection. The answers you receive to this selection of questions will give you a feeling for what to expect from a potential employee when you give negative feedback, and also of the level of professional maturity.

"What problems do you experience when working alone?" or *"How do the work habits of others change when the boss is absent?"* or *"Tell me about a time when there was a decision to be made and your boss was absent"* or *"How do your work habits change when your boss is absent?"* Any of these questions will tell you much more than the traditional *"Can you work alone?"*
What the mice do when the cat is away should be of concern to every manager. These questions examine both self-reliance and how far the candidate perceives his or her personal authority and responsibility to extend, thus indicating an understanding of systems and procedures. Often, there are no specifically right or wrong answers to these questions, because so much depends on your management style and the systems and procedures of your company. The answers that match your modus operandi and make you comfortable are the right ones; others are the red flags.

Finding the Team Players and Team Destroyers

There are people who have loyalty to their team and people who do not. You see this not so much in terms of job-hopping (some of a company's most disloyal employees can be lifers), but more regularly in the subtly disruptive influence such people can have over the general happiness and effectiveness of your department. Most jobs today require interaction with others, and depending on the level of interaction, your candidate's communication skills and "get-along-with-the-gang" quotient can be a vital consideration in making the right hiring decision.

Willingness to get along with the rest of the human race, especially those members who spend the majority of their waking hours in your department, is a key element that is easily overlooked in the hiring cycle. You will probably be working with the chosen candidate for fifty weeks of the year, so find out beforehand if the person in front of you will shorten your life expectancy with disruptions of your department and your life. In making a good hiring decision, you want to be able to differentiate between the team players and the team destroyers. You will already be getting good data from your manageability questions; the questions in this section will help you fill in the blanks.

"How important was communication and interaction with others on this job?" This is the first question in a sequence that can be coupled with others, such as, *"What other titles and departments did you have dealings with?"* and *"What were the challenges you encountered there?"* These questions together will establish how the candidate evaluates the importance of communication to the success of the job, and with whom and at what levels the interaction took place. The third question in the sequence recognizes that there are always difficulties with interdepartmental communication and seeks to gain insight into the candidate's sense of diplomacy and understanding of systems and procedures.

"How many levels of management did you interact with?" You might follow this with, *"What was the nature of your interactions?"* The first question seeks to understand the level of exposure a candidate has had in working in a multilevel business situation. The second question establishes whether the interaction was one-sided (between manager and worker) or on an equal basis (between colleagues). Finish this sequence with two questions that identify the candidate's comfort and intimidation

levels: *"What level of management are you most comfortable with? What levels are you most uncomfortable with?"*

Here is another short sequence using the same structure but tailored for a more specific answer.

"Tell me about a time when you had a project that required you to interact with different levels within the company—people above and below you. How did you do this?"

After the answer, follow up with, *"Who caused you the most problems in executing your tasks?"* and *"With whom were you most comfortable?"* The response will always be interesting for two reasons: If hired, the candidate will be representing you when dealing with lower levels or with upper levels of management; also, you are naturally concerned that this representation be adequate.

"Have you ever had to make unpopular decisions?"

Any professional job that requires interaction with different people, levels, and departments demands a professional with some diplomatic muscle. Unpopular decisions in such instances are invariably part of the job. Find out with the yes/no answer whether the person worked at a level at which his or her decisions affected the perceived well-being or comfort levels of other workers. If the answer is applicable, proceed with, *"Tell me about an unpopular decision you had to make,"* and layer it with, *"Whom did it affect? Why did the situation arise? How long did it take you to make the decision? How do you feel you handled it?"* Of course, this is a natural time to add at the end, *"What did you learn from the event?"*

"Give me an example of when you have convinced people, over whom you had no authority, of an approach to a task."

Apart from gauging the respect that the candidate offers to others, this is a useful question for any position in which verbal skills are integral job requirements.

"Tell me how you went about becoming a real member of the team when you joined your last company" and *"Have you worked with a group like this before?"* followed by *"What was it like?"* or *"How did you handle it?"*

The latter question is a little sneaky. It implies that the situation had its problems and needed "handling." The response will reveal emotional maturity and an adult approach to getting along, or else wave a big red flag for you when the person says, "Well, in the beginning, I always find

it necessary to tell people exactly how I feel about . . . and . . . and . . ."
Autocrats can make effective leaders at the very top of the food chain, but
they never make team players.

"How much of your work was done alone in that job?"
You might need to know whether the person, although part of a team,
can function on his or her own. While recognizing the value of teamwork,
we should also remember that every team is made up of individuals who
need to be self-starting and self-motivating. As a manager, you cannot
afford the time to crank-start each member of your team first thing every
morning.

*"Tell me about a time when you needed to get an understanding of another's
situation before you could get your job done. How did you get the understanding,
and what problems did you encounter?"*
How much does this person consider another's viewpoint? As well as
enlightening you about an ability to get along with others, this question
also probes listening and analytical skills and how the candidate weighs
individual needs against the institutional good.

*"In working with new people, how do you go about getting an understanding
of them?"*
Here is another option that addresses analytical ability and group interaction, and the way this is phrased might give you insight into how the candidate will assimilate during those early days on the new job. A follow-up
for this is, *"Are you able to predict the behavior of others, and if so, how?"* This
is a good question that can generate some interesting responses regarding
the candidate's overall perception of others.

"What is your role as a group member?"
Many managers find this open-ended question to be valuable in evaluating
a candidate's willingness to get along with others. These same managers
follow this opening with, *"Tell me about a specific accomplishment you have
achieved as a group member,"* and if necessary, tag on, *"What was your role
in this?"* The theory behind the three-part question is that the first reveals
intellectual awareness, the second demands a concrete example as proof,
and the third completes the loop by requesting the candidate to tie his or
her role and contributions into those of the group. Difficulty in answering

the question may demonstrate that the candidate lacks an awareness of his or her role as a part of the larger effort.

"What kinds of people did you have contact with on your previous jobs?"
This first part of a two-part question identifies the different levels and/or personality types with whom the candidate has been involved. The second question—*"What did you do differently with each of these different types to get your job done?"*—will tell you about the candidate's ability and range of response in dealing with divergent personality types.

"What type of person do you get along with best?"
This is the first part of a layered, three- or four-part probe. The second part is, *"What types of people do you find it difficult to get along with?"* The third is, *"How do you manage to get along with these types?"* You may even want to add, *"Tell me about a difficult situation you had with one of these people, and what happened."* You want to keep the response open, so this time do not give a lead in your question by adding, *". . . and how you handled it,"* because that could tell the candidate that you wanted to hear about a successful solution. It might even be appropriate here to add one of the generic probes: *"What did you learn from this experience?"*

"What difficulties do you have in tolerating people whose backgrounds and interests differ from yours?"
This one is somewhat of a trick, because there is the inference that naturally there are problems, and the question encourages the candidate to reveal them. You might find it a useful double-check if you are not quite satisfied with the sincerity of answers to earlier questions in this chapter. Employees who cannot tolerate differences can put you in the way of a hostile work environment lawsuit.

"When you joined your last company and met the group for the first time, how did you feel? How did you get on with them?"
Past actions can predict future behavior. The answer could well be a picture of what will happen when this person joins your company. Will it be a perfect fit, a case of "deep calling to deep" (as the poets say), or will it presage the start of Armageddon?

"Define cooperation."

This is a nondirective question that will help you build a case concerning the candidate's understanding of individual responsibilities as an integral part of a work group.

"How would you define a conducive work atmosphere?"

If the description is diametrically opposed to yours, it could be a sign of trouble. Unfortunately, we spend the majority of our waking hours at work, and an unpleasant atmosphere often contributes to employee turnover. Continue the sequence with, *"As a member of a department, how do you see your role as a team builder?"* If morale in your department is low for some reason, you might find out whether the candidate is a follower or a leader. Will he or she actively work to improve the atmosphere and build team spirit, or passively accept the current situation, or, even worse, become part of any negativism?

"Tell me about an occasion when, in difficult circumstances, you pulled the team together."

This can reveal the person who is willing to take responsibility for the well-being of the team. However, because the person who initiates such actions is the exception rather than the rule, this is not a question for which you should press the candidate for an answer. If a response is not readily forthcoming, move on to the next question, knowing that while the candidate may have many admirable skills and traits, he or she simply is not a natural born leader. This question does, however, have special relevance if you are hiring a manager; in that case, the inability to answer convincingly could well be a significant black mark against the candidacy.

"Tell me about a time when a team fell apart. Why did it happen? What did you do?"

Did the candidate make an effort? Where was the finger of blame pointed? Remember to look for patterns in answers. Beware of a candidate who consistently lays the cause of problems at others' doorsteps—management's in particular. He or she may blame others today; tomorrow, things could change, and the finger of blame might just be pointed at you. Again, this question has special relevance when hiring managers, where you expect a convincing and detailed answer.

"Have you ever had to build motivation or team spirit with coworkers?"
A positive answer might lead you to add, *"Tell me about the situation,"* and *"How did this situation arise?"*

"Tell me about an occasion when you felt it necessary to convince your department to change a procedure."
What gets his goat? How strong are her convictions? How valid are they? Follow with, *"How did you go about it, and whose feathers got ruffled?"* You need to know whether the candidate will adhere to systems and procedures in these circumstances and how he or she will go about getting the changes made—like a diplomat, or like a bull in a china shop?

"Recall for me a time when those around you were not being as honest or direct as they should have been. What did you do?"
This particular one is very difficult for a candidate to answer without sounding like Tom Sawyer's milquetoast half-brother, Sid. Try to be certain in your own mind what constitutes an acceptable answer before you ask the question; it is supposed to probe integrity in a very direct fashion, and it should be used sparingly. You may only want to use it if you suspect dishonesty in the department, or the company has recently experienced the same. Of course, some industries—retail goods and services, for instance—suffer continually from petty larceny, and in those cases the question has much greater relevance.

"What is your general impression of your last company?"
This can be followed by, *"Tell me how you moved up through the organization,"* and, *"How did this affect your peers?"* These three questions collectively have a single goal: to tell you about the candidate's prevailing attitudes toward his or her job, peers, and management. These together will spell out whether this person will have a bad or a good attitude once a team member.

"Give me an example of a time when management had to change a plan or approach you were committed to. How did you feel, and how did you explain the change to your people?"
You usually will ask this one only when the potential employee will be managing others. It is a complex and revealing question that tells you not only about manageability, but also about leadership, team building, and maintenance of the team under pressure.

The Breaking Point

We all have our good days and our bad days, our favorite moments and our pet hates. One of a manager's important roles within the department is to provide a conducive work atmosphere and reduce friction. So, it is helpful to know the flash points of your potential new employees. This is a sensitive area to examine, and nowhere is your tone of voice or the setup of your questions more important. For instance, it is no good coming right out and asking someone what makes him or her angry.

"Tell me about what makes you tick as a professional."
Listen to the explanation, but no matter where the conversation wanders (and it is all right to let it wander for a minute or two), bring it back to the following three questions about anger. Ask, *"What are your pet hates at work?"* layered with *"Why do you feel this way?"* and *"What situations can give rise to these problems?"* The responses will show you what will make each of your candidates really explode, and that's good for manageability and team player evaluation.

"When was the last time you got really frustrated/angry?" or *"Tell me about the last time you felt anger on the job."*
You might also inquire about frustration and anger more directly. It is important that whoever you hire is able to control and channel frustration. If the previous sequence doesn't quite give you all the information you need, you might try this question. If the cause of the anger doesn't surface in the explanation, follow with other probes—*"What caused it?"* for instance. Be sure to find out how the individual reacted to the situation: *"What did you do about it?*

Oh, the World Owes Me a Living

There are few things more rewarding in a professional's life than getting recognition for a job well done, for putting out effort above and beyond the call of duty. This seems fair and reasonable, so the prudent manager should take the time to see exactly what kinds of rewards and recognition are going to be expected by potential employees in order to keep them happy. As in all of the questions in this book, you hope to hear the positive, but will remain alert for the negative.

"Tell me about a time when you felt adequately recognized for your contributions." On the upside, the answer will show emotional maturity and understanding of the relevance of that contribution to the company's bottom line. On the downside, you could hear an expectation that a champagne brunch will be in order every time a deadline is met. Follow this one with *"What kinds of rewards are most satisfying to you?"* Ideally, you will hear that recognition and encouragement by management is most satisfying; such things are, after all, a validation of a person's career. Layer either of these questions with *"How does this affect what you do on the job?"* or *"How does this affect the effort you put into your job?"*

"How do I get the best out of you?"
This is different from earlier questions about how prior managers got the best out of this candidate. This question is future oriented and asks the candidate to define the ideal worker/manager relationship; it is a question that you will only ask of short-list candidates.

What'd I Do?

One of the biggest headaches of a manager's life is the unexpected resignation. It demoralizes the troops, puts extra pressure on everybody, and makes you look bad to your management. Time after time, people leave jobs because they did not feel appreciated for their efforts. Sometimes the one who leaves is the linchpin of the group, that person on whom you have come to rely, who in fact is so reliable that you take him or her for granted until it's too late. You can learn more about how bosses cause resignations unconsciously and thus reduce your turnover by asking, *"In what ways did your manager/past managers contribute to your decision to leave this job?"* The answers will naturally be subjective, and may once in a while rule out a particular candidate, but understanding workers' perceptions of you and your peers can be invaluable. You might also check out my companion career management book for lots of ideas about how to successfully manage others: *Knock 'em Dead in Management.*

Wrapping It Up

Now you know how to smoke out the candidates who are able to do the job, are motivated to do a good job, are comfortable working as part of a team, and who will be manageable by you, with all your warts and blemishes. To close the interview, you should give the candidate the opportunity to ask for the job or promote his or her candidacy: *"Are there any questions you would like to ask?"* or *"Is there anything we haven't covered that you think I should know about?"* As we've said before, the interview is a two-way street, and the interviewee needs the chance to get information from you, to make sure that your company is the right choice. After all, just as you are trying to hire the best, the candidate is also trying to hire on with the best for his or her future. You should be prepared to answer the candidate's questions clearly and succinctly, and be knowledgeable about the benefits, company mission, and so on.

If you have used stress questions and techniques during the interview, it can be a wise idea to address why you did this, and to let the candidate know that you are happy with the way he or she responded. This will make the candidate more comfortable in accepting a job offer from you.

After all of your short-list candidates have passed through the interview cycle, you move on to the decision-making process, perhaps scheduling a separate meeting to go over the job again, making sure that the candidate will accept your offer, and introducing him or her to team members and other levels of management. We are going to address that in Chapter 16, but first, to give you an even better handle on the selection questions and techniques, we are going to look at hiring specific types of people: management, sales, entry-level, and clerical/administrative personnel. From a personal career standpoint, you should be especially interested in the suggested questions to ask candidates for management positions.

The Management Hire

*A*ll management jobs have this credo: Get work done through others. When the people you hire must in turn hire and get work done through others, making the wrong choice can ruin your year.

While all management jobs hold certain responsibilities in common, not all management jobs are alike. Sometimes there is a mistaken focus on the technical skills of the profession rather than management competency.

A management selection cycle, like any other, needs to address the deliverables of the job, the problem-solving and other professional behaviors that help determine those deliverables, and a candidate's manageability and team orientation. If you accept that the key credo of any management job is to get work done through others, the deliverables that define an ability to do any management job focus on staff selection, training, motivation, and troubleshooting.

Management Competency

With this in mind, your first sequence of questions should deal with determining the size and scope of your manager candidate's job, and provide revealing insights into his or her management competency.

"How would you define the job of a manager?"

Over time, you have developed preconceived notions of what a manager does, and it is all too easy to project those ideas onto your candidates if you don't ask for this definition. The idea is to get an understanding of the candidate's viewpoint. You will continue this with, *"How many people do you manage now?"* and *"What type of positions are you responsible for?"* Answers to these questions will allow you to determine both the size and the scope of the individual's department and job.

"Do these people report directly and solely to you, or on a project basis?"

There is a distinct difference. The duties we traditionally associate with a manager are hiring, training, supervising, performance and salary reviews, and terminations as necessary. However, there are other definitions that a candidate might be using and which you must differentiate. The first is what is sometimes called project management: at its most elementary, you assign three members of your department to work under the guidance of a fourth on a particular project. That fourth person with project responsibility becomes in some minds a manager (titles being cheaper than raises), but this person might have no fiscal responsibility nor the right to hire, fire, or administer performance reviews.

"Who performed salary reviews on these people?" and *"Who terminated these people?"* will help clarify the level of management responsibility. If the candidate held these responsibilities, you may later want to hear how the performance reviews and terminations were executed, because both are watershed events in a department's life, with potential for significant impact on morale.

Hiring: The First Step in Team-Building

No sports coach survives by blaming poor performance on the team, and the same standards apply in your world. Because your management hires are in turn going to "get work done through others," the direct impact they have on your own performance is magnified. Although you may know how long this person has been in management, and how many people he or she manages and has hired and fired, you must never take the degree of competency for granted.

"How do you plan to interview?"

Here, you must watch out for those people who tell you they "like to get to know the person," or who laugh, saying that with all of their experience, they just "know 'em when they see 'em." These are the Unconscious Incompetents; they don't even know that they don't know what they are doing. Follow this with, *"On what criteria do you base a decision to hire?"* Naturally you will be looking for someone who understands the importance of defining ability, problem-solving skills, professional behaviors, motivation, team orientation, and manageability. You might ask, *"What questions do you ask when you want to know about [for example, motivation]?"* Then, determine what that person hopes to learn by asking those questions. If you get treated to responses of "What's your greatest strength/weakness?" and "Why do you want the job?" push with, *"Tell me what questions you would ask, or techniques you would use, to establish whether the person was willing to do the job."*

You might also pick a job title that your management candidate would be hiring and ask, *"What are the professional behaviors most important to the success of a _____?"* and follow it with a query as to why those behaviors are relevant. At the end of the sequence, always be sure to ask whether your candidate checks references, and if so, the questions that he or she typically asks. You might also structure questions around the number and duration of interviews necessary to make good hires, the number of second opinions that would be sought and why, and how a decision to hire is reached and a dollar offer determined and extended.

"How many people have you hired?"
This reveals the extent of practical experience in the skill area, and by asking you might learn that the interviewee's first and only management job included taking over a fully staffed department with little turnover; consequently, the candidate will have only light experience in the selection area. This is occasionally the case in mature and stable companies, in which managers invariably inherit a department as a "going concern." If managers in your company are involved in the recruitment process, you may also want to examine the candidate's knowledge in this area.

"How have you developed your skills in recruitment and selection?"
This provides an easy way to find out (a) whether the candidate has had any formal training, and (b) whether he or she has made the effort necessary for improving critical skills. The knowledge that comes from reading this book will supply you with plenty of other questions, as will the management interview skeleton at the end of the chapter.

Orientation of a New Employee

The orientation and training of new employees can be perceived as having varying importance, depending on the role of the Human Resources or Training and Development department in the process. In all instances, though, your managers are ultimately responsible for getting new employees settled in (orientation) and for getting them up to speed (training), so you need to examine this skill area.

"How important do you feel orientation and training are to the success of a new employee?" and "What steps do you take to get a new employee oriented to the new ways of doing things?"
The manager who lacks sensitivity to orientation and training is likely to lack team-building and motivational skills as well, which can lead to high employee turnover and all that it implies about your security.

"Have you ever had to train staff in new skills?"
This is a good opener for the area of training capabilities. It should be followed by such questions as, *"What skills have you trained?"* and *"How did you go about it?"* and *"What techniques did you use?"* There is a difference between teaching and having an employee actually learn. The answers you hear should reflect this awareness and reveal a manager who is concerned with sharing needed information and skills in a fashion most conducive to enhancing the employee's learning capabilities, rather than talking to hear his or her own lips flap.

"How do you analyze the training needs of your department, or of specific individuals?"
Training does not stop once the new employee has settled down, so you might finish the series with this question. It is particularly valuable, because the answer will demonstrate the analytical skills in determining training needs, and the commitment of the candidate to building overall team competency. You may well find the good manager tying the answer into his or her staff performance reviews—which, incidentally, should occur independently of, and more frequently than, the annual salary review.

Staff Communication and Motivation

Management philosophy recognizes that communication and motivation are interrelated skills in the competent manager's arsenal. The inability to communicate appropriately with staff usually leads to retaliation by those same staff members who apparently become unable to interpret directions correctly (you've no doubt seen this happen). Without adequate communication skills, staff motivation leaves by the early train.

"How do you keep your staff aware of information and company activities that might affect them?"
Small companies and growing companies depend largely on verbal communication; written communication comes more to the fore with larger, more mature companies. If management turnaround success stories are to be believed, too much formality leads to communication breakdown and an early symptom of corporate atrophy, which is definitely something to be avoided. Watch out for the manager who prefers memoranda to personal contact; it may signify a lack of people skills elsewhere in his or her management style (unless, of course, the memoranda are used to confirm and/or reinforce previous verbal communications).

"Have you ever had an employee suddenly start acting out of character?"
People problems—and everyone encounters them with staff at one time or another, whether they are psychological or emotional, drugs or alcohol—do intrude upon the workplace. Your managers have a direct responsibility to be on the lookout for such problems, because they affect productivity, morale, and employee turnover. Appropriate help or acknowledgment of caring can go a distance toward increasing motivation for a valued but troubled team member. Sensitivity to systems and procedures is also important here; for example, a manager who, without appropriate consultation, oversteps his bounds of authority by getting a drug counselor for an employee can land your company in a heap of legal trouble. So to determine the degree of sensitivity and an awareness of systems and procedures you should ask, *"Would you tell me about a specific situation and how you approached it?"*

"Tell me about a program you introduced to improve morale."
This question can be repeated to cover subjects such as saving money; increasing efficiency; decreasing turnover, tardiness, or absenteeism; or whatever other situations are relevant to your world. Layer them with how, what, where, who, and when questions. You gain valuable insights into the candidate, and even if you don't hire the individual, you just might come up with a first-rate program that your company could use.

"How do you motivate your staff?"

The answer will tell you about the candidate's management philosophy, and even a blank stare can be worth a thousand words. In the same sequence, you might ask, *"Have you ever had to meet tight deadlines?"* and then follow the unfailingly positive response with, *"Tell me about how you motivated your staff when faced with a specific tight deadline."* The relevance of these questions lies in the fact that tight deadlines invariably require extra effort from everyone in the department. Ideally, your candidate is a good enough manager that he or she can rely on the department's pride in a job well done to pull it together and do whatever it takes to meet that deadline. You are, however, always on the lookout for the manager who uses threats or bribery as a means to meet tight deadlines, because this behavior is symptomatic of other management inadequacies.

"Tell me about a time when a team fell apart. Why did it happen? What did you do?"

This question has appeared earlier in the book, but has a special relevance for management hires. You are looking for someone who can determine root causes and takes actions based on those causes rather than just their symptoms. Beware of a candidate who consistently lays the cause of problems at others' doorsteps—upper management's in particular. He or she may blame others today; tomorrow, things could change, and that finger of blame might just be pointed at you.

"Tell me about an occasion when, in difficult circumstances, you pulled the team together."

This is another question from earlier in the book with specific importance to management selection. You need a manager who is willing to take complete responsibility for the well-being of his or her team. When this question came up earlier in a different context, we noted that non-management staff members who step up to the plate in difficult circumstances could be the exception rather than the rule. Here in the management selection context, such skills and motivation need to be front and center.

"Give me an example of a time when management had to change a plan or approach that you were committed to. How did you feel, and how did you explain the change to your people?"

This is a complex and revealing question that tells you not only about manageability but also about leadership, and the building and maintenance of a team under pressure.

Authority and Discipline

An important consideration for how a manager keeps productivity high and turnover low is how authority is wielded and discipline implemented. These questions will also help reveal the candidate's "management personality" and its compatibility with yours.

"What methods have you found successful in setting job objectives for subordinates?"

Management is a continuous coaching and nurturing process. It requires far more than directing the employee to read the proffered job description and follow directions. Look for a manager who combines both a formal approach to setting objectives and a sensitivity to understanding the need for informal coaching on an individual basis.

"Have you ever had to make unpopular decisions?"

Setting objectives does not always make the manager a popular person. This is a simple, closed-ended question that sets you up for some good layering techniques: *"Tell me about a time . . ."* *"Why did you feel this was an unpopular decision?"* and so on. Most important, to reveal procrastination, ask, *"Having identified that a decision was necessary, how long is it before you take action?"*

Following naturally from your questions about unpopular decisions, you can ask, *"How do you maintain discipline in your department?"* and *"What special problems do you have with the day-to-day management of your staff?"*

The answers will shed new light on both disciplinary and management style.

You can continue with, *"What are the typical problems and grievances that your staff bring to you?"* and *"How do you handle them?"* Then develop the theme with, *"In working with others, how do you go about getting an understanding of them?"* Remember, an integral part of any manager's job is communication with other departments and managers. If necessary, rephrase the question as it relates to other departments, peers, and superiors. In the latter instance, this can tell you something about the candidate's likely interactions with you, which is the topic that we are going to detail in the next section.

Attitude Toward Management

Your managers are also your employees, and you need to know how they are likely to react to your management. Though there are questions elsewhere in this book that help you determine these aspects of an individual's manageability, the following few questions are particularly appropriate in evaluating management candidates.

"Tell me about a time when an emergency/directive from above caused you to reschedule your personal workload and the department's priorities."
This one can tell you about the ability to multitask and handle pressure, and it can also reveal possible irritants and management conflicts. Teams typically react to situations in the same way as the leader, so check the last answer with, *"How did the staff react?"*

"Tell me about a time when management had to change a plan or approach you were committed to. How did you feel, and how did you explain the change to your people?"
You will be interested to find out whether the candidate explained the situation to the staff in positive, negative, or defensive terms. It is a weak manager who in such times talks to the staff about "them" and "us," and sides with the employees rather than the company.

Employee Turnover

Time is money, and there are few things more costly to a manager or a company than the time and expense associated with employee turnover. Yet examining a candidate's performance in this area is a subject mostly ignored in management interviews. Tied to the questions about training and motivation (everything is interrelated with management jobs), these questions will help you pursue this neglected area.

"What was the turnover in your department over the last two or three years?"
Is the answer above or below industry norms? Whichever it is, as a competent interviewer you are rarely satisfied with the first snap answer to any of your questions. Instead, you use this question partly to obtain a quantitative answer but, more important, to give the candidate a focus for the rest of the questions in this sequence.

"What type of turnover was most frequent, terminations or resignations?"
A history of high turnover could be a problem, but at this point you do not have enough information about the reasons. Poor interviewing? Poor orientation? Unsafe or hostile working conditions? The reasons are limitless, so you'll have to determine which was the cause in this case by asking

these and similar questions: *"Why do you think this was the case?" "What have you done about the situation?"*

"How many people have you fired?"
This is another straightforward, quantitative question. It should be followed by, *"What is your most common cause for terminating an employee?"* The response—including the candidate's tone of voice—can tell you about management style and competency. For example, a manager who explains resignedly about the extreme difficulty in locating competent employees as reason for termination and turnover is really telling you that he or she doesn't know how to interview. In that case, you will recommend that the interviewee read *Hiring the Best,* and then say farewell. Whatever the answer, follow it with, *"Tell me about the last time you fired someone for this reason. What led up to it?"* Then, if the information doesn't come out in the story, ask, *"When did you first notice the problem?" "With hindsight, were there any steps you could have taken to rectify the situation?" "At what point did you make the decision to terminate?" "How long was it from this decision to implementation?" "Do you follow a formal disciplinary procedure leading up to termination?"* A candidate's awareness of and adherence to proper termination procedures will minimize lawsuits for wrongful dismissal.

"What are the common reasons for resignations in your area of responsibility?"
The saying that loyalty is a function of being appreciated has great relevance here. Pay people reasonably, recognize their contributions consistently and in different ways, give them a decent work environment and a positive atmosphere, and resignations will usually be few indeed (see my book *Knock 'em Dead in Management* for commentary on these topics). Because a competent manager can satisfy many of these requirements for low turnover with little effort, responses to this question such as "better opportunity elsewhere" and "more money" can sometimes be cop-outs, and you'll want to examine the issue further. *"How do you keep track of an employee's relative contentment?"* and *"What signals of discontent do you look for?"* will tell you about how a manager keeps in touch with individual staff members.

You might also wish to identify when resignations typically occur: *"Within three months, six months, fifteen months, two years?"* An answer in the short term will give you an indication that this manager's hiring and training capabilities need closer examination; an answer in the mid-term could be cause for probing management style and judgments.

"What contingency plans do you have in the event of unexpected resignations?"
In this last question, you hope to find a manager who is personally connected to the recruitment process and who recognizes, as you do, that having a ready conduit to talent is a management necessity.

As you ask this series of questions, remember that people often quit jobs no matter how good the management, so the answer to any single question should never rule a manager in or out. Rather, each answer is another argument in the complex case for or against selection.

Day-to-Day Management Skills

Here are a handful of questions that will help you evaluate how the candidate is likely to perform, on a daily basis, some of those responsibilities essential to every working manager.

"Describe the organization of the department and the responsibilities of each of the staff members."
Here you get good, solid data to give you a picture of the candidate at work. It will also shed light on delegation, organization, and planning skills.

"What methods do you use in planning and performing salary/performance reviews?"
You are looking for a logical and consistent approach that shows the ability to track employees' performances through the year against objective, predetermined performance criteria.

"How often do you administer performance reviews?"
With a good manager, this is almost an ongoing process, and not restricted to the annual salary review.

"How do you schedule projects, assignments, and vacations?"
Here, you will learn about planning skills and will also see whether your potential manager is reactive ("Well, I just have to cover for them if too many go away at once") or proactive ("I tell all new employees that the department must be adequately staffed at all times and that I require adequate planning notice for vacations").

"What responsibilities do you hold in relation to other departments?"
The answer to this can tell you about committee involvement and how the candidate sees the management role in a larger context. Any

interdepartmental coordinating responsibilities can be indicative of room for increased responsibilities. The answer should also give you an understanding of the candidate's awareness of his role as a team player, and display an awareness of how his role makes a contribution to the smooth running and profitability of the company.

Fiscal Responsibilities

These four mandatory questions probe the way the potential manager can handle money.

"Do you hold budgetary responsibility for your department?" "What is it?" Also, "What challenges do/did you have staying within budget?" "How do you go about meeting those challenges?"
There are many in management who claim that a manager without fiscal responsibility is nothing more than a hired hand. Whatever your feelings, the level of the candidate's budgetary responsibility and ability to deliver within its strictures are sure benchmarks by which to make a judgment.

"What was your involvement in short-/mid-/long-term planning?"
Budgeting and planning responsibilities go hand-in-hand, and the answer will indicate whether your candidate is a policymaker or implementer. This in turn defines another nice difference in management responsibilities: there are many managers who implement, but have no input into determination of company policy. This question will allow you to see which camp the candidate falls into and, consequently, whether he or she will be both capable and happy in the job you are looking to fill.

"How do you quantify the results of your activities as manager?
The answer should be straightforward, but it will be intriguing to see what the candidate does with it. The effect on the bottom line, of course, is how management judges performance. Simply put, this is determined by the ability to earn money and become more efficient by saving money and saving time. In the same vein, you might be interested in the response to, *"What would you say are the major qualities a manager's job demands?"* and *"How would you characterize your management style?"* All these questions help you develop a three-dimensional understanding of the management candidate. The result is that the picture which emerges may be different from the one initially presented by the candidate.

"Tell me about a time when people were making emotional decisions about your projects. What happened, and what did you do?"

Emotional maturity and judgment become increasingly important as people climb through the ranks of management. This question will help you get inside the candidate's head. When all other questions have failed to pierce the interview armor, this will often show you the candidate's surprisingly emotional reactions to perfectly sound business decisions. It is, after all, rare in business that decisions are ever made on anything but hard fact and profitability potential.

Remember that any manager you hire will in turn reflect directly on your competency. The care with which you pick such important players should be equally objective and practiced. Leave nothing to whim, nothing to chance. While reference checks are important for any job, they are mandatory with management hires.

You can use the management interview skeleton that follows as a check and balance after you have custom-built your own interview sequence. Of course, one sequence of questions, perfect for every position, does not exist. Each candidate is different, as is each company, interviewer, and position. These questions are meant as support to your own analysis of what is important, not to replace that analysis.

Management Interview Skeleton

Ability

How long have you been in management?

How many people do you manage?

What level and types of people do you manage?

How long have you held these management responsibilities?

Do these people report directly and solely to you?

Who hired and fired these people?

How creative do you see a management role to be?

How do you quantify the result of your job?

What do you perceive the responsibilities of this job to be?

How far in advance do you and management typically make specific decisions about directional changes?

Day-to-Day Management Skills

How would you characterize your management style?

Explain the limit of your management responsibility by explaining the types of decisions that are beyond your authority.

How often do you prepare reports?

With what other departments do you deal?

What responsibilities do you hold in relation to other departments?

How do you schedule projects, assignments, and vacations?

Tell me about a recent crisis.

Hiring

How many people have you hired?

How have you learned to interview?

How do you plan to interview?

What has been your biggest hiring mistake?

Employee Orientation

What steps do you normally take to get a new employee settled in?

How do you analyze the training needs of your department or of specific individuals?

Communication, Motivation

How important to you is communication and interaction with the staff?

What are some of the tasks you typically delegate?

How do you maintain checks and balances on employee performance?

What things cause the most friction in your department?

Do you feel it is your responsibility to adapt to your employees, or is it their responsibility to adapt to you?

Tell me about a time when morale was low. What did you do about it?

When have you seen proven motivational techniques fail?

Tell me some of the ways you have seen other managers demotivate employees.

Have you ever become involved in an employee's personal problems?

How do you keep the staff aware of company information and activities?

Have you ever faced a situation with a staff member who was being less than direct with you about his or her activities?

How do you organize and run department meetings?

Authority, Discipline

How have you been successful in setting objectives for your staff?

Have you ever had to make unpopular decisions?

What are some of the everyday problems you face with your staff?

Have you ever worked with a group that jointly resisted management authority?

What management situation is personally most difficult for you?

What employee behavior makes you angry?

What do you do when a team member breaks corporate policy?

Turnover

How do you handle poor employee performance?

What has been the turnover in your department over the last three years?

How many people have you terminated?

What steps do you take before deciding to terminate? How have you gone about forecasting manpower needs?

Have you ever experienced problems with company pay scales when trying to attract new employees?

Fiscal Responsibility

Do you hold budgetary responsibility in your department?

What has been the most expensive fiscal mistake of your career?

Manageability

How do you take direction?

How do you take criticism?

What have you been most criticized for as a manager?

What have you and previous managers disagreed about?

What do you do when there is a decision to be made and no procedure exists?

How have past managers gotten the best out of you?

How would you describe the best manager you ever had?

Tell me about the worst manager you ever had.

Tell me about a time when you felt that management had made an emotional rather than logical decision about your work.

When have you been described as inflexible?

How does your job relate to the overall goals of the company?

How often are you involved in making formal presentations or proposals to management or customers?

How do you define the difference between supervision and management?

How do you play the office politics game?

What kinds of things bother you most?

If you could make one constructive suggestion to management, what would it be?

The Sales Hire 11

With turnover higher in sales than in other professions, and considering the impact of the sales function on profitability, it's arguable that hiring the right sales staff is one of management's toughest jobs. The situation is complicated by the superior communication skills of salespeople and their tendency to regard the interview as a sales presentation to a prospect, representing the product that they know best: themselves. They know how to emphasize the good points and minimize or steer clear of the others.

You already have an appreciation of interview structure and evaluation techniques, and you also have plenty of useful questions. In this chapter, you will find additional questions to give you an edge in penetrating those superior communication skills and getting to the truth of each candidate's ability, professional behaviors, problem-solving skills, motivation, team orientation, and manageability.

"What do you know about our product line?"
Once you have walked a candidate through his or her work history, following the steps discussed earlier in the book, this can make a good opening question in the area of ability. Only an incompetent would go for a job in sales without a clear understanding of the company product or service line. Yet your question goes beyond this; you are looking for an overall understanding of how your product/services fit into the overall marketplace in which you compete.

"Describe a typical day." "How do you plan your day?" and "Why is it important to prioritize?"

The ego strength necessary for survival in sales can raise problems of manageability; consequently, a candidate's self-discipline and organization need to be examined. The Plan, Do, Review cycle of time management and organization that is common to all successful professionals is nowhere more important than in the sales process. You are looking for efficient time blocking of tasks to maximize the number of sales calls. Salespeople must organize their day around the behavior of the industry they serve. For instance, when you deal with the financial community, you keep bankers' hours; when the restaurant business is your field, you keep hospitality hours and would never call on a client between 11 A.M. and 2 P.M.

In this context of time management, you will want to examine the mandatory non-selling activities that allow sales to occur, such as paperwork: *"How much time do you spend doing paperwork and other non-selling activities?"* Remember to find out what time of the day these duties are performed, and to match that information with your business's prime selling hours.

"What steps are involved in selling your product/service?"

Good analytical skills must go along with excellent written and verbal communication skills. This question will sort out those who happen to be making a decent living in a good marketplace from those who will be able to sell regardless of the economic climate. The answer helps give you an understanding of the candidate's grasp of the building blocks that lead to consistent sales performance.

"What different types of customers have you called on, and what titles have you sold to in these companies?"

This question should be asked early in the interview process to tell you what experience the candidate has in dealing with your particular client base, and the relative sophistication of those individual customers with whom he deals. The higher the ticket on the item being sold, the more sophisticated the buyer and the longer the sales process.

"What percentage of your sales calls result in full presentations?"

This question examines a candidate's ability to get through to the decision-maker. It is unwise to accept the answer as it stands, because it is an easy statistic to fudge. This may be a suitable opportunity to develop the theme with a situational technique, and to role-play difficulties that are typical in your business. If the candidate habitually pitches the receptionist and then retreats, it is better to find out about this now rather than later, when he or she is destroying your sales projections. A natural follow-up to this is, *"What percentage of your sales calls result in sales?"* Watch for discrepancies: A sales rep, for example, who claims to close one of every two sales presentations and who isn't ranked very near the top among peers is either lying or has other performance problems such as absenteeism. So you can ask, *"Where do you rank in performance among your peers?"*

"How long does it typically take you from initial contact to close of the sale?" The answer, perhaps jogged with conversational follow-up questions, will tell you about the candidate's grasp of the sales process in your area of endeavor. The answer might also give you some help in evaluating whether the candidate likes to go for the close or merely jogs along, waiting until the prospect makes a decision. So this question could be followed with others about closing sales: *"At what point do you go for the close?" "What techniques do you find effective in closing sales?"*

"How large a client base do you need to maintain to keep sales on an even keel?" "Have you ever broken in a new territory/desk for your company?" "How did you approach the job?" "How would you go about identifying customers in a new market?" "How do you prefer to go about securing new prospects and clients?" All of these questions address the issue of market penetration and market development, those activities that keep the pipeline of sales prospects full. The responses give you specific information about preferred approaches and can also tell you about the candidate's motivation to treat sales as a real career. You also will learn more about creativity, analytical skills, and determination.

"How do you turn an occasional buyer into a regular buyer?" "Have you ever taken over an existing territory/desk?" "What was the volume when you started? What was it when you left?" These are all questions that take the focus from the individual sale to the larger picture of the marketplace; the answers will give you an idea of how your candidate is likely to accept the challenge. Any market, of course, that has been left as it was found denotes a lack of skill, effort, and/or knowledge of market penetration and development techniques. Questions such as these are ripe for phrasing with past-performance techniques: *"Tell me about the last time you turned an occasional buyer into a regular buyer."* Using techniques that require sales candidates to talk about specific events helps keep them honest.

"What kind of people do you like to sell to?"
This is really a setup question to be followed by, *"What type of people don't you like to sell to?"* and then *"How do you manage to sell to these people?"*

This question sequence is designed to help you examine the candidate's ability to deal with difficult customers. You can flesh it out with past-performance queries—*"So tell me about a time you had to sell to someone like this"*—or by role-playing a situation: *"Perhaps I'd understand better if I put myself in the position of that customer. How will you respond when I say _____?"*

"I'd be interested to hear about a difficult collection problem you have experienced."
Sales go wrong in postsales as well as in the sales process itself, and you can customize this question to fit your particular situation. You are looking for insight into this specific challenge but also to gain an understanding of how well the candidate executes the sale and thereby avoids postsale problems. You can follow this with, *"In hindsight, how could you have avoided this problem?"* After the answer, ask for another example of the same problem that has occurred since, to find out whether the individual learns from his or her mistakes.

"How involved should a company be with its customers?"
You are looking for the insight that allows a sales professional to get close to customers to understand and sell to their needs while also maintaining an objective distance. Customers have buying cycles that crest and then crash, so your best candidate is one who combines a hard head with a broad client base.

"Tell me about your most difficult sale and how you approached it."
In sales, as in other professions, you learn much about ability and motivation when you understand how candidates handle problems. The answer might well highlight specific areas of interest worth probing further. For example: *"So the sale was difficult because . . ."* *"Why do you feel that way?"* *"In hindsight, what could you have done earlier in the sale to have precluded the problem?"* Good sales managers know that the majority of tough, messy, or failed closes could have been avoided with better initial qualification of the prospect and attention to the details along the way; that's how they got to be sales managers. The question looks for this same kind of analytical ability, with the extra dimension of revealing areas suitable for professional development.

"What was the most surprising objection you ever heard, and how did you handle it?"

After the candidate's response, create a sequence of questions around the sales objections common in your business. A salesperson's lot is dealing with objections day in and day out, so you want to know about the analytical skills and poise that show he or she handles the unexpected. You might continue with, *"What are the three most common objections you run into?"* or *"What are the very toughest objections you have to meet in your job?"* Then, for all of the most interesting responses, ask, *"How do you handle that?"* You can easily simulate real objections by getting the candidate to role-play with you. A good way of doing it is to follow up on the previous question: *"I think I understand, but perhaps it would be better if you showed me. If I were the customer and I said, 'It's too expensive,' what would you say?"* Short of having the candidate make live sales presentations, situational techniques like this will get you closest to the real performance capabilities. Slip into the approach conversationally for best effect. The next example is a common but effective case in point.

"Sell me this pen."

This is such a wonderfully appropriate sales interview question I'm surprised it isn't asked more frequently. If you don't want to use the generic, you can always make the object/service specific to your company's product. At the root of every successful sale is the salesperson's ability to identify a need and subsequently demonstrate how the product will fill that need. This is commonly known as feature/benefit selling: Here is the feature, and this is what it can do for you. This question tests your candidate's awareness of an essential sales skill and his or her quick thinking. A salesperson is worthless if he or she gives up after your first objection.

"Tell me about a time when all seemed lost in an important sale. What did you do to weather the crisis?"

Look for a positive and resilient attitude. There is a saying in sales that the sale isn't dead until the client has said "no" three times. That's the kind of persistence you need to see in a candidate.

"Tell me about your most crushing failure."

Give the candidate all the time necessary to come up with an answer. We have all experienced defeat. You are interested not only in the actual circumstance but also in the spirit with which the candidate handled defeat. Alternatively, you might say, *"Give me a specific example of a time when you were rejected, and how you handled it."* Ego strength and self-image are important components of the overachiever, which is a personality type that many believe is particularly suited to sales. Salespeople must not only be able to handle stress; it needs to be a motivating factor in their lives. Most important, sales professionals need to able to emerge from stressful situations with their egos firmly intact.

Along with the response, look for that salesperson who has a strong listening profile coupled with analytical skills and who will draw your attention to the difference between refusal of product and rejection of self.

"Give me an example of a sale that was, for all intents and purposes, lost. How did you turn the situation around and then make the sale?"
Sales is a stressful profession, so your candidates need to be able to handle the tough questions. To keep any candidate malleable, though, you must intersperse the tough questions with easier ones. This question is easy for the candidate, but don't take time to tune out; you just might miss a salesperson who regularly closes sales with deep discounting as the lead tool. Look for original thinking and an ability to empathize with the client.

"All of us have failed to meet a quota at one point or another. When you don't meet your goals, how do you handle it?"
This question tests resiliency and can also be a springboard for probing where, when, how, and why the goal got off track. Because such a problem can often be one of prioritization, your next question could be, *"Why is it important to prioritize?"* The last in the sequence could be, *"Tell me about a time when you exhibited persistence but still couldn't reach a carefully planned goal."*

"Give me an example of a time when it was necessary to reach a goal in a short period of time and how you planned to achieve it."
Every salesperson in the world has lost business and approached the end of the quota period empty-handed. You are using the question to examine whether or not the candidate can come from behind. Hopefully, what you will get is a "when-the-going-gets-tough" answer, telling you how the salesperson keeps calm and keeps plugging. You are also likely to get good question fodder concerning how the emergency arose in the first place—was the candidate perhaps slacking off after a good quarter?

"For what have you been most frequently criticized, and by whom?"
This is an open-ended question, and the odds of getting a straightforward answer from a salesperson are not always good. Nevertheless, you'll never

know what you might dig up without asking, and the question doubles very adequately as a way of testing the quick thinking and poise so necessary in sales.

"How do you keep yourself going when everyone is having a bad day/is unorganized/is depressed?" and "Have you ever worked in an environment where people took advantage when management was absent? How did you handle it?"
These will tell you about emotional maturity, self-discipline, and drive. In the sales world, someone has always just lost a sale or a client. It's all part of the territory, and can be a downer. The last thing you need on the team, however, is someone who will be affected by the moods of others. In the responses, look for evidence of determination, a strong sense of self-worth, someone who is independent and not swayed by the group. Sometimes a candidate will tell what happens when he or she is having a bad day/is unorganized/is depressed. When this happens, you will of course want to probe the cause of the problem. Ask, *"What caused you to feel depressed in the first place?" "How often does this happen to you?" "What have you done to be more effective in your present position?"*

Here you look for that extra effort made outside of work hours and beyond company-sponsored programs. You are hoping to find those candidates who invest themselves in their professional future; perhaps a candidate has studied the technical side of the product line, or regularly attends seminars, or reads motivational books.

"How productive are you compared to your peers?"
This is the first of eight ego-strength questions, asking the candidate for a self-rating against peers. The others, which all finish with "compared to your peers," follow: *"How smart are you compared to your peers?" "How articulate are you . . . ?" "How well dressed are you . . . ?" "How witty are you . . . ?" "How do you rank professionally . . . ?" "How tenacious are you . . . ?" "How well do you accept disappointment . . . ?"*

Now, these are all questions that anticipate subjective responses. By the same token, you cannot possibly be expected to know the candidate's peers. So, don't take the answers at face value, because all you will get is an impression of whether or not the candidate can talk a good game. Take advantage, rather, of the fact that the candidate is willing to take a position on, for example, why he is more tenacious than his peers. Then, in the second part of the question, ask the candidate to defend the position, just as he or she must do in a tough sales presentation. You begin with, *"I'd be interested to hear of a time when you proved yourself to be more tenacious than your peers."* As you listen to the response, you can well be layering further probes of the event.

"What have been your highest and lowest rankings in your current/last sales force?" All salespeople know exactly where they rank, so don't let someone off with, "I can't remember." If that is the reply, tell the candidate to take his or her time; then shut up and wait. If you do have to elicit an answer in this way, and you intend to lend some credence to it, be certain to verify it with a reference check.

"Share with me an example of surpassing what was expected of you from your employer." or *"I'd be interested to hear about a specific time when you greatly exceeded the norm."*
This is a chance for a candidate to brag, perhaps, but it also gives you the opportunity to find out just what this person considers exceptional performance. Of course, if no story is forthcoming, you might be in serious trouble.

"What do you dislike about most sales?"
This will test quick thinking and creativity. There are many odious, but necessary, tasks in sales, and you need to know if a specific "dislike" will preclude his or her doing the necessary work. If the answer is unhesitatingly "prospecting" or "making cold calls," it may well be the last question you have to ask—successful sales are based on making new contacts. You will, at least, certainly have something to talk about.

"How do you feel about out-of-town/overnight travel?"
If travel or unusual hours are required to do the job, you need to know early on if personal circumstances preclude a candidate from doing the job. Where you place this question depends on the problems the company experiences with the necessary travel schedule.

Telemarketing Skills

While not all sales jobs are done over the telephone, almost all require at least part of the sales process to be executed that way. Here is a sequence of questions to help you evaluate the effectiveness of your candidates when they have to work over the telephone. Naturally, you will customize the questions to the telephone usage common in your sales process.

"Have you ever sold anything over the telephone?" or *"What part of the sales process do you conduct over the telephone rather than face-to-face?" "What special skills or techniques are necessary to be successful over the telephone?"*
To sell on the phone—even to facilitate sales—requires a set of skills separate from face-to-face sales. Because there are no facial expressions or body language to help the salesperson, he or she must rely on voice inflection, a highly developed listening profile, advanced questioning techniques, and conversation control techniques. Follow up with, *"Tell me about a time when you called a client on the phone for the first time. How did you establish rapport?"*

When telemarketing, it is necessary first of all to reach the decision-making individual. More and more, a company's clerical staff is warned to screen out sales calls. So, along the same tack, ask, *"When getting through to a sales prospect for the first time on the phone, what roadblocks can you expect the clerical staff to put in your way?"* You may even want to role-play one or two of those roadblocks.

"How do you go about gathering names of new contacts on the telephone?"
The answer to this question will tell you how an intelligent salesperson can identify new prospects quickly and cost-effectively with the telephone, and how prospecting, in the right hands, is an integral part of the many conversations a salesperson has during the day.

A Skeleton Interview for Sales

Using all of the knowledge and techniques you have picked up in this book so far, you need to custom-build interviews to address the needs of your specific sales positions. The following skeleton interview is not suggested for use as it stands; rather, you can check your entire, carefully prepared series of questions against it.

Of course, one sequence of questions that is perfect for every position does not exist. Each candidate is different, as is each company, interviewer, and position. You will probably find questions in this skeleton that do not meet your particular needs. You may want to add a few of your favorite questions, or you may want to replace some questions with others found in *Hiring the Best*. You will have to address the details of your particular position yourself.

When building your interview, you also should employ the interviewing techniques discussed elsewhere in this book. For example, you will find many questions here that beg for question layering, past-performance, or situational interviewing techniques.

Ability, Suitability

Why are you pursuing a career as a professional salesperson? What are your qualifications?

Of all your work in sales, where have you been more successful—in servicing clients or in developing a new territory?

Would you prefer to sell a big- or a small-ticket item?

When you consider your skills as a professional salesperson, what area concerns you most about your ability to sell?

What aspect of sales do you like most?

What do you find to be the most repetitive tasks of your job?

What bothers you most about sales?

How necessary is it to be creative in your job?

What makes you think you can sell consistently?

Tell me about your training. What have you done to become a better salesperson?

What do you know about our company and its products?

What do you like least about the job description?

What special characteristics should I consider about you as a person?

Willingness

Tell me about a sales project that really got you excited.

What do you consider a good day's sales effort?

Tell me about a time when you exceeded both your quota and your goals.

When the pressure is on, where does your extra energy come from?

How often do you find it necessary to go above and beyond the call of duty?

Do you ever take work home?

Give me an example of your initiative in a challenging situation.

What are some of the things in sales that you find difficult to do?

The Indomitable Salesperson

Tell me about a sale that was, for all intents and purposes, lost. How did you turn the situation around?

What are the three most-common objections you face?

What would you say if the customer said, "It's too expensive"?

Tell me about your most difficult sale. How could you have prevented problems from arising?

It is sometimes difficult to get an immediate yes from customers. What do you do in these situations?

When do customers really try your patience?

Tell me about a sale you couldn't close because of lack of information. What did you do?

How do you feel when you get rejected?

Tell me about an important sale that went on the rocks. How did you weather the storm?

How do you react when you miss a sales quota?

Self-Image

Do you consider yourself successful?

What do you feel are your personal limitations?

What sales achievement are you most proud of?

What do you consider your greatest strength?

How do you rank among your peers?

Communication

What types of people do you sell to in your current job?

Tell me how you made an "impossible" sale.

Tell me about a time when your timing was good.

Tell me about a time when your timing was bad.

What do you do when you can't get a word in edgewise?

Sell me this pen.

How do you get a fix on people in the first few moments of meeting them?

How do you turn things around when the initial impression of you is bad?

Tell me about how you dealt with an angry or frustrated customer.

How often do you prepare sales reports? How detailed are they?

When and where in the sales process have you found silence to be a useful tool?

How do you approach getting an understanding of a customer's needs?

What business or social situations make you feel awkward?

Telemarketing

How much time do you spend on the telephone in your job?

What services or products have you sold over the phone?

What special skills and techniques are required to be successful over the phone?

How do you go about establishing rapport with a stranger on the phone?

What kinds of roadblocks do you expect from clerical staff over the phone? How do you handle them?

How many phone calls do you make in a day?

Time Management, Organization

How much time do you spend doing paperwork and non-selling activities?

How do you organize yourself for day-to-day activities?

Describe a typical day.

Tell me about the planning for an important project.

Tell me about the problems you face in getting all of the facets of your job completed on time.

What are the component parts of your job, and how much time do you spend on each?

How many accounts do you like to handle at one time?

Do you set goals that are easy or difficult to reach?

Tell me about some long-term working goals and how you are getting along in achieving them.

Market Penetration

What steps are involved in selling your product?

How long does it typically take from initial contact to close the sale?

What percentage of your sales calls result in full presentation?

What kind of people do you like to sell to?

What kind of people don't you like to sell to?

Have you ever broken in a new territory for an employer?

How do you turn an occasional buyer into a regular buyer?

What was the most important account you have worked on?

Tell me about a difficult collection problem.

What are you most proud of in your ability to develop a market-place?

Sales Maturity

What would you feel are the major personal characteristics of a successful salesperson?

What have you learned from the different sales jobs you've had?

What aspects of your work do you consider most crucial?

Why do people buy a product or service?

What kind of rewards are most satisfying to you?

What are some of the things you have found especially motivating over the years?

What do you dislike most about sales?

Problem Solving and Decision-Making

What kinds of problems do you have to solve as a salesperson?

Do you regard them as complex or overwhelming?

Have you ever made a quick decision that cost you money?

What kinds of decisions are most difficult for you?

What is the biggest mistake you have made in your career?

Do you discuss important decisions with anyone?

Teamwork

Explain your role as a group member of a sales force.

How would you define a conducive work atmosphere?

How do you deal with disagreements with others?

Have you ever had to change your behavior to work successfully with others?

Have you ever been with a sales team that fell apart?

Manageability

How does your boss get the best out of you?

How do you get the best out of your boss?

Describe the best manager you ever had.

Describe the worst manager you ever had.

Tell me about the last time you really got angry about a management decision.

If you could make one constructive suggestion to your current management, what would it be?

How do you take direction? How do you take criticism?

What are some of the things your boss did that you disliked?

What types of decisions are beyond your level of authority at your current job?

If a coworker came to you with a complaint about the job, how would you react?

Do you feel you are adequately recognized for your contributions?

Salespeople regard the interview as a sales presentation, and you as a hot prospect. Most salespeople know that it is easier to sell to a friend—someone who wants to speak with them in the first place—than to a stranger, and that makes your job doubly hard. Be sure to remain objective and methodical in your approaches to interviewing sales personnel, or you may buy something that you don't really need.

People Futures: The Gentle Art of Hiring Entry-Level Workers 12

*H*iring workers with no track record is an underappreciated challenge. You are hiring raw, untested talent with little or no real-world experience that would allow you to judge ability. Still, good hires have to be made on more than grade-point average.

Potential ability to do the job has to be based on all facets of academic performance and whatever scant work experience exists. A recent graduate who has any work experience gets points for the effort; that experience also gives you openings for examination of the candidate's understanding of the professional workplace. Although you have to accept that the entry-level worker must develop the ability to execute a job's responsibilities, the more desirable candidate will already have begun development of professional behaviors and will bring to the table good listening, verbal, and written skills; technological adaptedness; initiative; energy; and an analytical approach to problems. There are ways that you can judge the motivation to work and to learn and evaluate the manageability and team orientation factors from the academic experience and any limited work experience.

In this chapter, you will find some additional considerations and questions to give you that extra edge in determining real potential when buying people futures. Just as for other positions, your interview structure will be custom-designed for each opening and tailored to the particular technical competencies of the profession; the analytical and other professional behaviors that go along with the job; and the candidate's motivation, manageability, and team orientation.

When there is work experience, it won't very often be relevant to your profession and industry. This shouldn't really be a problem, because if we strip jobs down to their essentials, every job is at some level about problem solving; every job demands the same learned professional behaviors to succeed; and every job requires that you are motivated to take the rough with the smooth and get along with others. Use the techniques and questions from throughout the book to understand how the candidate has performed in these areas, on whatever jobs there have been. The result will be a reasonable predictor of how he or she will perform on your payroll.

The interviews will start with general questions about education and experience to date, to get the candidate comfortable with talking. Then, if there is little or no professional work experience to evaluate, you can tailor some of these questions about the educational experience to give you insight about performance to date and potential for the future. Start with an interview outline you have used for junior people in this position, but who have a little experience, and then customize it to the entry-level situation and add any of the following questions, as they fit your needs.

"How did you spend your vacations while at school?"
Perhaps the greatest challenge in hiring recent graduates is that they are extremely difficult to judge because they don't have real-world experience. Those candidates who have some work experience will stand out because you immediately have more in common with them: their experience demonstrates a basic understanding of the relationship between effort and money. Although college co-op work programs, carefully geared to the chosen profession, are obviously desirable, any work experience is valuable. Even the level of the job is not as important as what and how much the student learned from the experience. This is where your questions should lead.

"What did you learn from that job?" "Where you ever bossed around? How did it feel?" "What did you like the least about the job? Why?" "What hours did you work?" "How many days a week did you work?" "What did you dislike most about the routine of regular work?" "Did the job include repetitive tasks?" "How did you feel about doing the same thing time and time again?"
In reality, no entry-level jobs are very exciting, once you scratch the surface. They all carry a fair amount of repetition, so understanding how the young

candidate feels about regular hours and repetitive tasks, once the initial excitement has worn off, is important. The candidate's answers will tell you about willingness and manageability.

"What have you done that shows initiative and willingness to work?"
The answer is valuable because you are giving candidates an opportunity to share their orientation toward motivation and making a difference with their presence.

Along with the examination of any relevant work experience, you can also learn a great deal from how a candidate has handled the educational experience.

"Which of your school years was most difficult?"
The answer is only important in that it gets the candidate to focus on a tough time. Your data banks fill up when you follow with, *"Why do you feel that was the toughest year?" "What were some of the problems you faced?"* Then, concentrating on them one at a time, ask, *"What caused this to occur?" "What did you do about it?" "If you had to face the problem all over again, would you do things any differently? If so, how?"*

The answers begin to tell you how the individual approaches life and its challenges: head-on, procrastinating, taking responsibility, laying the blame elsewhere, rushing blindly ahead, or planning strategy in a difficult situation. Analyze the answers for pointers toward likes, dislikes, and causes of stress, as they would apply to your job.

"Do you think grades should be considered by first employers?"
Whatever the answer is, look for someone who can back up his or her beliefs. The question is not that valuable with a straight-A student, but is very revealing with those who may feel an understandable amount of guilt because his or her grades weren't perfect. With those who have perfect grades, as well as those who don't, you might ask, *"Do you feel you have anything else to learn?"* This question allows you to gain insight into potential manageability problems.

"So, these are the best grades you are capable of? How do we know you are good enough for our company?" or *"Your grades aren't all that good. How do I know your capabilities?"*
These questions take on the topic of grades and ask candidates to promote themselves from a defensive position. There is obviously a distinct intimidation factor here, which is most suitable when the candidate in

mind will have to face intimidation on the job or when it is someone for whom you have high hopes. Your voice inflection plays an important role in determining the degree of stress you want to create; these two examples can lose much of their sting when customized to your own speech and asked in your most sympathetic voice.

"What kind of work interests you most, and why?"
This brings the interview back to the present and gives you an overall view of the career that the candidate feels would be fulfilling. Once the candidate is finished, follow with, *"What are the disadvantages of your chosen field?"* Complete the sequence with, *"How do you think you will handle that?"*

Also include such probes as, *"Why do you want to work here?" "Where else are you applying?" "Do you prefer working with others or alone?" "Define cooperation." "How long will you stay with the company?" "Will you go where the company sends you?" "How long will it take you to make a contribution?" "Why should I hire you?" "Tell me about an event that really challenged you. How was your approach different?" "Tell me about a time when your work or an idea was criticized."*

"Are you looking for a temporary or permanent job?"
This is a good knockout question to ask at any point in the interview process, if you start to get a sneaking feeling that the candidate may not be around too long.

The Future

Having looked at past performance, it is logical to look at the future.

"Do you plan further education?"
The knowledge that you gain from this question can indicate a certain degree of dedication to learning and improving professionally. If the courses are relevant to your business, it could be a good sign. But always be aware of that gap between dreaming and doing. This is especially true with recent graduates, who perhaps don't always understand the extra effort required to work full-time and pursue academic studies. Ask what educational goals the candidate intends to pursue, and why; you can then ask how those goals relate to a career in your profession.

*"Can you put your education behind you and start from scratch in the profes-
sional world?"*
This one takes a slightly different tack toward relating education to the
workplace. The question usually comes as somewhat of a shock to the
candidate, so the degree of turmoil or confusion it causes can give you
an indication of self-control. Occasionally, it flushes out aggression and a
know-it-all-already attitude, which gives you early warning of some tiring
times as a manager while you acclimate this person to the harsh realities
of business.

*"What job in our company would you choose if you were free to do so?" "What
job in the company do you want to work toward?" "What would you like to be
doing five years from now?"*
A candidate who has a real idea of how the profession works demonstrates a desirable degree of focus. These questions help you determine a
candidate's sense of direction, inner strength, ambition, and confidence.
A recent graduate may not have much practical experience, but that can
be overcome with energy and drive. Regardless of the answer, ask for it to
be justified: *"Why that job?" "Tell me what you think a person in that position
does on a daily basis?"* You will find out how much the neophyte really
understands about the nuts and bolts of his or her chosen career goal.

Of course, one sequence of questions that's perfect for every position
does not exist. You may find some questions in the following skeleton that
do not meet your particular needs; you may find yourself saying, "That
wouldn't work for me, but if I twisted it this way or that way it would."
You will find many questions here that beg for question layering, past-
performance, or situational interviewing techniques.

Entry-Level Interview Skeleton

Educational Background

Why did you enroll at your university?

How would you describe your academic achievement?

How did you choose your major?

What college subjects have you enjoyed most?

What school year was most difficult, and why?

What changes would you make in your school?

Tell me about your most rewarding college experience.

What are your plans for further education?

What extracurricular activities did you enjoy?

How do you think college contributed to your overall development?

Do you think first employers should consider college grades?

How do I know your capabilities?

What have you learned from your mistakes in school?

Work History

How would you describe the ideal job for you?

What kind of work interests you most?

Explain your understanding of this job's responsibilities.

Do you feel you still have anything to learn after all your years of academic study?

Which summer job did you enjoy most?

How many levels of management did you interact with?

What was the job's biggest challenge?

Tell me about a responsibility you have enjoyed. What has been your least valuable work experience?

How would your references describe you?

Are you looking for a permanent job, or do you plan to return to school?

Motivation, Leadership Potential

If you were hiring a graduate for this position, what would you be looking for?

What have you done that shows initiative and willingness to work?

What would you look for in potential leaders for this organization?

What experience have you had in leadership positions?

As a leader, have your decisions ever been unpopular?

When the pressure of work is high, where does your energy come from?

Tell me about a time when unexpected events demanded that you reschedule your time.

Future Career

Why are you interviewing with us?

What do you know about our company?

What do you expect out of this job?

What do you think you would like best about this job?

What do you think you would like least?

How will this job help you reach your long-term personal and career goals?

What is more important at the start of your career, money or the job?

What do you feel are the disadvantages of this field?

Where do you think you could make the biggest contribution to this organization?

What do you see yourself doing five years from now?

How long would you anticipate staying with the company?

How do you define a successful career?

What can you do for us that someone else can't?

What special characteristics should I consider about you?

Goals, Organization

What are your long-range goals?

How do you plan your day, your week?

How do you determine your priorities?

An overwhelming, time-sensitive task has just been assigned to you. How do you plan a strategy for meeting your deadline?

What happens when two priorities compete for your time?

When short-term goals clash with long-term ones, which takes priority, and why?

Communication

Getting the job done involves gathering information and input from others. How do you do this?

What is the toughest communication problem you have faced?

Tell me how you have verbally convinced someone of an approach or an idea.

Tell me about a time when you have compromised successfully.

In what situations are you inflexible?

How do you overcome objections to your ideas?

When have your verbal communications been important enough to follow up in writing?

Are there situations better suited to written communication?

What is the most difficult paper you have written?

Stress, Flexibility

Tell me about a time when someone lost his or her temper at you in a business environment.

Have you ever worked in a place where it seemed to be one crisis after another?

What makes you feel tense or nervous?

What is the most frustrating work-related experience you have faced?

What do you do when you are being pressed for a decision?

Decision-Making

How will you evaluate the company for which you hope to work?

What makes you think you have what it takes to be successful in this business?

Do you take an intuitive or a logical approach to solving problems?

What kinds of decisions are toughest for you?

Developmental Issues

What do you see as some of your most pressing developmental needs?

What have you been involved with that you now regret?

What is the biggest single mistake you have made?

What have the disappointments of life taught you?

Tell me about something you started but couldn't finish.

Teamwork

Define cooperation.

What is the difference between a friend and a colleague?

Can you think of a time when you have successfully motivated friends or colleagues to achieve a difficult goal?

How will you establish a working relationship with the employees in this company?

How would you work with the various different opinions in a team in order to reach a goal?

Define a good work atmosphere.

What are some of the common friction areas you watch for when working with others?

Manageability

What qualities should a successful manager possess?

What do you feel should be the relationship between the manager and the staff?

How have past managers gotten the best out of you?

Describe the toughest manager you ever had.

How do you take direction?

How do you take criticism?

Tell me about an occasion when school or employer policies have been unfair to you.

For what have you been most frequently criticized?

The hiring decision you make regarding a recent graduate is ultimately a judgment call. You are betting on the future with less than adequate information about the past. As a prudent manager, with the best interests of your company and career at heart, you can reduce the long odds by careful evaluation of each candidate against the considerations addressed in this chapter.

The Clerical/
Administrative Hire

13

*T*he glue that holds many departments in our companies together is
the clerical staff. However, new technology is reducing the ranks
of administrative staff, placing responsibility for self-administration more
squarely on the shoulders of the individual, and making superb administrative hires compulsory for the productive manager. With more people
relying on fewer administrative staff in a far more complex work environment, a bad administrative hire can really slow down your department.

How do you make the right clerical/administrative hiring decision?
What questions should you ask? Much clerical/administrative work can
be measured in functional ability, but a willingness to do the work is also
critical, especially when that work is not "exciting," so the ability and motivational aspects of a candidate must be coupled with a real understanding
of how his or her job relates to the overall success of the department. At
the same time, the personal chemistry among boss, team, and support staff
can make the difference between a productive and a depressing workplace,
so teamwork and manageability are likewise paramount. You can harvest
relevant questions addressing ability, willingness, and manageability from
the other chapters as they relate to your specific needs, and then check
your interview structure against the questions here to make sure you have
all the bases covered.

The Clerical/Administrative Career Path

The need for more productivity and cohesive teamwork is critical in all companies, but you can find yourself hard-pressed to find an administrative assistant who will burn the midnight oil on your behalf. One of the reasons for this is that we still consider secretaries, receptionists, and general administrative assistants in their traditional role, as functionaries without the ability to take on increasing responsibility. However, technology places more and more responsibility for the smooth running, and therefore success, of a department in the hands of support staff. Without the opportunity for growth, and absent professional respect from the team, why would anyone stretch for an employer?

You will want to determine understanding and ability to do the job, which given the nature of administrative jobs has some special considerations in the areas of understanding priorities, getting the job done, and demonstrating reliability and flexibility.

"Explain your understanding of the job's responsibilities." "What aspects of your work interest you the most?" "What aspects of your work are the most frustrating?" "Describe a typical day at the office." "What do you see as the priorities in your job?" "What do you do when priorities conflict and there is no clear procedure for the situation?"

Beyond matching specific skills to your particular needs, these questions all seek to gain an understanding of how each candidate multitasks an ongoing flood of responsibilities while being constantly interrupted with urgent requests. You can expand and customize these questions with requests for past-performance examples: *"Tell me about a time when . . ."* You can also use real-life crises from your world posed as hypothetical situations: *"What would you do in a situation in which . . . ?"*

Reliability

Reliability is a major concern when it comes to hiring admin/clerical staff, and this concern becomes greater as the workload and job responsibilities increase. Poor work habits can have far-reaching repercussions. Some of these questions might help:

"Tell me how you handle your multiple responsibilities." "How do you plan and organize your workload?" "How do you prioritize responsibilities?" "What do you see as your role within the department?" "How do you think your job relates to the overall goals of the company?"

"How do you get along with all the different personalities that are part of your daily interactions?" "What types of people are difficult for you? How do you deal with them?"

"Tell me about a time when, rather than following instructions, you felt it better to go about a task in your own way." "When have you worked on a project of little enough importance that you let it slide?"

"Have you ever found it necessary to come in early or stay late?" "In what ways do you find that work interferes with your personal life?" "Have you ever found it necessary to sacrifice personal plans in favor of your professional responsibilities?"

Some of these questions are a little pointed, but they can help give you a three-dimensional picture that shows the candidate's ability to organize, self-start, and juggle responsibilities.

Flexibility

Clerical and administrative personnel must be flexible in ways not always necessary in other jobs. Here are some questions that examine this willingness to be flexible:

"How do you prioritize your responsibilities?" "Do you prefer handling one task at a time, or multiple responsibilities?" "How do you handle a crisis where it is clear that priorities have to be changed?" "Tell me about a time when you had an overwhelming number of urgent requests to handle. How did you prioritize?"

"Your boss is going on vacation for a month, and although it isn't in your job description to do so, she asks you to work for another manager in her absence. What would you say and do?" "Are you prepared to fill in for someone who has different responsibilities?"

These are all good questions for an administrative candidate who will be working in a dynamic environment, where situations continually change.

Judging Career Orientation

Like everyone else, most administrative professionals have career goals, which, for a good hire, have to match your realities. Here are some basic but revealing questions that can help you define a candidate's career orientation in a professional area in which upward mobility isn't always a clear path:

"What are your professional goals for the future?" "Where do you see yourself six months from now?" "Where do you see yourself a year or two from now?" "What do you see as your responsibilities in achieving professional growth?"

"What new skills have you developed in the last year?" "What new skills are you developing right now?" "What skills do you plan to develop in the coming year?" "What commitments do you make to your profession outside of work?" "What job would you like to work toward in our company?" "If you could have any job in our company, which would it be?" "How would this job help you reach your professional goals?" "How do you define a successful career?"

The answers you get will tell you what will motivate each candidate over the long haul, and in the process you will also learn about his or her personal commitment to professional growth.

In the following clerical interview skeleton, there may be questions that do not meet your particular needs, but you may find that reading them generates completely new and relevant questions for your situation.

You certainly should employ the interviewing techniques discussed elsewhere in this book when building interview scripts for admin/clerical hires. For example, you will find many questions here that beg for question layering, past-performance, or situational interviewing techniques. Just like the skeleton interviews for management, sales, and entry-level positions, this skeleton is intended as a tool against which to check your own carefully developed question sequences.

Clerical Interview Skeleton

Work History

Describe a typical workday.

Tell me about your responsibilities.

What skills can you bring to this position, other than the ones required in the job description?

What accomplishments are you most proud of?

What aspects of your job give you the most enjoyment?

What aspects of your job cause you the most problems?

Ability, Suitability

What would you change about your current job?

How do you handle repetitive tasks?

What are you looking for in your next job?

What are the personal qualities that this job demands?

What aspects of your job do you consider the most crucial?

How would you describe yourself in terms of your work?

Tell me about your role in a crisis situation.

Have you ever worked for more than one manager?

How does your job relate to the overall success of your department and your company?

Tell me about a time when the boss was absent and you had to make a decision.

What special responsibilities or assignments have you been given?

Tell me about an occasion when you chose, for whatever reason, not to finish a particular task.

Have you ever found it necessary to sacrifice personal plans in favor of your professional responsibilities?

Are you prepared to perform duties that may not be part of your routine?

Describe what you think a typical day would be like on this job.

Tell me about a time when your performance did not live up to your expectations.

Where do you see yourself six months from now?

What kind of work interests you most?

If you could have any job in this company, what would it be?

How would that job help you reach your long-term personal and career goals?

How do you define a successful career?

Motivation

Do you ever find it necessary to go beyond the call of duty to get a job done?

What role do you play in ensuring a smooth working environment when your boss is away?

What have you done to become more effective in your career?

If you went to your boss for a raise, why would you be doing it?

Flexibility

How many levels of management do you deal with?

What type of people do you get along with best?

How do you get along with people whom you don't like?

How necessary is it to be creative in your job?

Describe the toughest situation you have ever faced.

How many projects can you handle at a time?

How do you prioritize your projects?

When have you rescheduled your time to accommodate an unexpected workload?

Have you ever been affected by communication problems between two managers?

Have you ever dealt with the general public?

Do you handle personal matters for your boss?

When was the last time something or someone got you really upset at work?

Tell me about a time when you put your foot in your mouth.

The receptionist has gone home sick. Are you prepared to fill in for her, even though the job is beneath your level of responsibilities?

Communication

Tell me about the kinds of communication you type at work.

Do you ever compose letters for others?

How do you set up a letter? An invoice?

What was the most complex document you ever produced?

What forms or documents have you developed for your department?

Planning, Organization

Describe your method for keeping track of important matters.

How do you plan your day?

How would you plan for a major project?

Do you set goals for yourself?

Tell me about a time when, despite careful planning, things got out of hand.

Teamwork

Have you ever worked with a group like this before?

How do you establish a working relationship with new people?

Tell me how you see your responsibilities as a group member.

What kind of people do you like to work with?

What kind of people do you dislike working with?

What do you do when you have to work with these people?

Have you ever had to stifle your normal behavior to get along with someone?

How do you feel about people who don't like their jobs? How do you define a conducive work atmosphere?

Manageability

How does your boss get the best out of you?

How do you get the best out of your boss?

What do you think of your current boss?

Describe the best manager you ever had.

Describe the worst manager you ever had.

What made those managers stand out?

How do you react to criticism?

How do you take direction?

Describe the toughest manager you ever worked for.

Tell me about the kinds of rewards that make you feel adequately recognized for your contributions.

How do your work habits change when your boss is out of the office?

How could your boss do a better job?

In what ways has your boss contributed to your reasons for leaving your job?

The hiring decision you make regarding an administrative staff member is as important as any you will ever make. Not only are these professionals responsible for the smooth flow of work in your department; they have considerable impact over your ability to function as you must. As a prudent manager, with the best interests of your company and career at heart, you can increase the chances of making good hires by carefully developing the job description and not skimping on the selection procedure. These are important positions that have a direct impact on your peace of mind and your success.

Interviewing Within the Law 14

*I*n *Hiring the Best* we sensibly structure interviews to discover a job candidate's ability, analytical skills, professional behavioral profile, motivation, team orientation, and manageability. These principles are based on common sense and the necessity of making consistently productive hires; they also keep you from breaking the law and getting your company sued—something never very conducive to beefy year-end bonuses.

This chapter addresses the legal considerations of hiring. It is intended as a general primer and is not meant to be a legal guide.

The federal and state laws addressing equal opportunity and discrimination in job opportunity and the workplace began to be enshrined in corporate culture with Title VII of the 1964 Civil Rights Act, whose reach was extended by the Equal Employment Opportunity Act of 1972, the Age Discrimination Act of 1975, and the Americans with Disabilities Act of 1990.

State and federal laws involving individual and worker rights seem to be undergoing a sea change at the highest levels of government in the first decade of the new century; in turn, the letter of the law is constantly interpreted by case law. To cover every detail of employment law as it applies to your situation, and on the day of your need, is beyond the scope of this book. Whenever you are in doubt about a question or an approach, please consult company counsel.

Employment Discrimination

The laws, amendments, and court decisions that define and clarify employment discrimination are directed toward the elimination of discrimination in the workplace; toward equal opportunity for all in the land of opportunity. In broad terms, when you make a hire, you may not discriminate on the basis of age, race, national origin, religion, disability, or sex; many states additionally forbid discrimination on the basis of sexual preference. Consequently, you may not ask questions at the interview that are seen as examining these issues.

But what questions are clearly illegal? That is not an easy one to answer. A general measure for a legal question is this: Is the question necessary to determine the candidate's ability to discharge the responsibility of the job satisfactorily? In other words, if the question doesn't have anything to do with the job, don't ask it. When your objective is simply to find the most qualified person for the job, you don't need to ask questions unrelated to job performance.

As a general rule, questions about height, weight, age, marital status, religious or political beliefs, dependents, birth control, birthplace, race, and national origin are strictly out of bounds.

National Origin

You should not ask:

▶ about the candidate's or the candidate's parents' or spouse's nationality, ancestry, lineage, or parentage

▶ whether the candidate's parents or spouse are native-born or naturalized citizens

▶ the name of the next of kin

▶ the candidate's or the candidate's family's birthplace

▶ how the candidate learned a second language

You can usually ask:

▶ whether the candidate is a U.S. citizen or a resident alien with the right to work in the United States

▶ the various languages he or she speaks (as long as the question is relevant to the job)

Religious and Political Beliefs

The Civil Rights Act of 1964 was amended by the Equal Opportunity Act of 1972, and in it, all matters relating to the examination of religious and political beliefs and affiliations are designated as impermissible.

You should not ask about a candidate's:

▶ political beliefs or affiliations

▶ religious beliefs, affiliations, denomination, his or her parish, synagogue, church, and so on

▶ religious holiday observances

You can usually ask about a candidate's:

▶ willingness to work on Saturdays or Sundays (if the job so requires)

Even when it comes to character references, you must be circumspect. I have heard of employers who ask for references from a candidate's pastor or religious leader, and that's absolutely discriminatory.

Race

You should not ask questions regarding a candidate's race, country of origin, complexion or skin color, or those of the candidate's family. If you still think there's a good reason for asking about race—if you feel it has anything to do with performance in a job, for example, such as with international positions for which cultural diversity can be argued as a "must have" skill—you are advised to clear all questions through legal counsel.

Sex

The lion's share of sexual discrimination in the interviewing process is directed toward women.

You should not ask about a candidate's:

▶ change of name, maiden name, or original name

▶ current or previous marital status

▶ preferred form of address (Miss, Mrs., or Ms.)

▶ spouse

▶ number, names, or ages of children or dependents

▶ method of birth control or reproductive ability

You can usually ask:

▶ whether the candidate has ever worked for your company under another name

▶ whether any of the candidate's relatives currently work for your company

Age

The Age Discrimination Act of 1975 prohibits discrimination in employment against candidates between the ages of forty and seventy. Ultimately, the only question you should ask concerning age is whether or not the candidate is eighteen years old. And if you are ever tempted to discriminate against older workers (as many employers are), ask yourself whether you wouldn't rather hire someone who has already made the big mistakes on somebody else's payroll.

Convictions

In some states, it is illegal to ask about arrests and/or convictions. Whatever the prohibitions, it is extremely risky to inquire about convictions unless you can prove without a shadow of a doubt that the information has a direct relevance to the job at hand. For example, a company whose employees enter people's homes may well be warranted in inquiring about convictions for violent crimes, but you would naturally seek company's counsel before proceeding.

Military History

Most questions concerning military history are illegal, unless the job specifically requires a military background.

You should not ask:

▶ in what branch of the military the candidate has served

▶ what type of discharge he or she received

You can usually ask:

▶ whether the candidate has military experience in the Armed Forces of the United States

Education

You should not ask, "Are you a high-school graduate?" However, you can usually ask the candidate to detail his or her educational history.

People with Disabilities

The 1990 Americans with Disabilities Act (ADA) has changed forever the way we must view hiring of the disabled. The act, though undeniably well intentioned, has effectively doused a potentially explosive issue with regulatory gasoline—and sent a firestorm of legal repercussions through every nook and cranny of the U.S. employment market. If you can get a grasp of the issues at stake here, you'll have a firm foundation for understanding most employment discrimination issues.

Signed into law by President George H. W. Bush in 1990, the ADA is a mammoth legislative document that reads like Chaucer and has all the clarity of a weather forecast for late December. Contained within its enormous bulk are enough definitions, prohibitions, exemptions, and enforcement mechanisms to keep people on every side of the equal opportunity issue groping blindly through a semantic fog for years to come.

Not surprisingly, a passel of lawsuits have been filed as a result of the ADA's seemingly boundless ambiguity. Ironically, many of the legal riddles crying out for adjudication have remained unsolved because ADA suits are being settled out of court at a rate three to four times that of other discrimination suits.

This, unfortunately, leaves everyone except the lawyers in the lurch when it comes to making sense of the complex question of an organization's ADA compliance. About the best you can do as an employer, it seems, is to remind yourself of the law's good intentions and muster up all the caution and common sense you can.

Although the law can be extremely difficult to deal with, what's truly tragic is the attitude of many companies when it comes to taking advantage of the untapped human resource of 43 million disabled Americans. People with disabilities have suffered from discrimination throughout recorded history. And even today, despite the countless studies that document their exemplary productivity and on-the-job attendance, disabled workers remain the victims of shortsighted employers who fail to take full advantage of this vast source of talent and competency.

Driven by a relentless desire to overcome stereotyping, disabled workers have consistently proven their ability to meet or exceed the standards set by their nondisabled coworkers.

How the Law Affects You

Simply put, the ADA represents a comprehensive set of guidelines that mandates the end of discrimination against people who, from birth or as the result of injury or accident, have a physical or mental disability that substantially limits a major life activity such as hearing, seeing, speaking, breathing, performing manual tasks, walking, caring for oneself, learning, or working. The ADA also protects persons who have a record of such a physical or mental impairment, and those who are regarded as having such impairment.

If you employ fifteen or more people for any consecutive period of twenty weeks during the year, then your company is bound by the ADA. The ADA forbids discrimination against disabled persons in all aspects of employment, including the application process, hiring decisions, promotions, assignments, and termination. Employers must also provide reasonable accommodation in the workplace for disabled employees and job applicants. Reasonable accommodations might include making physical changes to the building in which your organization is located, job restructuring, schedule modifications, or providing a disabled employee with special equipment or even a reader or interpreter as an assistant. Additionally, state regulations often pick up where the ADA leaves off. Some states have requirements that are substantially more stringent.

There's one exception to the law, however. If you can show that a proposed accommodation would be "excessively costly, extensive, substantial, or disruptive," or would "fundamentally alter the nature or operation of the business," then your company may be granted an exception based on undue hardship.

Let's say, for example, that you find yourself in Diane's situation. Diane runs a business in a building she bought several years ago, a building that has twelve water fountains, all too high to be used by Dave, one of her employees. Dave is a cost accountant who uses a wheelchair.

After agonizing for weeks over her employee's need for accommodation (and the enormous expense that would surely accompany a dozen separate plumbing reinstallations), Diane finally approached the cost accountant himself for suggestions.

"No problem," he replied. "All we need to do is hang up a paper cup dispenser next to each fountain, and I'll be fine."

Clearly, there are different ways to approach the many challenges of providing access and accommodation. Before you make any assumptions, remember that the size, structure, function, and financial resources of your company will ultimately determine your ability to make changes—and these factors may exempt you from certain provisions of the ADA altogether.

Legal Discrimination

According to the act, there are three conditions under which you, as an employer, are allowed to discriminate legally. You may do so when the employee's disability will:

▶ threaten the public health

▶ risk the safety of others

▶ restrict the execution of the essential functions of the job

For example, if your company manufactures food products in open vats, then the law (and plain common sense) dictates that you may discriminate when it comes to hiring people with infectious diseases. Likewise, you wouldn't be in violation if you were to deny employment to a person with one leg who applied for a job as a firefighter, if the resulting lack of mobility might risk the life of an infant trapped in a smoke-filled room.

However, the law is very clear when it comes to judgments based on perceived, rumored, or past impairments. You can't reassign, for example, a receptionist who has controlled high blood pressure to a less stressful position simply because you're afraid she might have a heart attack, or exclude an engineering candidate from consideration due to her past history of mental illness, or because she was at one time misdiagnosed as having a learning disability.

Remember that a disability is defined as an impairment that substantially restricts one or more major life activities. Forms of social expression, minor neuroses, temporary afflictions, and sexual disorders, however, are not protected disabilities. For that reason, an environmental extremist with a broken arm that would eventually heal itself would be excluded from ADA protection, as would a cross-dressing psychedelic drug user or a voyeur with a compulsive gambling problem.

The Essential Functions of the Job

In any hiring decision, the first and most important question should always be: Is the candidate qualified for the job? That is, from a purely objective standpoint, does the candidate possess the requisite skills, educational credentials, work experience, motivation, licenses, and/or certifications in order to be seriously considered for employment? If the answer is yes, so far so good.

But if the person also has a disability, you need to go one step further and answer the next question, which is paramount in the eyes of the ADA: Can this candidate perform the essential functions of the job, whether with or without a reasonable accommodation?

This is where things get complicated, because most of us aren't accustomed to quantifying job duties in such a precise manner. According to the ADA, there are three reasons why a job function could be considered essential:

1. *The position exists solely to perform the function.* That is, if you need someone to transcribe handwritten documents eight hours a day, and that's all the job entails, then transcribing is an essential function.

2. *There are a limited number of other employees available to perform the function.* This is a corollary situation to the first reason in that it specifies the need for versatility, especially in smaller businesses with

fluctuating demands. If transcribing is the usual job, but peak periods of intensive activity require answering the phone and shuttling out-of-town customers to and from the airport on short notice, then the versatility itself becomes an essential function of the job.

3. *The function requires special expertise.* If the rest of the staff and all the customers only speak Lithuanian, then fluent Lithuanian language skills may be considered an essential job function.

In determining exactly what's essential and what isn't, the ADA suggests that you look for evidence that would either prove that the new hire will actually be required to perform the function or prove that removing the function would fundamentally change the job. Evidence may come from written job descriptions, observations of past or current employee performance, the amount of time normally spent performing various functions, or the consequences that may arise from not requiring a person to perform a required function. If neither the requirement nor the removal conditions can be proven, then the function has to be considered nonessential.

The Total Hiring Picture

The provisions of the ADA cover a broad range of employment-related activities. If you think that your nondiscrimination responsibilities are limited to the interviewing, offering, and managing processes alone, think again. Your legal obligations extend to every conceivable aspect of the hiring picture, including these:

▶ *Application procedures.* If you run a classified ad in the Sunday paper, or a job posting on an Internet site with a phone number but no address, you must also provide a telecommunications device for the deaf (TDD) or telephone relay service to accommodate inquiries by the hearing impaired. Similarly, you must ensure accessibility to your facility for the purpose of conducting an interview.

▶ *On-site recruiting.* If your company exhibits at a job fair or visits a college campus looking for recruits, you will want to ensure physical accessibility for those with disabilities who may wish to attend.

▶ *Personal associations.* If you deny an employment opportunity to someone because he or she has a relationship with a disabled person, you run the risk of being held liable under the ADA.

▶ *Activism.* If you retaliate against someone who has a past, present, or pending ADA-related grievance, or attempt to coerce someone who gives aid to a person seeking protection under the provisions of the law, you could also be headed for trouble.

▶ *Third-party representation.* If the search firm, employment agency, or college placement office you use in your recruiting or screening efforts fails to comply with any ADA provision, then you could *both* be held accountable.

▶ *Succession planning.* If you're interested in long-term team building, be careful. You can only evaluate a candidate's qualifications based on what the job currently is, not on what it might be in the future.

ADA and Interviewing

In addition to making sure that disabled candidates are given equal consideration during the interviewing process, you need to adhere to certain ADA guidelines for the interview itself.

For example, the ADA explicitly forbids you to ask a candidate during an interview whether he or she is disabled, or to inquire about the nature or severity of the disability. However, it is the candidate's responsibility during the interview to inform you of a disability that may not be noticeable, since you are only required to provide reasonable accommodation for a disability of which you are aware.

Once the disability has surfaced, it's permissible to ask questions about the candidate's ability to perform specific job functions, or allow the person to describe or demonstrate how he or she would perform these functions. To be on the safe side, though, you should always try to phrase your questions so that they center on "if" rather than "how."

What do I mean? Well, let's suppose the candidate is a quadriplegic, and apparently needs some sort of special transportation to get to work. You may be tempted to ask, "How do you plan to get to and from the office every day?" A more appropriate (and legally defensible) question would be, "The hours of work here are 7:30 A.M. to 4:30 P.M. If you were an employee of this company, is there any reason you can think of that you wouldn't be able to fulfill your essential duties during those hours?"

Another no-no: asking the candidate to take a special medical exam at any time during the pre-employment process. A tactic like that will get you sued faster than a hungry programmer can fax or e-mail a Domino's pizza order.

The only exception is a standard medical examination given after an employment offer has been made. However, if a standard exam reveals the existence of a disability that was previously unknown and you end up hiring someone else, then you must show that the exam played no part in your decision. Any skill or aptitude evaluation can only pertain to job-related activities and has to be consistent with business necessity.

To Test or Not to Test

A few more words on the issue of essential versus nonessential as it relates to testing. If you design a test used to assess a candidate's ability to create illustrated letterhead on Macintosh computers using the latest version of Adobe Illustrator, then you have to make certain that all job candidates are tested in this way, and that the tested skills represent an essential function of the job, not a peripheral activity.

Such a test would be perfectly appropriate (and legal) for screening the qualifications of a graphic designer who uses Adobe Illustrator on the job—but totally inappropriate for screening a receptionist who answers calls all day but needs to address an occasional envelope on the same equipment.

To comply with the act, you must guarantee that all pre-employment tests can be taken by a disabled person, even if it means making a reasonable accommodation by providing special access or a trained helper. And above all, you must avoid any type of test that might unwittingly screen out a disabled but otherwise qualified person.

The goal of these guidelines is to ensure equal opportunity for everyone, not to engage in reverse discrimination. As far as the law's concerned, you're under no obligation to employ a person *because* he or she has a disability. Your duty is simply not to discriminate against that person because of the disability.

To cover all the bases, it's a good idea to keep a written job description on file for each position you plan to fill. Even though it represents only one form of evidence, a clear and accurate job description is a good defense should you ever be accused of discrimination. I advise that you run any job descriptions or job description manuals by your organization's legal counsel.

Recruiting the Disabled

One way to attract disabled candidates is through your recruitment advertising. Although it's illegal to solicit for any particular group, the following statement will let all qualified job seekers know that they're welcome to apply, and that your company promotes equal opportunity for all:

"We are an equal opportunity employer. We do not discriminate on the basis of race, religion, color, sex, age, national original, or disability."

(*Note:* Other categories may be protected from discrimination under the laws of your state.)

In addition to advertising, you can ask for referrals from state and local vocational rehabilitation centers, local Independent Living Centers, the U.S. Department of Veterans Affairs, ADA regional Disability and Business Technical Assistance Centers, and the Job Accommodation Network. The organizations can also provide you with valuable information pertaining to specialized training programs, architectural compliance guidelines, and the legalities of equal opportunity. Check your phone directory for contact information.

Agencies such as these are more than eager to refer qualified applicants, and may even share in certain expenses needed to help their disabled clients play on a level field.

The Incentive to Hire

From a financial perspective, there are a number of tax incentives offered to businesses that hire the disabled. These include:

▶ *Tax Credit for Small Business (Section 44 of the Internal Revenue Code).* If eligible, your company can receive up to $5,000 a year in tax credits if you make special accommodations to comply with the ADA.

▶ *Tax Deduction for Architectural and Transportation Barrier Removal (Section 190 of the Internal Revenue Code).* After all, the more your work force reflects your customer base, the better they will understand, capture, and service it. If qualified, your business can deduct up to $15,000 per year.

▶ *Targeted Jobs Tax Credit Program.* If you hire disabled individuals referred by certain state or local agencies, you may be eligible to receive a tax credit of up to 40 percent of the first $6,000 of a disabled employee's first-year salary.

The cost of accommodating the disabled can be surprisingly low. According to the Job Accommodation Network, many assistive devices (such as indicator lights, telephone amplifiers, customized headsets, large-display computer screens, and redesigned tools) can be purchased affordably. Sometimes, with a little creative thinking, costs can be passed along or shared with those outside your company.

Consider this example. Craig is the Human Resources manager at a retail organization. He was able to convince his company's supplier of forklift trucks to absorb the cost of training a driver who was hearing impaired. Working with a sign-language interpreter from the local United Way, the driver was able to acquire the skills he needed in order to perform the job. Total cost of the accommodation: less than $600, picked up by the vendor.

Hiring Within the Law

As you can see, you tread a fine line when it comes to employment discrimination during the interview. The laws in each state differ, and they change all the time. If you are concerned about the bent of some of your interview questions, consult the Equal Opportunity Commission, your state employment organization, your own human resources department, or legal counsel.

Hire Consciousness at the Executive Levels

*J*ust as people grow and change during their professional lives, so do companies. The needs of companies change as they pass through different stages of growth, and your ability to make successful hires at the higher levels can depend on your being able to identify the dislocations between the corporate growth-cycle position of both your company and your candidates.

Depending on their success, companies pass through five stages of growth: they are *start-up*, *growth*, *maturity*, *atrophy*, and *turnaround*. A company's nature and its manpower needs at the more senior levels can change quite dramatically at each stage.

Start-up

The start-up company can begin on a kitchen table or in a garage, comprising just its founders as employees. The founders struggle with an idea, a service, or a product, its development, and its initial "bringing to market." From this point the company may continue to struggle for survival and stay with few or no employees, or it may begin to grow. At this stage, any employee may be in direct daily contact with the company owner; there is little in the way of systems and procedures; and the mission is relatively simple: "Pay the phone bills and the rent to stay in business while we find a market." With venture capital financing growing exponentially over the last couple of decades, this start-up phase can rapidly accelerate into the growth phase with the influx of capital.

Growth

The company finds its market (or sometimes just its funding), and begins to grow. The focus is on gaining customers and then market share, rather than just struggling to keep the doors open. Staff is hired in response to overload rather than planning. At least in the early days, the founders are still involved in every aspect of the business, and communication is largely verbal. The main focus of a growth company is the marketing process to enhance that growth. Many growth companies never grow beyond a size that the founders can manage personally. An entrepreneur's inability to let go of even the tiniest detail is seen as the Achilles' heel of many growth companies; they stall out because the founder is the only individual with any authority, overseeing perhaps seventy-five personal assistants, and there is no management structure.

Companies that successfully pass through the growth phase to that of a mature company emerge from the "cult of the founders" to institute a management structure and the basic systems and procedures common to all mature companies. This is, in fact, the rite of passage that the growth company navigates to become a mature company.

The Mature Company

The third phase of growth comes when the company is stable and at the top of its stride. All communication necessarily becomes formal, with more emphasis on written communication. More and stricter systems and procedures are implemented; the Human Resources department moves into ascendancy; there is less room for individual creativity; the company is unlikely to be alone in its market; and that market might even be reaching the saturation point. The aggressive investments in marketing that typify growth-cycle companies begin to be replaced by a greater focus on operations. While in earlier stages a company worried more about getting the job done and making sales, the mature company, finding it more difficult to increase sales and profit margins by increasing volume, begins to look more seriously at cost containment as a viable profit generator. Automation, downsizing, outsourcing, and offshoring of jobs and processes come to the fore.

The company's larger size necessitates more levels of management. It becomes possible for careers to flourish simply by avoiding mistakes, and as the mature company relies more on committees than on individual initiative, such avoidance becomes easier. Risk-taking changes, too, partly because now any risk is so much greater and partly because of the increasing "analysis paralysis" practiced by ever-growing numbers of managers and administrators. The once-vibrant concern has become a bureaucracy, sluggish with overhead. It behaves like an institution, swelled with self-importance, blind to maladies that it believes to be strengths. The mature company under all these pressures eventually begins to stagnate.

Atrophy

Here begins the decay stage of the corporate life cycle. Early signs are an acceptance of the same old profit margins and standards; excuses that the market, the economy, or the numbers of competitors now flooding the field make it impossible for anyone to make a living; and complaints about the lack of competent employees. The focus is on cost cutting. The finger of blame points outward, and no one sees where the other three digits on the hand are pointing.

Turnaround

The fifth stage is recognition of atrophy and sustained, concerted action to achieve turnaround. Consultants are everywhere, turnaround experts are brought on board, and the focus becomes one of returning to the vibrancy of the growth company.

Hiring and the Life-Cycle Challenge

At the higher levels, the suitability of a candidate for a position depends in part on the corporate life-cycle history of the candidate, and, in part, on the personality of that candidate. A person from one phase of the cycle may, or may not be, appropriate for a company in another phase. Consequently, the lesson you learned about selection at the lower levels applies in the upper echelons too: *The most apparently qualified person you can find may not be the best person for the job.*

Take the example of a young company transitioning from start-up through the growth phase of the cycle, looking to bring on its first PR director. Their ultimate choice was acknowledged as one of the top people in the industry; he headed the publicity department of one of the country's premier companies. He had wanted a new challenge, and a start-up company in the field seemed the answer to his prayers. The company principals were pinching themselves to check that they weren't dreaming. Who would have thought they could land the best in the business? The honeymoon lasted six weeks, and the marriage six months, before the "resignation" was accepted. Our top man was used to managing an established team—the best money could buy—and controlling multimillion-dollar budgets, while at the new company, his budget was loose change and his staff even smaller. Although no one was better at driving the train once it was out of the station, this particular hotshot had neither the skills nor a real desire to create and stoke the corporate image from a cold start. His skills had passed many years ago from those of a doer to those of a delegator. While this is an important executive transition, the life-cycle demands of the company necessitated an executive who still wanted to, and had the ability to, roll up his sleeves and climb down into the trenches. The moral is that what you see isn't always what you want to get.

Our example tells us that there could be problems when executives from mature companies join start-ups. These same executives can have problems when they join growth companies, too, except at those times when the executive can ease the growth and transition of the company into its next stage. An awareness of the different stages of the corporate life cycle, with appropriate questions during the interview, can bring these matters to light and save everybody considerable aggravation.

Start-ups will frequently benefit most from executives who have seen their prior employers at least through the growth phase and possibly into the calm waters of organization and maturity. Growth-stage companies benefit from a combination of executives with experience in that stage and from those who have seen the successful transition into maturity.

Companies in the fourth and fifth stages need fresh blood, executives who can raise the dead. These people come mostly from start-up and growth companies, yet sometimes they and the turnaround experts (who often have experience throughout the different stages) just do not fit into the mature and wilting company. The bureaucracy drives them crazy, and they upset everyone else on the train. Of course, that is really why they are there in the first place.

Finding someone who has successfully operated in all these phases is rare indeed, as each demands different approaches and skills. While a senior-level professional may, over the course of years, have practical experience with a number of different corporations—each in a different phase of development—it is more common to find senior people whose experience has been entirely with companies within one phase of the cycle. For companies in transition from one phase to the next, broad corporate life-cycle experience can be eminently desirable. On the other hand, an individual with a track record in companies from a single phase may have become indoctrinated by the behavior patterns common for that phase. This is by no means always the case, but being aware of this possibility will lead you to fruitful areas of inquiry during the selection process.

Now, what does all of this mean? It means that in the selection of important positions, you need to have an awareness of where your company stands in its evolutionary cycle, and where it is headed:

▶ When you are in start-up mode or in the midst of strong growth, you are wise to look for someone who comes from a similar cultural environment—unless, of course, your strong growth is tilting you toward the need for order and organization that typifies the mature company.

▶ If your company is approaching transition, you could well benefit from someone grounded in the next phase of the corporate life cycle.

▶ If your company is in a state of atrophy or turnaround, you will want people from the earlier stages of growth and vibrant maturity to re-energize your corporate situation.

None of this means that you should reject otherwise qualified candidates out of hand. But it does mean that when you know where your company stands on the continuum, and therefore the type of management it needs, you are likely to make more productive hires. This is especially true when you are able to identify the life-cycle stages of companies that a candidate has been with; you use these two realities as a focus for discussion. When hiring, never assume. The trick is to identify where your company stands and which environments the candidate's experience stems from. Then you can examine the questionable areas.

To this end, you will want to know how long the candidate's company has been in business, and its recent and projected growth rates. You need to identify the dollar volume and the number of employees in relation to management ranks—usually, the more mature the company is, the greater the number and levels of management deemed necessary to run the operation.

Likewise, you need to know the ratio of administrative assistants to management, and whether the company encourages verbal or written communication. The approaches to planning and project management endorsed by the candidate's company can also indicate mismatches or necessary learning curves.

Examination of these considerations can be done effectively over food and drink, which gives you an opportunity to evaluate the social graces so important to a successful executive.

Here are some questions that will help you examine these areas and avoid hitching yourself to a star from the wrong universe.

"What is the size and role of the HR department in your present company?"
Human Resources becomes increasingly powerful as companies grow and mature, so the answer here will give you a general idea about the stage of the corporation. Also, knowing the responsibilities of Human Resources can lead you into fruitful discussions about the extent of influence of HR as it affects the day-to-day operations of your candidate's department; this in turn will tell you something about a manager's attitude toward systems and procedures. These insights, coming on top of your careful evaluation of the candidate's other attributes, can help you picture that person functioning *in situ.*

"Describe in detail your impression of the day-to-day responsibilities of this job."
You probably asked this question, quite appropriately, earlier in the interviewing cycle, but following our recent discussion, the answer takes on a new relevance. This is where you will catch the misconceptions before they cost either of you time, money, and reputation. The earlier example of the experienced top dog in the start-up company would perhaps never have occurred if this question had been asked, instead of the answer being taken for granted. This question should be a must in every final interview, so that even the smallest misunderstanding is cleared up.

"What interests you least about this job?"
Again, you may have asked this at an earlier stage, yet here it takes on a new relevance because you have been able to describe the day-to-day responsibilities and deliverables of the job. It is another reality check on the candidate's perception of the job and his or her suitability to your needs.

"What kinds of management rub you the wrong way?"
An awareness of the corporate life cycle might make the candidate's people skills worthy of some re-evaluation. For instance, putting a successful bureaucrat among the entrepreneurial types common in start-up companies is to ask everyone to suffer needless frustrations. Follow the subsequent conversation to its natural conclusions.

"With the wisdom of hindsight, what was the least relevant/fulfilling job you have held?"
The response will tell you how clearly the person sees the sum of his or her experience. If the "least relevant" job turns out to be one from, say, a company in the growth stage, and your company is about to enter that stage, then you have gained some valuable information. The emotionally mature and truly competent professional will find that something of value can be gained from every job.

"Wouldn't you feel happier in another company?" and *"I'm not sure that you are suitable for the job."*
Earlier in the book, we addressed the judicious use of stress questions such as these. At that point, they were being used exclusively to test poise and quick thinking, and you learned to employ them as the stress of the job demanded. Here, however, you are using the probes in a far more straightforward manner when you notice a life-cycle and attitudinal misfit between the candidate and your needs. Using the questions in this context, any ensuing conversation will be geared to making the candidate aware of your concerns.

The considerations addressed in this chapter only have impact at the more elevated professional levels. An awareness of the challenges that these realities present can enable you and a top candidate to put those concerns to rest and go on to experience a mutually beneficial relationship. Your discussion may also save both of you from professional embarrassment.

Hiring the Best 16

What is the most difficult responsibility in the life of a manager? Some think it is making the decision to hire, but the rest of us know that it is living with that decision.

When your job's primary responsibility is defined as "getting work done through others," making the right hiring decisions has a direct positive impact on your entire career, while failing to make the right decisions has the equal but opposite effect. In this final chapter, I'll summarize how you can advance your career by hiring only the best.

Understand the Position You're Hiring For

Good hires always depend on an accurate real-world analysis of the job. Only when you clearly understand the day-to-day challenges of that job, and the small role it plays in the overall success of the company, can you recruit a suitable slate of candidates or develop the right questions to ask them at interview time.

You begin with analyzing the specific functions of the job, and the skills, education, and professional background required to discharge those functions. However, you don't box yourself in with, for example, a definition that demands "five years' experience in sales," because you realize it isn't so much the quantity of experience as it is the quality of that experience. So you then think about the job in terms of its productivity—the results you expect to be delivered in return for steady employment.

To help with these determinations, you consider the job in terms of its problem-solving responsibilities, both for the problems it is there to anticipate and prevent, and those problems that arise in the natural course of the job's functions. You recall that every job is at some level a problem-solving job, doing its small part in solving the ongoing challenges that every corporation shares: making money, saving money, and saving time, the latter of which is the double whammy that both saves money and makes time to make more money. Tying each job to its specific problem-solving responsibilities and identifying its contributory role in the bigger picture is always an important step in defining ability and suitability for the job.

Your next step is to match the job's responsibilities and deliverables against a sequence of desirable professional behaviors (communication skills, time management and organization, determination, and so on), which, when present in a candidate, help determine that the job will indeed get done.

When ability is defined in this way, you move on to a consideration of motivation. To make a good hire, a candidate not only has to have ability in the ways you have defined it; he or she also has to have the motivation to do a good job, no matter what it takes. Your final considerations in analyzing the needs of a job opening require that you look forward to daily work life, creating a profile of a candidate who is a team player and manageable by you, with all your warts and blemishes. You do this when you are objectively focused on the nuts and bolts of the job, because it completes the three-dimensional picture of your target candidates and helps you develop the right questions and evaluative frame of mind for the interview and selection cycle.

Screen Candidates Efficiently and Effectively

With the position analysis completed and a recruitable job description developed, you move into the recruitment and selection cycle. With benefit of the analysis and selection skills you polished working through these pages, you learned to weed candidates out at the resume-screening stage, and through judicious use of telephone interviews as a time management tool, you only schedule in-person interviews with those who fulfill your basic requirements.

Once the face-to-face interviews commence, you are ready with a logical approach for determining ability, motivation, team orientation, and manageability. Based on your specific needs, you create a structured interview format that guarantees you will compare apples to apples, in terms of developing a slate of questions that enable you to fairly judge each candidate against the others. This structure employs a sequence that focuses first on ability. Your interviews are organized along these lines: you determine ability first, and if a candidate cannot do the job, you bail out. If the ability is there, you move on to motivation, because you know that it is one thing to be able to do the job; it is another to be willing to take the rough with the smooth so necessary to success in every professional endeavor. Only when you determine a candidate's ability and motivation will you proceed to examine issues of teamwork and manageability.

By keeping a clear picture of the job in mind and following this logical selection process, you will easily separate the real contenders from the pack. Then, because you are going to be hiring people for many years to come, and you cannot possibly know your needs for tomorrow, you recognize that today's "also ran" might be an ideal candidate for another job down the line. You reject that person's candidacy with respect for personal dignity, and then store the resume in your personal recruitment database for possible use another day.

Make a Well-Considered Final Decision

Depending on the complexity of the job, you employ second opinions intelligently, and you may invite the short-list candidates back for second, third, and perhaps even fourth interviews when a choice between top candidates is difficult. In narrowing down the final contenders, you will naturally lean toward those who have the most experience, but you will also be aware that someone with all the skills of the job is likely to come in at the higher end of your approved salary range. If there is no room for professional or financial growth through further skill development, raises, and promotions, this can be cause for concern; you have to ask yourself just how long such a candidate is likely to stay with the company. Sometimes, when there is clearly no room for such growth, you might do well to consider the candidates who come in a little lower down the experience and salary scale.

It's easy to make errors in judgment at decision time. For instance, the practice of hiring in the perceived image of yourself or an existing group member is common. "This is the guy we should hire; he's just like Jack, my best salesman." When a particular candidate reminds you of a good employee, it's all too easy to project a transference of that good employee's skills onto the candidate. When you see such parallels, be sure that they are based on performance and behavior rather than physical appearance, speech, and mannerisms.

When the skills, motivation, and manageability factors allow, it is a good idea to look for balance and to strive to add depth to the team, because the more your department mirrors your employer's customers, the more connected you will be to those customers, and the better the job you will deliver as a team. With this in mind, a team staffed with young Turks should look for maturity, and hire people who can share with new generations the practical solutions and know-how that experience can bring; a team dominated by one particular sex or race should encourage diversity; and so on.

This logical approach to selection will usually deliver one clearly top candidate, but unfortunately, "usually" isn't "always." You may come down to a couple of final contenders and need to decide between the two. Should that be the case, following is another selection of questions that might help you break the deadlock.

In evaluating the answers, and coming to a decision between such top contenders when there is little or nothing to differentiate them, you need to consider what they say, how they say it, and in turn what this demonstrates about both their understanding of your company and their commitment to the profession. Putting these considerations together, you are looking for the undercurrent of excitement about the profession, and motivation about the job and the company. When all other considerations are equal, the most professionally committed candidate, the one who is most knowledgeable about your company and enthusiastic about the job, will always turn in the better performance. It's that motivation factor coming into play again.

"What do you know about our company?" "What can you do for us that someone else cannot do?" or "Why should I hire you?" or "What excites you about this job?"
These questions ask the candidate to pitch for the job. You can't expect objective answers to them, but that isn't what you are after; you are looking for motivation, understanding of the job, and professional commitment.

You can also ask questions such as, *"Do you have a career path mapped out for yourself?"* and *"What commitments have you made to following this path?" "Are you willing to go where the company sends you?" "What are your reservations about living/working here?" "How would working evenings affect you?" "How would travel affect you?"*
When relevant to the job, such questions can help define the candidate's willingness to handle a required travel schedule and to make the commute or the move that the job requires. Please note that these questions should

be asked only if they have direct and important relevance to the job. Also, if it is necessary to ask such questions, be sure to ask them of each and every candidate; to do otherwise would be allowing your prejudices to come into play, and it could also be construed as discriminatory. Likewise, you are courting trouble if you ask any candidate how working late or being required to travel would affect others in his or her family, or how such a family might feel about these requirements. Such questions are illegal, and they open you to a lawsuit.

It is a common error to assume that every candidate applying for a job is desperate for the privilege of coming to work for you. As a prudent manager, you will be interested in your candidates' motivations for applying, because that knowledge helps you make appropriate offers only to individuals who will actually accept them. You could put together a sequence of questions like this.

"Why are you interested in this job?"

"What interests you most about it?"

"What interests you least about it?"

"For what have you been most frequently criticized?"

"How long will it take you to make a contribution?"

"Should you be offered the job, how long will it take you to make a decision?"

"Why should I offer you the job?"

"What can you do for us that someone else cannot do?"

"What special characteristics should I consider about you as a person?"

"How have past managers asked you to improve?"

"How have past managers gotten the best out of you?"

"Are you able to provide me with references and the permission to check them?"

With final candidates, even if you have done so before, you should always carefully review performance responsibilities and expectations during the final interview, when he or she is likely to be most receptive. Do it in the context of the department's mission, because *its* goals and objectives form the umbrella for the future employee's responsibilities. Clear expectations from you at this time will build the candidate's confidence in your leadership, the job, and the company. Most workers want to succeed, and want to work for managers whom they feel can lead them to success. The fact that you know where the troops are heading and why, and how you are going to reach your destination, breeds confidence in your followers and attracts people to your banner.

Final Considerations

In extending an offer, you will have existing company guidelines by which to abide, but it certainly helps to ask, "*How much money are you looking for?*" or "*What are you looking for in an offer?*" in order to get an idea of salary requirements. If you followed the advice for determining salary progression from job to job as discussed in the sections about initial screening and using second opinions, you will already have a reasonable idea of the kind of offer that is likely to be acceptable.

At this point, any aptitude testing that is part of your corporate hiring procedure will have already taken place. Now, it is time to discuss drug testing and background and reference checks.

Drug Testing

While drug testing is on the increase with employers, it faces quite strong objections from a majority of workers. If you have a drug testing policy, adhere to it; if you don't, stick with your program. If you are undecided, there is a huge amount of information available on the Internet as to whether you should drug-test or not.

Background and Reference Checks

Background checks conducted by third-party companies allow you to inexpensively verify a person's educational history, criminal record, credit history, driving record, and so on. Depending on the nature of the job, this is not only a good precaution to take, but it can also provide some protection in the event of a lawsuit. For example, when a moving company didn't do background checks, and one of its employees with a violent crime history committed a customer rape in that customer's new home, the moving company was held liable. Background checks could have prevented both the crime and the ensuing liability. There are also countless cases of banned drivers on delivery routes causing accidents and subsequent lawsuits for their employers. You will find resources for third-party background and reference checks in the Background Checks and Reference Check Companies sections of the Appendix or at knockemdead.com.

In all instances, the privacy of the individual whose background and references you are checking must be respected. This privacy is protected under the Fair Credit Reporting Act of 1970, which essentially requires that in order for you to check background and references, you need the candidate's written approval. This is usually covered when an employee fills out the application form and signs it on the line above a paragraph, in fine print, that grants such authority.

Many companies have a formal policy about background and reference checks; in these instances, HR most frequently implements it. At the same time, I do recommend that you become personally involved in checking references of potential employees, and that if you use a third-party company to check references, you require a rundown of the questions it intends to ask, amending that list with appropriate questions of your own.

Sometimes companies have a policy of not providing references beyond confirming dates of employment and leaving salary. They have done this to minimize lawsuits; however, this is another of those employment law issues that is in a state of turmoil. Currently, companies are gaining more protection in the provision of accurate references, so the odds of your getting meaningful references is once again on the increase. From a perspective of personal protection, you will want to check with HR/counsel to see where your company stands on this issue before you provide references for an ex-employee.

With all of these considerations in mind, you do want to check past manager references yourself, whenever possible. Given the appropriate permissions, this is a last and valuable step to take in making sure that you hire only the best. Bear in mind that even your peers can be subjective when giving references, and the ones you get will reflect, to a degree, that manager's personal approach to management.

In preparing your reference-check questions, you will first go back to the job's performance analysis and recall the specific skill sets, deliverables, analytical requirements, team orientation, and manageability that you determined to be important to success.

These are questions you should ask when you check references:

"Can you tell me the starting and leaving dates of employment?"

"Can you tell me starting and leaving salary?"

"Were there any performance bonuses involved, and did _____ receive them?"

"How would you rank _____'s skills in _____?" You will repeat this question to cover all the relevant areas of performance.

"What attendance record did _____ maintain?"

"How would you rate _____'s motivation?"

"How would you rate _____ as a team player?"

"As a manager, how did you get the best out of _____?"

"What would you say was _____'s greatest strength?"

"What would you say was _____'s biggest weakness?"

"How would you say _____ took direction?"

"What management problems, if any, did _____ cause you?" If necessary, follow up with, *"How did you resolve these issues?"*

"What parts of the job did _____ have the most problems with?"

"What was _____'s attitude toward developing needed new skills?"

"How adept was _____ at developing new skills?"

"Would you describe _____ as task oriented or goal oriented?"

You can repeat this question for all of the professional behaviors that are most important to you.

"What advice would you give me, as a potential manager of _____?"

Getting answers to such questions as these will on occasion save you from making the wrong hire. However, if you have applied the lessons in *Hiring the Best*, you will most likely have uncovered any skeletons in the closet long before this. You should check references partly to verify what you have already discovered, partly to give you peace of mind, and partly to give you a greater understanding of how to get the best out of your chosen candidate once on board.

In Conclusion

As you'll remember, a myth in corporate America makes people think that upon promotion into management, you somehow become mystically endowed with all of the skills of the successful manager. However, as we noted, you must separate the myth from reality, recognizing that management skills don't come as a gift from the heavens; they come from study, effort, and application. You know that it is impossible to *manage* productively without first *hiring* effectively, and that this skill is the bedrock of your success as a manager.

With *Hiring the Best*, I hope you have learned that employee recruitment and selection isn't brain surgery; it is just a series of logical steps and sensible techniques that enable you to make consistently good hires.

In this book, I have tried to synthesize all of the most practical recruitment and interviewing techniques currently available, so that you will always have access to a wide selection of candidates and the tools to make hiring decisions that will reflect well on your professional management skills.

In closing, I want to wish you well in your career, and suggest that while possession of good selection skills *is* the bedrock of your success, it is far from the only management skill you will need to survive and prosper. Over the last twenty years I have written eleven books about different aspects of career management, each with a different focus on the tools necessary to survive the twists and turns that come into everyone's half-century work life. If you are on the management track, reading *Knock 'em Dead in Management* will help you in polishing many of the other skills you need in order to be successful in the management ranks of the corporate world.

I hope this book will prove helpful to you over the years. I am always available at knockemdead.com to help with your career management issues.

Appendix A
Drug Testing

*I*t is safe to estimate, based on figures from the National Institute on Drug Abuse, that at least one out of every fifty employees uses illicit drugs. Even bearing this in mind, I cannot in good conscience recommend that any company begin a comprehensive drug-testing program, for reasons I will detail in this section.

Our country's ongoing drug problem needs no documenting here. As employers, we are of course concerned about the dangers of drugs in the workplace and their adverse effects on productivity, attendance, morale, and health care costs. For the most part, society seems willing to support private sector efforts to alleviate the problem, yet some significant obstacles remain. In a survey by the Employment Management Association, less than half of all workers polled supported drug testing.

The fact is your organization's reputation as a good place to work can be jeopardized by an ill-conceived testing program. Many managers fail to see the implication of mistrust that can accompany the question, "Are you willing to take a drug test as a condition of employment?" As employers, we must accept that answering that question is likely to be difficult, even if the applicant responding has never used drugs.

The Message You Send

Here's the translation of that query from the prospective employee's point of view: "Yes, we'd like you to work here, but unfortunately we don't think you can be trusted too far. In fact, we have so little faith in the image you have presented to us that we think you might even be a drug fiend. Consequently, we'd like you to take this drug test."

I want to note for the sake of background that I speak here not as one with a particular policy agenda to advance but as a professional in the employment industry who has dealt with this issue first-hand as it affects both employers and employees. Every year I talk to job seekers who are confused, angry, or both about how to handle this issue. During one recent twelve-month period, I made over two hundred radio and talk show appearances on job search and career management issues; a number of them featured call-in segments that focused on drug tests. Many calls came from people who had been asked to take the tests and who vehemently objected to them.

These people did seem to me to be drug fiends singing the praises of crack cocaine. They seemed to be rational professionals and solid citizens who object to the suspension of the presumption of their innocence. They object to the fact that, often, it is the workers on the bottom of the totem pole—the assembly line workers, the secretaries, the receptionists, those who do not have a college education—who are chosen for testing, while the directors and vice presidents somehow slip by. They object to the hypocrisy of ignoring alcohol abuse on the job, and they see management as prime abusers almost every afternoon of the week. They object to a system that ignores a solid work record and sound references, apparently on the belief that past history is no indicator of whether a worker will wreck valuable equipment, destroy morale, and generally turn the company into a crack den.

They object to all that, and it is difficult to blame them. What's more, they have questions to which few employers have ready and sufficient answers. What are the tests really being used for? Will the applicant also be tested for, say, epilepsy, asthma, diabetes—or pregnancy? Who will have access to the information? What guarantees are there that it will remain confidential? What safeguards exist against false positives?

The bottom line is this: When it comes to drug testing, current and potential workers simply do not trust management. (The Center for Organizational Effectiveness found in a survey that only 30 percent of workers feel that employers have their best interests at heart.) Given the current atmosphere that surrounds this question, it is essential to proceed with the utmost caution, tact, and evenhandedness, and not simply issue edicts from on high.

"Damn the Torpedoes!"

Having said my piece on the subject, I should note that, despite all of the problems outlined above, drug testing in the workplace appears to be a trend that is likely to become more, rather than less, common in the foreseeable future. For example, federal government guidelines from the National Institute on Drug Abuse and from the Substance Abuse and Mental Health Services Administration require that companies employing commercial class drivers as employees must have a testing system in place. Following are some guidelines for companies instituting testing programs despite the risks and uncertainties I have outlined here.

1. Use a reliable test. Many are wildly inaccurate, and the cheaper the test the more inaccurate it is going to be. There are five primary types of drug tests: urine, sweat, saliva, hair, and blood.

▶ **Urine Tests**—The least expensive of the test methods, and generally argued to be the least accurate, urine tests are considered an intrusive method of testing.

▶ **Sweat Patch Tests**—This is also considered an intrusive method of drug testing, because a patch needs to be worn for an extended period of time. Sweat patch tests are controversial in terms of accuracy and are not commonly used.

▶ **Saliva Tests**—These are more expensive than urine tests, but less expensive than hair or blood tests. Saliva tests are considered unobtrusive and are becoming more common. However, saliva tests have no nationally accepted standards for detection. This could possibly make results problematic in court cases.

▶ **Hair Tests**—Several times more expensive than urine tests, these tests cost in the range of $100 to $150. They are considered unobtrusive, as they only require a lock of hair that is about 1 1/2-inches long and the thickness of a pencil. Hair tests are considered reliable.

▶ **Blood Tests**—These tests are the most expensive, most intrusive, and most accurate means of drug testing. They are also the least common, possibly because they are the most expensive.

2. Reduce the odds of a lawsuit by consulting with your attorney before implementing the program. He or she might tell you, for instance, to test all applicants rather than just the final contenders (many firms do this).

3. Work with a reputable firm that has done work in the field for some time. By doing so, you will increase your chances of conducting the tests with accuracy and sensitivity. You can find a selection of reputable drug testing companies in the list of Internet resources in Appendix B.

4. Use a back-up test for all positive findings. It should be a different test to avoid the possibility of the same error repeating itself. The back-up test is likely to be more costly than the initial screen, but it should nevertheless be built into your program's budget.

5. Select a laboratory only after obtaining strong references. The recommended minimum is three positive recommendations. Be

extremely wary of "hard sell" techniques from sales representatives.

6. Talk with other employers using drug testing programs. Listen and learn.

7. Establish strict guidelines for administering and processing the tests, and for protecting the confidentiality of the results. One company I know gives every job applicant a registration number, and the telephone number of their chosen laboratory. The candidate is informed that the result will be identified only by the number on the jar. After two or three days, the candidate may phone the laboratory and learn the result; at his or her discretion, a second application, which is mandatory for all applicants regardless of the test results, may be made.

8. Make sure the right people are administering the test. Their approach should be personable; they should be able to answer any and every question the test-taker might have. Do everything possible to remove the implication that the test-taker is guilty of something.

9. Provide test-takers with all relevant information about the foods and medications that can lead to false positives. Ask them to list all medications and suspect foods they may have ingested in recent weeks.

10. Give adequate notice. You will reduce the impression of coercion if you allow a reasonable lead-time. Avoid the humiliation of requiring a job candidate to give the test in front of a third party.

Appendix B
Hiring the Best *Reference Sites*

*R*ather than laboriously type in the URLs in this resource section, you can come to knockemdead.com, go to the management page, and link directly to any of these site pages.

Aptitude Tests

www.gneil.com/newhiretesting/default.asp

www.wonderlic.com/

www.psychtests.com/professionals/hr/index.html

www.analyzemycareer.com/index.cfm?auid=256&action=signup&test= aptitude

www.worldwidelearn.com/career-assessment.htm

www.prospects.ac.uk/cms/ShowPage/Home_page/Applications_and_ interviews/Interviews/Test_yourself/Aptitude_tests/p!ejcig

www.assessment.com/mappmembers/welcome.asp?accnum=06-5185- 000.00

Aptitude Tests (Sales)

www.salestestonline.com/default.asp

Aptitude Tests (Management)

www.funeducation.com/products/bmat/ (both aptitude and assessment)

www.pearsonps.com

Aptitude Tests (Technical)

www.psionline.com/industry_tech.htm

Background Checks

http://global-verification.com/

http://gobackgrounds.com

www.arrin.net

www.accufacts.com/

www.backgroundsonline.com

www.choicepointinc.com/business/pre_employ/pre_employ.html

www.empfacts.com/employee-home.html

www.esrcheck.com/about/index.php

www.informus.com/

www.informationresources.com

www.personnelprofiles.com

www.staftrack.com/

www.absolutehire.com/

www.hrscreening.com/

www.employeescreen.com

www.infolinkscreening.com/infolink/index.htm

www.disa.com/background_screening.htm

www.xukor.com/Services.aspx

Background and Reference Check Companies

http://global-verification.com/

www.jobreference.com/index.htm

www.references-etc.com/employment_reference_checks.html

www.resumagic.com/r_ref_check.html

www.xukor.com/

Diversity Recruiting

www.LatPro.com

www.IMDiversity.com

www.HireDiversity.com

www.bilingual-jobs.com

www.blackcollegian.com

www.bwni.com

www.diversitylink.com

www.taonline.com

www.diversitysearch.com

www.eop.com

Drug Testing Companies

www.datia.org

www.disa.com

www.corporatedrugtesting.com/cdtfeedb.htm

www.drugtestingnetwork.com

www.choicepointinc.com/business/pre_employ/pre_employ_5.htm

www.hrscreening.com/drug_testing.html

www.arrin.net/index.cfm?action=drugtesting

www.employmentdrugtesting.com

www.sgdrugfree.com

www.norchemlab.com

www.drugtestingnews.com

Employee Referral Program Resources

www.allbusiness.com/articles/content/23775.asp

www.peopleclick.com/knowledge/ind_lefkow.asp

www.angami.com

http://hr.cch.com/default.asp?subframe=/issues-answers/tips-to-reap-rewards-of-employee-referral-program.htm

www.us.manpower.com/uscom/contentSingle.jsp?articleid=58

http://articles.findarticles.com/p/articles/mi_m0FXS/is_6_80/ai_75916197

www.hrzone.com/topics/employee_referral.html

www.itworld.com/Career/1893/ITW3349/pfindex.html

www.erexchange.com/articles/printer.asp?d=H&CID={7E006D7A-1873-4E41-BF06-5C68D0093353}

www.wetfeet.com/employer/articles/harnessing.asp

http://employers.gc.ca/gol/recruitment/interface.nsf/engdocBasic/9.2.html

Human Resources Services

www.blissassociates.com

www.cambriaconsulting.com

www.competencymanagement.com

www.ddiworld.com

www.donphin.com

www.hamsher.com

www.haygroup.com

www.hhrconsulting.com

www.hrstore.com

www.hradvice.com

www.hralliancegroup.com

www.hrsynergysolutions.com

www.hresults.com

www.innovative-hrsolutions.com/generali.htm

www.valueinsights.com

www.management-advantage.com/about-us/about-us.htm

www.mgtamer.com

www.pacificbridge.com

www.humanresourcesplus.com

www.personnelsystems.com

www.praxishr.com

www.resumeminers.com

www.shlusa.com

www.the-williams-group.com

www.mercerhr.com

www.hr-guide.com/data/009.htm

www.webhire.com

www.hrservicesinc.com

www.accenture.com

www.strategichr.com

www.thechoiceint.com/hr.htm

Job Sites, Headhunters, and Associations
For more than 200 general and specialist sites for recruitment, head-hunters, and associations, go to knockemdead.com. Go where the job hunters go.

Outsourcing Companies

www.keane.com/index.php

www.ezgoal.com/outsourcing/

www.rttsweb.com/services/outsourcing/onshore.cfm?pc=94

http://itonshore.com

www.administaff.com/why_hr_outsourcing_works.asp

www.coefficientsolutions.com

www.alvaka.net

www.csc.com/industries/financialservices/

www.vanguardms.com/?EZGoal.com/Outsourcing

www.diversified-credit.com/?EZGoal.com/Outsourcing

www.cambridgeoutsourcing.com

www.askhello.com/

www.seneca.com/

www.hudsonsoft.com/

www.databasesystemscorp.com/

www.experexchange.com/

www.pfsweb.com

www.probusiness.com/

www.onepointbpo.com/Group/OnePointGroupDetail.shtml

www.trinet.com

Index

A

Abilities
   of candidates, 127–30, 238
   of clerical hires, 210–11
   of management hires, 176–77
   of salespeople, 190
ADA. *See* Americans with
   Disabilities Act
Administrative hire. *See* Clerical
   hires
Advertisements
   creating, 40–47
   days to print, 47
   headlines, 41–42
   including salary, 46
   Internet ads, 36–39, 48–49
   job description, 43–46
   message, 42
   newspaper ads, 36–39
   in pennysavers, 47–48
   placement of, 48
   radio advertising, 49–50
   responses to, 47
Age Discrimination Act, 215, 218
Age questions, 218
Alumni associations, 33
Americans with Disabilities Act
   (ADA), 68, 215, 219–27
America's Job Bank, 39–40, 53–54
Analytical skills, 13–14
Aptitude tests, 39, 225, 253–54
Atrophy stage, 231–33

Attitude issues, 171–72, 178
Authority, 171, 178

B

Background checks, 39, 242–43,
   254–55
Bailey, F. Lee, 102
Basic Compensation, 19
Behaviorally based questions, 111
Benefits for employees, 20
Boschert, Bob, 71
Breaking point, 162
Broadcast letters, 81–83
Bush, George H. W., 68, 219

C

Career fairs, 50–52
Career orientation, 209–10
Career resiliency, 4–5
Careerbuilder.com, 37
Certified International Personnel
   Consultant (CIPC), 57
Certified Personnel Consultant
   (CPC), 57
Chronological resume, 74–75
Civil Rights Act, 215
Clerical hires, 207–14
   abilities, 210–11
   career orientation, 209–10
   communication skills, 212–13
   flexibility issues, 209, 212

About the Author

Martin Yate has exemplary credentials in the field of career management, with a career grounded in an unusually comprehensive understanding of the challenges we all face in surviving the twists and turns of a half-century-long work life. This understanding comes from three decades spent in management and technology recruitment, human resources, training and development, public speaking, and executive career coaching.

With a personal career vision focused on helping professionals of all levels survive and prosper throughout their professional lives, Martin Yate has published ten books in the last twenty years. These include:

▶ *Knock 'em Dead 2006: The Ultimate Job Seeker's Guide*
▶ *Business Presentations That Knock 'em Dead*
▶ *Hiring the Best: A Manager's Guide to Effective Interviewing and Recruiting*
▶ *Knock 'em Dead in Management*
▶ *Resumes That Knock 'em Dead*
▶ *Cover Letters That Knock 'em Dead*
▶ *CareerSmarts*
▶ *Beat the Odds*
▶ *The Ultimate Internet Job Hunting Book*
▶ *Keeping the Best*

Each of these books addresses a different aspect of career management, from finding jobs and growing professionally, to reaching and succeeding in the ranks of management. A *New York Times* bestseller, Yate's books are published throughout the English-speaking world and in seventeen foreign languages.

When not writing, Martin Yate runs a career management practice, supporting the career growth plans of upwardly mobile executives and those in transition.